The Religions of Oceania

More than a quarter of the world's discrete religions are to be found in the regions of Australia, Melanesia, Micronesia and Polynesia, together called Oceania. This is the first book to bring together up-to-date information on this great variety of traditional religious beliefs and practices, which have been profoundly influential on the theories and understandings of religion in general.

A comprehensive survey of the changing and various religions in the Pacific zone, *The Religions of Oceania* documents traditional cultures and beliefs and examines indigenous Christianity and its wide influence across the region. It covers the backgrounds to and development of traditional religions, and includes analysis of the new religious movements generated by the response of indigenous peoples to colonists and missionaries, the best known of these being the so-called 'cargo-cults' of Melanesia.

The authors present a thorough and accessible survey of the diversity of religious practices in the area, and provide clear interpretative tools and a mine of fascinating information to help the student better understand the world's most complex ethnographic tapestry.

Tony Swain is Lecturer at the School of Studies in Religion, and **Garry Trompf** is Associate Professor in the School of Studies in Religion and Fellow of the Research Institute for Asia and the Pacific, both at the University of Sydney.

The Library of Religious Beliefs and Practices
Edited by John Hinnells
University of Manchester
and Ninian Smart
University of California at Santa Barbara

This series provides pioneering and scholarly introductions to different religions in a readable form. It is concerned with the beliefs and practices of religions in their social, cultural and historical setting. Authors come from a variety of backgrounds and approach the study of religious beliefs and practices from their different points of view. Some focus mainly on questions of history, teachings, customs and ritual practices. Others consider, within the context of a specific region or geographical region, the interrelationships between religions; the interaction of religion and the arts; religion and social organization; the involvement of religion in political affairs; and, for ancient cultures, the interpretation of archaeological evidence. In this way the series brings out the multi-disciplinary nature of the study of religion. It is intended for students of religion, ideas, social sciences and history, and for the interested layperson.

Already published

Zoroastrians
Their Religious Beliefs and
Practices
Mary Boyce

Theravāda Buddhism
A Social History from Ancient
Benares to Modern Colombo
Richard Gombrich

The British
Their Religious Beliefs and
Practices
Terence Thomas

Mahāyāna Buddhism
Paul Williams

Muslims
Their Religious Beliefs and
Practices. Volume 1: The
Formative Period. Volume 2:
The Contemporary Period
Andrew Rippin

Religions of South Africa
David Chidester

The Jains
Paul Dundas

Hindus
Their Religious Beliefs and
Practices
Julius Lipner

The Religions of Oceania

Tony Swain and Garry Trompf

ROUTLEDGE

London and New York

First published 1995
by Routledge
2 Park Square, Milton Park, Abingdon, Oxon, OX14 4RN

Simultaneously published in the USA and Canada
by Routledge
270 Madison Ave, New York NY 10016

Transferred to Digital Printing 2006

© 1995 Tony Swain and Garry Tompf

Phototypeset in Times by Intype, London

British Library Cataloguing in Publication Data
A catalogue record for this book is available from the British Library.

Library of Congress Cataloging in Publication Data
A catalogue record for this book has been requested

ISBN 0–415–06018–4 (hbk)
ISBN 0–415–06019–2 (pbk)

Publisher's Note
The publisher has gone to great lengths to ensure the quality of this reprint
but points out that some imperfections in the original may be apparent

for Eric J. Sharpe

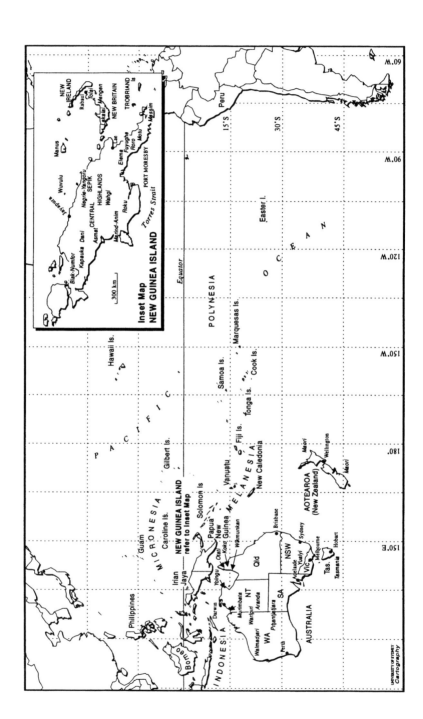

Inset Map
NEW GUINEA ISLAND

300 km

Contents

Acknowledgements

The authors especially wish to thank Ron Crocombe, Sibona Kopi, Sione Latukefu, Renaldo Pakarati, Maroti Rimon, Joel Taime and Esau Tuza, who provided valuable information, and Ruth Lewin-Broit, Dany Falconer Flint and Judith Lauder for their help in the production of this volume.

This book is affectionately dedicated to our esteemed colleague Professor Eric J. Sharpe, who held the first Chair in Religious Studies in the region spanned by this work, and who has constantly encouraged and supported research into the indigenous religious traditions of the south-west Pacific.

Introduction

This is the first book ever to be published in English on the religions of the south-west Pacific as a whole. Almost a quarter of a century ago, Hans Nevermann, Ernest Worms and Helmut Petri published *Die Religionen der Südsee und Australiens* (1968), and a French translation was made soon after. Worms and Petri's section on Aboriginal religion, which constituted a little more than half of the original, has only very recently appeared in English, but alas, their material, always disjointed and uneven, is now also thoroughly dated. A new work, such as this volume, is the only answer.

Why, it may be asked, a book on the religions of Oceania at all? We are tempted to reply with those mountaineers determined to scale remote peaks – 'because it is there!' The religions of Oceania – Australia, Polynesia, Melanesia and Micronesia – provide a colourful, informative and rewarding area of study. It is a region, furthermore, which despite having been neglected in its own right has been profoundly influential, perhaps more than any other area, on our theorizing upon and understanding of religion in general.

There remains, however, another angle to the question of why a book on the religions of Oceania. For unlike lofty mountain peaks standing boldly against the horizon, it might be asked to what extent Oceania is really there to be scaled. After all, the south-west Pacific has hundreds of language and cultural groups, not to mention an immense history which will mostly remain forever concealed. In what meaningful sense can all these things be brought together as a reality embraced by the word 'Oceania'?

This query must be squarely faced. Certainly, the traditions of the Pacific islands and Australia are quite distinct; so much so that, like Nevermann *et al.*, we have kept them quite separate in this book, although our chapters correspond and interrelate (as our table of contents indicates) far more than those in our predecessor's book.

There is, furthermore, an undeniable diversity *within* Australian and islander traditions. Since this is so, we are obliged to offer some explanation for the horizon which our book spans. This is the task of our Introduction.

Below, we consider the integrity of 'Oceania' in two ways. First, there is the indigenous *reality* of the south-west Pacific, which we briefly explore in terms of the prehistory of this rather culturally isolated part of the globe. Nonetheless, it is self-evidently true that until lately the original inhabitants of this area did not have anything approaching an identity of themselves as 'Oceanians'.

This brings us to the second part of our Introduction: the arrival of European investigators who created the *idea* of Oceania (or the South Seas, etc.). A major part of the intellectual legitimacy of our domain of enquiry lies in the history of Western thought, our understanding of 'otherness' and of Europe's encounter with world cultures. This is not, of course, just a history of ideas, for ideas take political shape and so Oceania does emerge as a socio-political reality in recent centuries. This in turn has reshaped the identity of the original inhabitants of this region, so that today there is indeed much substance to the notion of religions of Oceania as a whole, for example in the form of Pacific Black liberation theologies. All this forms a part of our story.

To begin, however, we must turn back some hundred thousand years to the peopling of Oceania.

THE PEOPLING OF OCEANIA

Indigenous peoples were present in Australia as early as *ca.* 60,000 BP. It is even possible that 'the modern human type' known now as *Homo sapiens sapiens* first developed on the Australian continent, or more correctly, on the continental shelf called Sahul (including mainland Australia, Tasmania and New Guinea). The renowned Charles Darwin once speculated that such a biological isolation might have been necessary for humanity to evolve, and new evidence about the immense antiquity of the Australian continent has thrown previous, if competing theories about human origins into the balance. The lowest level of a site on the Arnhem Land escarpment in the Northern Territory contains two ochre 'crayons' recently dated to 65,000–60,000 BP, and there are two controversial datings – one of (allegedly) human bone from central Australia put at 120,000 BP, and the other a stone tool from the Nepean River banks near

Sydney recalibrated to 120,000–80,000 BP – which are currently under scrutiny.

During the last two decades scholars have differed over whether there was a single or two-stage movement of peoples from the South-East Asian region. Two stages would make the ancient Australian population 'dihybrid', implying that we should be looking for signs of two types of peoples, rather than one so-called 'Australoid' stock. Among the puzzles to be solved is the apparent difference between most mainland Aborigines (with wavier hair and characteristically slender build) and the Tasmanians (who were comparatively stocky, with crinkly hair like the Melanesians). Older theories conflicted as to whether the more numerous mainlanders pushed the Tasmanians southwards, or whether some groups sailed down from the Tropics to reach the southernmost reaches of the eastern Australian seaboard (the earliest occupation date for Tasmania thus far being 30,000 BP, and the date of the severance of a land-bridge across Bass Strait being 7,000–6,500 BCE). While great lacunae in the archaeological evidence still prevent satisfactory answers to many questions, we can be sure now that Australian prehistory is of fundamental importance for understanding the emergence of the human species as a whole.

Upon contact with the outside world, Australia proved to be very diverse ethnologically, with up to 550 culturo-linguistic groupings – some of which were territorially confined, as along parts of the lush eastern seaboard, and some very scattered indeed, as were the desert Aborigines of central and western Australia. The prevailing picture of the Aboriginal socio-economic scene is that of semi-nomadic band societies; lineages or small kin groups engaged in hunting and gathering across land they recognized as shared with bands of the same ancestries or language(s). Bands usually camped and rarely settled permanently in the same location, although there were seasonal and ceremonial places where they came together for feasts, exchanges and rite. Mobility in sensitive eco-systems made for long-term survival, although snippets of archaeological evidence – about the firing of forests for game and the extinction of such a large mammal as the Tasmanian wolf (*thylacinus*) – suggest greater modification of environments during the early human occupancy of Australia than was at first supposed. But here one must remember regional variations and thus different potentialities of Sahul's landscape: on south Australian plains the spread of grass was encouraged to attract kangaroos, while on islands only just off Cape York some desultory steps in horticulture were taken. Along the north coast of

Arnhem Land, Aborigines used canoes to negotiate the seas between islands (perhaps being first inspired into such adventuring by Macassans), and in the centre is the genius of Black wanderers to try to find water when none might seem available.

By comparison with New Guinea, however, Aboriginal populations were much more spread out on European contact (about 1 million over 7,687,000 square kilometres), and the technologies and cultural configurations were relatively more homogeneous. Tool types, instruments, skills, institutions and beliefs tended to diffuse over large regions (occasionally over virtually the whole continent), and when it comes to phenomena of religion it is thus easier to generalize about the major themes of ritual life and the broad features of belief. In contrast, we find that in New Guinea and its outliers, as Sahul's northern component, the ethnographic complexity is sharper than anywhere else on earth; about a quarter of the earth's discrete cultures, languages and thus religions are documented in this region alone.

Some would argue – at least from DNA analysis – that New Guinea was populated as early as 72,000 BP; but archaeology has so far only yielded the firm date of 40,000+ BP (from raised beaches on the Huon Peninsula). New Guinea's greater archaeological fascination lies in its hortico-agricultural prehistory, for there are signs that tuber crops were curated as early as 30,000 BP and impressive evidence that humanity's first 'agricultural revolution' or systematic gardening occurred in the New Guinea highlands from *ca.* 9,000 BCE. The northern coast and the island outliers of New Guinea have been rightly identified as the spine along which the earliest known sea-faring explorers moved further and further eastwards, along the Solomons' chain to San Cristobal and thence across some 200 nautical miles to the next stepping-stone of Melanesia. The oldest known boat, dating to 33,000 BP, hails from a New Guinea coast.

'Melanesia', meaning the 'black islands', was named in 1832 by the French *savant* Dumont d'Urville to classify the occupancy of New Guinea, the Solomons, the New Hebrides, New Caledonia and Fiji by crinkly haired black peoples, who were distinct from mainland Black Australians and from the lighter coloured populations of Micronesia (the 'small islands' or atolls north of Melanesia) and Polynesia (the 'many islands' scattered across the rest of the Pacific). Although the classification is crude, it has, strangely enough, weathered criticisms over the years and will remind one that the peopling of central Oceania can hardly be explained solely in terms of the Black peoples of Sahul.

The human occupancy of the Pacific islands has long been a subject of controversy and competing speculations. The current consensus among scholars, in the light of technological, linguistic, cultural and genetic evidence, is that the islands were peopled through migrations from the Asian rather than the American side of the Pacific (though with Rapanui/Easter Island experiencing some South American impact). Older theories giving the Americas a much more important role (Thor Heyerdahl's view, for instance) have been discarded, and the debate (generated by Andrew Sharp) about whether voyagers found new islands more by accident or by 'being swept off course' than by deliberately organizing exploratory expeditions has tended to lose its point. A consensus among the present generation of prehistorians has it that the most inaccessible islands were populated by movements out from a regional centre, first from 'frontier Melanesia', east from Vanuatu, New Caledonia and Fiji between 3,000 and 2,000 years ago, and then from western central Polynesia (Tonga and Samoa) during the first millennium AD – fanning out, not just to Aotearoa/New Zealand and wider Polynesia, but also to Micronesia, and even to some extent doubling back into Melanesia.

The key evidence for this prehistoric pattern is the distribution of finely decorated Lapita pottery from northern New Guinea to Samoa, leaving us a vivid record of highly mobile sea-borne colonists and explorers moving steadily through Melanesia and out into Polynesia in the mid to late second millennium BC. It makes sense to believe that these migrants spoke Austronesian languages and were the ancestors of the present-day Polynesians and eastern Micronesians. During their movements through Melanesia they were typically coastal-dwellers who eventually became absorbed into the Black populations preceding them (but with darker-skinned groups getting no further east than Fiji). Some consider the processes to be more complex than this; a slow migratory wave through Micronesia is not to be ruled out, given the early date of 3,500 BP for the occupancy of the central Marianas (though non-Austronesian) in western Micronesia; while a great many Austronesian traditions speak of diminutive occupants of the islands before the ancestors of the present inhabitants arrived (in Polynesia usually *menehune*, in Fiji *leka*, in Rennell *hitihiti*, etc.). But for the time being the postulate of a single rather than binary or multiple entrance into central Oceania holds good, and squares with common Polynesian and eastern Micronesian traditions of a homeland (often *Hawaiiki*) somewhere in the regional 'spring-board' between Vanuatua and Samoa. This postulate also goes some way towards explaining techno-cultural differences between (relatively older) western and (relatively younger) eastern Polynesian societies.

Islander subsistence was based on fishing, horticulture and the domestication of animals. The newcomers brought with them dogs (as did the early Australians), pigs (reaching New Guinea around 3,000 BP) and fowl; they mildly modified their environments through shifting cultivation and animal domestication. As in Australia, their technology was lithic, yet with more developed techniques for grinding and smoothing stones. Rice-growing was unknown except in western Micronesia (Guam), and iron-forging was introduced only in far western New Guinea – after the Islamic presence at Tidore. Of the new crops introduced to the islands, the sweet potato is of much interest, since it may well have entered the Pacific from South America (in 500–1,000 CE).

What of the prehistory of Oceanic religions? In the chapters which follow we consider religious life from the time of the earliest contacts with 'the outside world' to the present day. We eschew speculation about the prehistoric character of Oceanic religion – there has been too much theorizing, even 'cult-archaeological' imagining about it – here we offer a few basic comments on the reconstruction of religio-cultural life from the distant past.

Australia is of great fascination in that it yields every major method of disposing with the dead: bodies extended or flexed, bones of the dead placed in rock crevices; interred jumbles of bones; platform disposals; grave goods present and goods absent – all these practices are known. From Lake Mungo (in western New South Wales) comes some of the earliest evidence for cremation anywhere in the world (25,000–24,000 BP); at Green Gully Victoria one even finds the corpse of half a woman set beside half a man in a mysterious unity; at Broadbeach, Queensland, there is evidence of cannibalism; at Cooma (near Canberra) a man was buried some 10,000 years ago with a magnificent kangaroo-tooth necklace. Australian art, too, has its extraordinary prehistory; currently cation-ratio dating suggests that the Olary engravings (in a semi-desert area of South Australia) could be as old as 30,000 BP, while stencilled hands in Tasmanian caves studied with Accelerator Mass Spectroscopy appear to have been repainted over 20,000 years of occupancy. All this confirms the likelihood of religion and something of its continuities in Aboriginal life, but it does not prove its existence, nor tell us anything precisely about its nature and mutations over eons of time.

Both Australian and wider Pacific archaeology provide evidence for the diffusing of human groups over wider and wider portions of the earth. The new places encountered were bound to have had an affect on responses to 'the supranormal' or 'spirit-world' – from the blow-holes of the Nullabor Plain to geyser and vapours at New Zealand's Rotorua, from the great Ayers Rock (*Uluru*) in Australia's very heart to impressive volcanoes on Tanna or Hawaii. Socio-religious institutions for group defence and consolidation grew up in a great multiplicity of small territorial domains, as did procedures for group negotiation to which the widespread use of ceremonial kava-drinking – from the Samoas to the Samo (the Western Province of Papua) – intriguingly testifies. If by 1700 an estimated 1 million persons occupied Australia, twice that number were distributed over the Pacific islands. No significant island groups were uninhabited before European contact; mutineering Mr Christian's arrival on an uninhabited Pitcairn Island may seem an exception, yet trowel and spade have revealed earlier occupation.

Now the populating of the islands in itself betokens the prepared-ness to make new discoveries, and as we shall see below (p. 146) the religious factor looks to be crucial for the spirit of adventure, including the transmitted knowledge to voyagers of 'letting nature be your guide' (as Harold Gatty's famous book suggests). The fre-quent heroicization of 'vanguard explorers' corroborates this, and occasionally prehistoric investigation points to the sacral and appar-ently charismatic character of great expeditionary leaders. On Efate (Vanuatu), for example, archaeologists followed up local traditions about Roy Mata, evidently the greatest of the high-ranking indi-viduals who had arrived just before a well-remembered volcanic eruption and who introduced the matrilineal social structuring to Efate, Makura and Tongoa. So significant was Roy Mata that a number of his faithful followers agreed to be buried with him on the islet of Retoka, an oral record substantiated by one of the most startling archaeological discoveries of the Pacific. Closely surround-ing the skeletons of a chieftain and his wife lay twenty-two men and women buried as couples, with radiocarbon dating to 1265 CE supporting prior estimates by genealogy.

This remarkable case indicates the importance of group solidarity in both finding and then managing island worlds. Maori traditions set great store by the arrival of a 'fleet' of eleven canoes, which provides the genealogical starting-point for the known tribes, and if the descent lists only take us to the thirteenth century – which, being around 300 years after the earliest known human presence in New Zealand, may possibly mark a second wave of immigrants –

they nonetheless reflect the significance of *collective* exploits and possession. At times the Austronesians appeared to have achieved larger unities transcending tribal differences. The Tongans held sway over a kind of inter-island dominion during the sixteenth and seventeenth centuries, for example, colonizing as far west as the Isle of Pines (New Caledonia) and parts of Fiji, and as far north as Wallis. We can presume that a sense of their own cosmic uniqueness, and that of their sacred king, Tu'i-Tonga, legitimated their activity. Into recent times there also existed the so-called 'Yap Empire' in western Micronesia, in which religious offerings of coconut oil, sennit, pandanus sails and mats were sent as tribute to Yap from islands to the east (Ulithi, Woleai, Ifaluk, etc.), which were themselves locked into an exchange system yet ranked in decreasing importance the further they were from paramount Yap (or Gagil).

We have arrived at modern times; yet before considering recent developments in the indigenous religious history of Australia and Oceania, it will be of value for introductory purposes to assess the manner in which the Western world discovered, or conceptually invented, Oceania, and the way in which the religions of its original inhabitants were envisioned by outsiders.

THE INVENTION OF THE RELIGIONS OF OCEANIA

What we now identify as the south-west Pacific has long fascinated the great cultural and intellectual speculators of the northern world. These imaginings go back long beyond the time of discovering the islands and cultures of the region. The ancient Roman Axiochus, for example, believed the Isles of the Blest, where the dead and the infernal gods dwelt, was in the Antipodes. Similarly, the Chinese novelist Li Ju-chen (b. 1763 BC), in his famous *Ching Hua Yuan*, describes island-hopping navigations until the Land of the Immortals is reached, an island which seems to lie in the direction of Tahiti, Fiji or even New Zealand.

Later, when we read of the early explorers' 'factual' accounts of their experiences in the south-west Pacific, it is clear that such lofty imaginings were still a part of intellectual traditions. We do not, in fact, know who were the first northerners to reach these parts. It is only recently that the sixteenth-century Portuguese presence in Australia has been acknowledged; interestingly, a Portuguese map of that century, believed to represent Australia, contains pictures of all kinds of fantastic humans, having the faces of dogs and monkeys. It is also possible that Chinese vessels had reached the Great South

Land at an early date – a notion cherished by eminent historians and prehistorians of both Australia and China, but as yet lacking any definite proof.

For our purposes, however, the advent of non-indigenous reflection upon the region of Oceania properly begins with the records of early European explorers to the regions. The most ancient work of this kind is the journal of Antonio Pigafetta (1521), who had accompanied the voyages of Magellan. Not surprisingly, his descriptions of the people of the island of Guam are superficial and dwell on the type of obvious physical and cultural features that could be observed, these days, by the casual tourist. This type of report was the norm for this period in accounts by those such as Alvaro de Mendaña de Niera, Francis Drake, Louis-Antoine de Bougainville and William Dampier; the last named, having said that he saw two signs of religion among the Australian Aborigines, added that 'setting aside their Humane shape, they differ but little from Brutes'.[1]

The initial impressions of these explorers were heavily coloured by an emerging intellectual orientation in Europe which increasingly used reason and observation as a means of discovering the true and essential nature of humankind. This was a time of internal strife, which led to a race to establish new colonies and to develop scientific knowledge (e.g. in navigation) to make such expansion possible. The new scientific spirit also shaped the understanding of humanity itself; instead of holy decree or divine monarchical right, reason and nature became the locus of truth. So it was that thinkers like Thomas Hobbes, John Locke and Jean Jacques Rousseau became fascinated by 'savages' as evincing what people were truly like in their allegedly 'natural' state.

These thinkers were divided as to whether they believed people to be essentially good (Rousseau and Locke), or, in Hobbes' famous phrase, apparently confirmed by Dampier's views quoted above, that the lot of 'savages' was a life 'solitary, poore, nasty, brutish and short'.[2] The protagonists of the 'Noble Savage' ideology admittedly invited rebuke with their overly romantic imaginings. When Rousseau was confronted by the details of a Maori massacre, he replied: 'Is it possible that the good Children of Nature can really be so wicked?'[3]

The interest in resolving these questions about human nature, and in the parameters of nature more generally, led in 1768 to the Royal Society promoting Captain James Cook's first voyage to the South Seas, the last great ocean region to be explored, yet, following

Cook's three expeditions, a region whose indigenous peoples had fully captured Europe's imagination.

Cook himself, while voyaging just after Rousseau's publications exhalting the 'Noble Savage', was not so faint-hearted as the great French philosopher. He certainly praised the Pacific islanders, those people primarily portrayed by earlier primitivists as living in an Eden-like state of bliss and innocence, but, if anything, the harder lifestyle of the Australians was even closer to Cook's ideal. Unlike his botanist Joseph Banks, who in his journals eulogized the Tahitian lifestyle, Cook saved his best for the Aborigines; a people who, without clothing or houses, were equally without want and, in all, 'far more happier than we Europeans'.[4]

Cook had little to say of Aboriginal religious life, but he was responsible for introducing two profoundly influential words from the Pacific islands. In 1777 he was the first European to comment on the Polynesian term *mana*, to which we will refer again shortly. The other word he introduced us to is *tabu*. He wrote:

> The people of Atooi [Atui] . . . resemble those of Otaheite [Tahiti] in the slovenly state of their religious places, and in offering vegetables and animals to their gods. The *taboo* also prevails in Atooi . . . For the people here always asked, with great eagerness and signs of fear to offend, whether any particular thing, which they desired to see, or we were unwilling to show, was taboo.[5]

Mana and *tabu* have been central to our understanding of Oceanian religions, and indeed to theories of religion generally, but before we consider this we need to follow our narrative a little further into the nineteenth century, for Cook was not only observing the South Seas but also claiming large parts of it, such as the continent of Australia, for George III. In succeeding years, waves of colonization began.

The most useful information on Oceanian religion from the early nineteenth century comes from long-term administrators or residents, missionaries and explorers who had encountered more fully the indigenous people of an area. An example is George Grey, who in 1845 was appointed Governor of New Zealand. Much of his time was spent trying to pacify the Maori people, and in this context he learned their language and translated a large body of their myths. His *Polynesian Mythology and Ancient Traditional History of the Maori as Told by Their Priests and Chiefs* (1855) was greatly influential on the rise of the then young discipline of anthropology, and has remained a standard source for students of Oceanian myth ever since. Grey, however, has another claim to fame, for some years earlier, as an explorer of internal Australia, he had discovered the Aboriginal term *kobong*, which he instantly associated with the *totam* (totem) of the Ojibwa Indians. While the term is derived from Native North America, ever since Grey's account 'totemism' has been pre-eminently associated with the Australian Aborigines.

Mana, tabu, totemism: where would the comparative study of religions have been in the nineteenth and early twentieth centuries without these concepts? How much, we must ask, have the religions of Oceania shaped our understanding of religion in general? The answer is difficult to overstate.

Were these concepts not enough, we must recall also that the rise of the academic study of religion occurred during the heyday of evolutionary thought, and so eyes turned to the south-west Pacific in search of 'the primitive'. E. B. Tylor, usually considered the founder of anthropology, redefined religion as a belief in spiritual beings primarily so as to embrace the Australian Aborigines within his 'animistic' theory of the origin of religion (animism = a belief in spirits). Sir James Frazer wrote volume upon volume on totems and tabus and none influenced his theories more than the first Australians. Indeed, his theory of magic preceding religion virtually hung on Australian data, as is revealed in his lengthy correspondence with the noted ethnographer of the Aranda of central Australia, Baldwin Spencer.

The 'animists' did not pose their ideas without contest, however. R. R. Marett put forward a most influential 'pre-animistic' theory of the origin of religion in which he drew public attention to the Pacific island concept of *mana* as recorded in missionary anthropologist R. H. Codrington's *The Melanesians* (1891). This, says Codrington:

is a power or influence, not physical, and in a way supernatural; but it shews itself in physical force, or in any kind of power or excellence which a man possesses. This *mana* is not fixed in any thing; but spirits, whether disembodied souls or supernatural beings, have it and can impart it.[6]

So, concludes Marett, this *mana*, this basic feeling of powerful awe, precedes and underlies any belief in spirits proper. In turn, Marett's ideas were applauded in Rudolf Otto's celebrated *The Ideas of the Holy* (1917) and, even more importantly, were incorporated as an essential part of Emile Durkheim's monumental *The Elementary*

Forms of the Religious Life (1912), in which he takes the *mana* idea as a starting-point in his investigation of Australian totemic systems.

No book in the history of the sociology or anthropology of religion has been more influential than Durkheim's, but the Oceanian connection does not stop there. Consider, for instance, Sigmund Freud's work, published in the following year. Even his title, *Totem and Taboo*, is unthinkable without the south-west Pacific, and his argument naturally rests on ethnographic data from the region.

During the late nineteenth and early twentieth centuries, when comparative theories of religion were in a period of vigorous growth, Oceania was the region which promised answers to the elusive, if misguided, quest for the origin of religion. Noted theorists read the available ethnographies written by missionaries and amateur fieldworkers, and when they were still unsatisfied they engaged in long correspondences with researchers. It was inevitable, however, that the time would come when the theorists would leave their studies to venture out and actually observe for themselves the people about whom they wrote.

At this point, our attention turns to the formation of the first Chair of Anthropology in the south-west Pacific at the University of Sydney. Plans were already being laid along these lines in 1913, although World War I soon disrupted them. Attending the meeting on that occasion were two young men who were to inspire the next generation of anthropological research world-wide – Bronislaw Malinowski, who had that year published *The Family among the Australian Aborigines*, and A. R. Radcliffe-Brown, who three years earlier had engaged in a turbulent but not profoundly fruitful bout of fieldwork in Western Australia. Soon after this meeting, Malinowski, a Pole and technically an alien, set off for the Trobriand Islands in east Papua New Guinea to see out the war performing the first ever piece of intensive long-term fieldwork. Malinowski's subsequent rich and detailed publications on Trobriand life became an ethnographic benchmark for future field-researchers, although his theories of religion (e.g. *Magic, Science and Religion*, 1948) were not always received with equal enthusiasm.

In 1926, Radcliffe-Brown returned to Australia as Sydney's first Professor of Anthropology, and under his guidance a multitude of researchers took to the field in Australia and the Pacific islands. To publish their findings, he founded the journal *Oceania* in 1929.

The period between the wars is marked by long-term field expeditions and the application of 'functionalist' theory, either that of Malinowski or the more sophisticated, structural-functionalism of

Radcliffe-Brown. In Australia, the works of A. P. Elkin (who was soon to take over the Sydney anthropology department), Phyllis Kaberry and W. L. Warner stand out, while in the Pacific islands one should note in particular the publications of Raymond Firth (who briefly succeeded Radcliffe-Brown at Sydney), Reo Fortune, Gregory Bateson, Margaret Mead and F. E. Williams.

This type of research continued until after World War II, but more recently, while the emphasis on fieldwork continues, theoretical fashions have turned to structuralist, Marxist and phenomenological models. The works of Claude Lévi-Strauss, which developed to some extent out of Radcliffe-Brown's later thinking, have drawn heavily upon Australian Aboriginal traditions. His methodology in the study of myth began something of a fad in Oceanian research, as it did elsewhere. More enduring, however, have been some profoundly sensitive studies of symbolic worlds in the Pacific islands and Australia. One which stands out is W. E. H. Stanner's *On Aboriginal Religion* (1959–61), which is an inspired analysis of Murinbata myth and ritual. Another is K. O. L. Burridge's *Mambu: A Melanesian Millennium* (1960), which brilliantly considers cargoism in the Madang region of New Guinea as part of a symbolic quest for the moral European.

Hundreds of works could be mentioned for the period which began with Malinowski's fieldwork and Radcliffe-Brown's professional chair, but our task here is not to provide a detailed inventory but a very general map for the inexperienced student. Something should be said here, however, about the politics of theory in Oceania.

It must never be forgotten that our theories have grown in a colonial environment on the one hand, and with a fascination with exotic cultures on the other. This should be evident from our discussion thus far. The ideas of noble and ignoble 'savages' not only served Western thinkers seeking to define the essence of human nature, they were also used, sometimes brutally, to justify the actions of Europeans in new-found colonies. The evolutionary notion of the 'primitive' was certainly rooted in an ongoing investigation to find the basic defining qualities of humanity, but how many deaths were justified by saying this was the law of 'the survival of the fittest' in operation? Even functionalist theory, seemingly innocuous at first glance as it documented the complex internal balance of 'native' cultures, has been heavily criticized for presenting an image of indigenous cultures as stagnant and inflexible, and hence requiring the guiding hand of colonial social engineering to ensure adaptation to change. One need only read A. P. Elkin, Raymond Firth or Hubert Murray (then Lieutenant-Governor of Papua) in the early volumes of *Oceania* to recognize how tightly anthropology and 'native administration' were interwoven.

One recurring failure in the study of religions of Oceania even today (although, thankfully, the exceptions are increasing) has been the neglect of history. The savage, the primitive, the native – those preconceptions that have accompanied the observations of people in the south-west Pacific all have overtones of immutability or time-lessness. The reality, however, is that our investigations have been carried on well behind a staunch, sometimes bloody, colonial frontier. Research has tried to rediscover or reconstruct what Oceanian societies were like before colonization, and publications so often ignore the fact that the people being investigated no longer practise the traditions described. What does this silence about present realities say? Simply that we will not acknowledge cultures in transition; that if 'primitive' societies become dynamic societies we will ignore their longings, their aspirations and their hopes for the future. Clearly, such a state of scholarship should not be allowed to continue.

If there is a lesson to be learned from looking back over the centuries of investigating religion in Oceania, it is that our fascination and theories tell us as much, if not more, about ourselves as about the people being encountered. This is a stark truth to confront, but dialogue takes time, and we need not therefore throw up our hands in despair. One of the best prescriptions for future study, we feel, is a sensitivity to the changing and shifting notion of religion in Oceania so that we deal not with the pallid relics of past cultures, but with representations of ongoing and vital traditions.

It is thus that our chapters are set within the context of history. Certainly we devote chapters to what seem likely to be the religions of pre-contact times (always remembering *all* our sources were written well after contact), but about two thirds of the book considers the history of religions in the south-west Pacific over the past few centuries. Some readers will ask why we have spent a good deal of time on the impact of Christianity in Oceania. It is because there are in the region fascinating new religious movements – crucial ones for the general study of religion – that cannot be understood without considering Christian missionization, and also because most 'first peoples' of the south-west Pacific have come to embrace Christianity, while expressing their identities through it in distinctively indigenous ways. Hence the sets of parallel chapters on 'cults of invasion' – covering various adjustment movements, including the famous Melanesian 'cargo cults' – and on 'Christianization', which is fast becoming the subject of a new industry among anthropologists, historians, missiologists and sociologists.

This book's methodological orientation is that of the newer discipline of Religious Studies, which lends itself in fact to a polymethodic approach. 'Religion', a term lacking a lexical equivalent in almost all the traditional cultures of Oceania, is employed typologically to cover the many life-ways and ancestral traditions that preceded the arrival of 'world religions'. Our approach is by and large historicophenomenological; we present an open-ended and flexible understanding of the religious dimension (avoiding its confinement to belief, for instance, or just to ritual); we are concerned to trace developments from the traditional to the more rapidly changing contemporary scene; and we do not intend to privilege any tradition so much as to report, assess and analyse with critical acumen the social realities we have experienced and researched. Work done on religion by scholars in a variety of social sciences has been utilized, without deferring to the conceits or special methodic protocol of one or another discipline and school. In moving through Aboriginal to wider Pacific materials, it should also be noted that this book has been designed to ease the reader from a more immediately manageable approach to more complex data and analysis.

Returning, then, to our opening question, we have shown that Oceania does indeed have a prehistoric integrity as a somewhat isolated cultural pocket, but, further, we have demonstrated that the religions of Oceania are equally the invention of colonial thought and practice. This makes them no less 'real', but we must be honest enough to acknowledge the context of our understanding and to reveal in our survey the constant fact that the people being observed were in truth being observed in a state of imposed transition. To put this another way, no book can say what the religions of Oceania *are*. What we reveal in the following pages is what, for the last few centuries, the religions of the south-west Pacific were in the process of *becoming*.

NOTES AND REFERENCES

Note the references at the end of chapters in this work are only connected to quotations in the text. For various other (and sometimes more important) publications, readers are advised to consult the Bibliography.

1 W. Dampier, *A New Voyage around the World*, London, 1937 (1697), p. 312.
2 T. Hobbes, *Leviathan*, London, 1975 (1651), p. 65.
3 Quoted in B. Smith, *European Vision and the South Pacific 1768–1850*, London, 1960, p. 87.
4 J. C. Beaglehole (ed.), *The Journals of Captain Cook*, London, 1955, vol. 1, p. 508.
5 Quoted in F. Steiner, *Taboo*, Harmondsworth, 1967, p. 22.
6 R. H. Codrington, *The Melanesians*, Oxford, 1891, p. 118 n.

Part 1
Australia

1 Tradition

THE DREAMING

Many people would admit they know little or nothing about Australian Aboriginal religion, but even among them few would not have heard of the notion of the 'Dreaming' or 'Dreamtime'. It is an evocative word which on the one hand we readily equate with the very essence of Aboriginal religiosity, and which on the other conjures up a host of inappropriate images from Western folk culture to psychoanalysis and the New Age. In brief, it is an important concept which is more often than not totally misunderstood.

To begin our discussion of Aboriginal religious life we will first clarify some basic features of the Aboriginal worldview and their conceptions of time and space. We can then ask just what kind of time is the so-called Dreamtime, and our answer will provide a point of departure for the remainder of this chapter.

Opinion on Aboriginal conceptions of time varies considerably. One school of thought, which has captured the imaginations of romantics and racists alike, is that Aborigines are a 'time-less' people. More recently, there have been those (mostly psychologists) who suggest that while Aborigines have a weak sense of historical time, the difference is a quantitative rather than a qualitative one. And finally, there are those who maintain that Aborigines have a different sense of time which is cyclical rather than lineal.

Each of these views attempts to grasp the same reality, but that reality is indeed elusive. We must be appreciative of those who have questioned the hackneyed image of the time-less Aborigine who is either invariably late for appointments or lost in an awareness of the infinity of existence. Such notions simply do not square with the very practical and worldly awareness of Aboriginal people. Nonetheless, it remains true that Aborigines in traditional culture did not recall events beyond about two generations back and did not have the means of reckoning events in terms of some measured calendar. It is important to note that Aborigines did not count (although they had words meaning 'duality' and 'trinity' as qualities rather than numbers) and so did not have a means of reckoning multiples of events (days, months, years, etc.). In this sense, it remains quite evident that they did not nurture a lifestyle based on a temporal philosophy.

While some scholars today are suggesting Aborigines saw time as looping back upon itself in ever-recurring cycles, it is vital to recall that Aborigines themselves do not speak of these occurrences as cyclical, and we should be most careful not to confuse Aboriginal outlooks with those, for example, from India, in which time is bent into gigantic (and measured) cycles which at the end of great spans of time return to the beginning. Indeed, insofar as cyclical and linear time are often, and wrongly, presented as the only possible contenders in an either/or choice, it is probably safest to attempt to locate another, more precise, term.

Following a suggestion of Paul Ricoeur, we will suggest Australian Aborigines have a *rhythmic* understanding of *events*, which really requires no reference to time. This way of understanding the world can be not only precise and most serviceable but also aesthetically pleasing. The Aranda of central Australia, for instance, could name at least thirty qualitative changes that occurred over what we would call a period of twenty-four hours. They included:

> The Milky Way is stretched out across the centre of the sky.
> Bandicoots back into their burrows.
> The shadows are variegated.
> The sky is aflame with red and yellow.[1]

This is a precise and poetic means of ordering life, but insofar as it refers to concrete *events* it is not strictly speaking a form of time, and insofar as the patterns recur but are not said to go back to some beginning it is *rhythmic* rather than cyclical.

This discussion of time or its philosophical absence bears fruit when we turn to the Dreaming – called, so often, the Dream*time*. The latter, as the Aboriginal linguist Eve Fesl says, is 'a compound word "dreamed up", by an English speaker who couldn't understand the Aboriginal language'.[2] One should not think of the Dreaming as a different type of time, but rather as a different class of events. In English, we might best call these 'Abiding Events' (abbreviated hereafter simply to Events), insofar as the word 'Abiding' on the one hand conjures up the idea of being eternal, yet on the other gives the connotation of being place-specific and belonging to an 'abode'.

The English word Dreaming was originally employed as a translation of the Aranda root *altjira*, which signifies 'eternal, uncreated, springing out of itself'. *Altjira rama* – literally, 'to see the eternal' – was the evocative phrase used to describe sleeping dreams, but the so-called Dreaming was actually a different compound, *Altjiranga ngambukala*, or 'that which springs from its inherent eternity'. Clearly the concept of eternity is not a time past, present or future, but only implicitly so; for in fact the real reference is not to time but to space or, more correctly, places.

Linguists who have cast a careful eye over the words translated as Dreaming have noted the term is used in two main contexts. One is when referring to certain Events which are embodied in stories, songs, emblems, etc. The other is when referring to the places which house the sacred power of which the stories tell. If we cling to the idea of Dreaming, then rather than Dreaming *time* we should speak of Dreaming Events and Dreaming *places*.

All the preceding discussion may at first appear to be over a semantic quibble, yet it is important in order to emphasize that Aboriginal peoples' worldview is not one based on time and history but, at an absolute level, on sites and places – a theme which can now be developed throughout this chapter. Our enquiry into the Dreaming is thus one which will focus on a class of Events which are on the one hand beyond the normal rhythms of life and eternally unchanging, while on the other they are embedded in the land. They, as we have said, are Abiding Events.

It is inevitable that some will feel reluctant to concede, without qualification, that the Dreaming lacks some temporal qualities. After all, do not Aboriginal people themselves speak of it as residing in the past? The answer is yes, but they also say Dreaming Events exist now, and in this regard ritual performances do not so much perform a past Ancestral action as make manifest something eternally enduring. The seeming 'pastness' of the Dreaming might best be understood in terms of an analogy. If a view from a mountain is obscured by broken clouds below us in the foreground, we reasonably say in describing what we see that we see clouds and then, beyond them, land. Does this mean that there is no land close to us? Obviously not, as we not only know it must be there but can actually see it through the broken cloud. What we mean is that in the distance we observe land alone but closer to us it is overlaid by cloud. Likewise, it is true that the Dreaming is ever present, an eternal now, but its Events are overlaid by the day-to-day rhythms (and chaos) of life if we look at it from the perspective of an individual human. It is thus the Aborigines give the impression that the Dreaming is always about two or so generations behind people now living; in other words, it is most clearly manifest at a point just beyond the memory of specific human lives, yet insofar as (from a Western perspective) it advances behind each successive generation, it is not fixed in time but rather endures like that landscape with lives like clouds sweeping across it.

COSMOLOGY

Thus far we have merely attempted to ensure that the emphasis of our interpretation of Aboriginal religion is firmly placed on the enduringness of place rather than the passage of time. Having argued so generally, we must now consider more specifically how Aborigines envision the structure of their cosmos.

Aboriginal cosmologies are never systematized into some grand doctrine but are instead always implicit within a multitude of stories. This lack of centralized mythic co-ordination is essential to the nature of Aboriginal religious life, and thus anyone attempting to orchestrate a single unified cosmology, even within one Aboriginal community, will succeed mainly in obscuring the very fabric of their worldview. We simply cannot even consider the matter of specifying *a* primary Aboriginal Ancestral story. What we can do is take an example, almost at random, and try to generalize something from its structure.

A story which we collected from central Australia will suffice for our purposes. Our field-notes read:

> *Ngarlu* is the name of a site and also the ceremonies performed, just south of Mt. Allan [a remote cattle station in central Australia]. *Ngarlu* is the name of the flower of the *ngarlkirdi* [witchetty grub tree].
>
> There was a Dreaming man named *Linjiplinjipi* of the Jungari subsection at this site. He had adorned his body with *Ngarlu* and was spinning hairstring. The whirling sound of his spinning tool [made of crossed sticks] attracted a woman of the Ngapangardi subsection [and therefore his mother-in-law]. He climbed the hill and as he was watching her she stopped to urinate. Sexually aroused, he continued to attract her with the noise. Finally, he

caught her, forced her legs apart and raped her. Upon ejaculation, however, she closed her legs and her tight vagina dismembered his penis.

Today, at *Ngarlu* her vagina remains transformed into rock and the severed stone-penis is still embedded in it. *Linjiplinjipi* himself, in agony went to the other side of the hill where he turned into a large boulder which has paintings upon it depicting his hairstring cross and his erect penis.

Yilpinji ['love magic'] is performed modelled on *Linjiplinjipi*'s methods of attracting his mother-in-law, using sticks from *Ngarlu* and adorning the torso with the flowers of the witchetty grub tree.

While this story's narrative, like all Aboriginal stories, is specific and unique, some of its underlying structure reveals something universally present in Aboriginal mythology. We should note that we do not intend to attempt to delve for the *true* latent meaning of myths (as generations of psychoanalysts and anthropologists have sought to do), for this at best yields disputable results, but rather we will be content merely to note something very basic yet significant in its pattern.

At a most elementary level, the Linjiplinjipi story has four elements. First, *something exists*. We are not told here or in other Aboriginal myths where the Ancestors first came from. In some accounts they are said to have been lying in a state of semi-sleep. In other words, all this potential to act is already present, waiting to be used. In many stories, like that of Linjiplinjipi, it is just stated that the Ancestor was there. Such openings are disconcerting to Westerners, but for Aboriginal religious thought the Ancestors' existence is the base line. Second, that something *becomes active*. In a sense, Aboriginal myths deal with a passage in which inactive Ancestral potentials move and act and then become immobile again. Third, through the activity, certain aspects of life are given *order and shape*. There are several instances of this in the Linjiplinjipi myth, which embraces elements belonging to what we might consider as moral, economic, ritual and geographical domains. The story evidently is related to the issue of mother-in-law tabus, it establishes a model of activity of spinning hair, it introduces a ceremony for attracting lovers (but *not*, for rather obvious reasons, mothers-in-law) and it establishes the Ancestral presence which constitutes the sacred immanence of the site. This last matter leads on to our fourth point, which is that the myths invariably end with Ancestors taking on an *enduring form*, as a terrestrial or celestial place.

In all this it should be observed that cosmic order is derived from a multitude of events in which countless Ancestors travel and transform themselves into sites. This is markedly in contrast to cosmologies which focus upon a single Godhead or other ultimate principle of sacred authority upon which the universe was and is dependent. Strictly speaking, there is in traditional Aboriginal Australia no creation nor a first creator. The myths avoid questions of first origin and instead begin from the assumption that the life-potential of the Ancestors simply exists. Likewise, the issue of who made the Ancestors or world is not addressed. In other words, Aboriginal cosmologies do not regress in either time or structure to a single point (as monistic traditions do), but rather are in their very essence always pluralistic.

If we appreciate the fact that Aboriginal cosmologies avoid first origins and Supreme Beings, we are still left with the question of why their Ancestral pluralism requires that the very pre-existent sacred powers move and ultimately transform into places. There are at least two answers to this query. The first is that Aboriginal people did not develop a philosophy which accepted a distinction between mind and matter. Earlier generations of scholars have said that Aborigines projected human intellectual and social attributes on to an inanimate world, but from an Aboriginal perspective this actually inverts the truth. In their view, humans are the moral and intellectual beings they are because all existence, as laid down by Events, has *consciousness*. Ancestors must have a conscious intentionality revealed through their actions, so that all that exists might also be conscious.

The other important factor to be observed in the movement of Ancestors is that it provides for a plan of cosmological *relatedness*. While Aboriginal traditions are pluralistic and hence local religious Law has a high degree of autonomy and independence, they also contain networks of relatedness at both internal and external levels. Without some cosmological principle of relationship, the Aboriginal world might tend towards highly isolated pockets, but in reality the Australian continent is criss-crossed by a network of pathways which employ the pathways established by Ancestral beings. In this regard, it is worth noting that while the Ancestors move, they do not move *from* one place *to* another place. Rather, their essence remains simultaneously throughout the entire pathway, so that at a basic level Aborigines conceive of pre-established lines of cosmological relatedness permeating their world. In brief, then, Aboriginal cosmologies might be characterized as establishing a pluralistic pattern of semi-autonomous and conscious places which are related through pathways representing the movement of Ancestral Beings.

One final phenomenon we must now consider is so-called totemism. Throughout the history of this concept prominent anthropologists, not least of them E. B. Tylor and A. R. Radcliffe-Brown, have asked if the term has any true substance. It was the French anthropologist Claude Lévi-Strauss, however, who in his *Le Totémisme aujourd'hui* made a sustained attack on the notion of totemism, arguing it was but a 'moment' in Aboriginal (and other) mentalities. In this he was certainly correct, although his broader interpretation of Aboriginal mentality is questionable. Totemism can be understood as a consequence of the Aboriginal understanding of the potentialities of place. If all existence shares its essence with that of lands which are conscious, then obviously all existence is related. Thus, says Mussolini Harvey, a Yanyuwa elder from central-northern Australia, 'No matter if they are fish, birds, men, women, animals, wind or rain ... All things in our country here have Law, they have ceremony and song, and they have people who are related to them.'[3] We must add, however, that insofar as Aboriginal cosmology is truly pluralistic it cannot portray each place as containing the full potentiality of all life-forms. The myths relate that sites are associated with specific species or natural phenomena and specific powers. Totemism can thus be thought of simply as an outcome of the fact that all existence has its place and those who share a site with other forms of life will naturally consider themselves to be identical to one another in essence, although this identity might be reckoned in many and various ways. It is thus that Aborigines assert they *are* their land and they *are* their totemic species; that is, they share the same localized Ancestral spirit.

MAINTAINING THE COSMOS

The logic of Aboriginal ritual is embedded within their cosmology and is foremostly a maintenance of that link between lands and the peoples of a land. Insofar as other species or natural phenomena are also land-linked, this process is one which maintains segments of the cosmos.

The quintessential Aboriginal ritual is referred to in the literature as the 'increase' ceremony, but this is a total misnomer. In some parts of Australia, there are in fact ceremonies to *decrease* the population of over-abundant things, and in general the concern is to ensure the continuation of a *cosmic balance*.

Cosmic balance rituals are present throughout all of Aboriginal Australia, although their form and context vary. Without doubt, they have a pragmatic and subsistence facet, for often the motivation for performing the ceremony will be someone else in the community saying something like, 'You make it, father; I want to eat.' Nonetheless, the act of bringing species populations up to their full and balanced abundance is an act whose significance is broader than mere economics. Rather, it is a process of ensuring the continual emanation of the life-potentialities of a particular place imbued with the power of an Ancestral Being.

The best known form of cosmic balance ritual is the Aranda Intichiuma first reported by Baldwin Spencer and Frank Gillen. In its simplest form, a person who shares a site's spirit visits that place and in particular a focal area, which may be a simple pile of stones or rock painting. The song of the Ancestor is sung while uncomplicated ritual acts, such as rubbing the stone, are performed. In more elaborate forms of these rites, the spiritual custodian may be decorated with red and white vegetable down and a headdress so that he in fact embodies the Ancestor in animal form and makes manifest the behaviour which leads to cosmic balance. Spencer and Gillen briefly describe the Intichiuma of the *unjiamba*, or Hakea flower, as follows:

> At a place called Ilyaba the ceremony is performed by men of the Bulthara and Panunga classes, and the exact spot at which it takes place is a shallow, oval-shaped pit, by the side of which grows an ancient Hakea tree. In the centre of the depression is a small projecting and much worn block of stone which is supposed to represent a mass of Unjiamba or Hakea flowers, the tree being the *Nanja* tree of an Alcheringa woman whose reincarnation is now alive.
>
> Before the ceremony commences the pit is carefully swept clean by an old Unjiamba man, who then strokes the stone all over with his hands. When this has been done, the men sit around the stone and a considerable time is spent in singing chants, the burden of which is a reiterated invitation to the Unjiamba tree to flower much, and to the blossoms to be full of honey. Then the old leader asks one of the young men to open a vein in his arm, which he does, and allows the blood to sprinkle freely over the stone, while the other men continue the singing. The blood

flows until the stone is completely restored, the flowing of blood being supposed to represent the preparation of *Abmoara*, that is, the drink which is made by steeping the flower in water, this being a very favourite beverage of the natives. As soon as the stone is covered with blood the ceremony is complete.

This stone is regarded as a Churinga, and the spot is *ekirinja*, or forbidden to the women, children and uninitiated men.[4]

In contrast to agricultural communities which have times of harvest, storage to span unbountiful times of the year, and a new beginning to an annual cycle often celebrated by some grand and co-ordinated moment of the New Year, Aboriginal cosmic balance rituals are performed continuously (for hunters and gatherers require constant fertility), lack any conception of a single moment of renewal and at first glance seem to be rather parochial. They consist of specific individuals (occasionally only one) performing many independent rites to ensure the maintenance of specific sites. Upon closer inspection, however, it is quite apparent that Aboriginal traditions are designed to ensure strong ties of relationship between the myriad ritual units.

The first thing to be noted is that in many parts of Aboriginal Australia, although only a person who shares the Ancestral spirit of a site can perform the rites, this does not mean that they can do so unaided. In Aboriginal English, a distinction is made between 'owners' of a site (those who have a direct spiritual link with the Ancestor) and 'managers' or 'policemen' who belong to the opposite patrimoiety and who, while having rights and responsibilities for the site, do not embody its spiritual essence. 'Policemen' is a nice gloss (although, given Aboriginal experiences with police, one should not miss the irony), for these people are overseers to ensure 'owners' obey the Law. In more elaborate cosmic balance rituals, they and they alone must decorate the custodian so that he becomes the Ancestor and they will direct through constant instruction given in authoritative or firmly humorous tones. The mutual roles of 'owners' and 'managers' ensures that, while certain people embody Ancestors, they cannot exploit this as their own exclusive individual power, for they must depend upon others to release the fecundity associated with their own lands.

A second conspicuous check against parochial autonomy is a widespread but not universal prohibition against individuals eating their so-called totemic species. In other words, in the areas where these tabus are operative, the resources that a person can maintain through cosmic balance rituals are *not* open to them as a part of their subsistence. The rites, therefore, are performed for the economic benefit of people outside their ritual group, who in turn enact their own ceremonies for the good of others' subsistence.

This structurally enforced interdependence between ritual and land groups is so marked that it is surprising to realize its implications have been largely neglected by scholars. One exception is David H. Turner, who in his book *Return to Eden* has recently attempted to draw out the socio-political significance of such a worldview. In a detailed investigation of the relationship between land and ritual rights and economic resources on Amagalyuagba (Bickerton Island) in the Gulf of Carpentaria, he began with the hypothesis that people's lands are actually deliberately demarcated around scarce economic resources. This would mean that the people of one land would perform rites for the balance of resources existing only within their territory, but because these were tabued to them they would do so for the benefit of others who lacked such species in their own lands. Upon closer investigation, however, it was discovered that although Aboriginal people of the area implied such an arrangement existed, there were very few areas on the island that in fact lacked all of the essential subsistence resources. It seems, therefore, that the arrangement and distribution of ritual groups with lands and species depends more upon Aboriginal *ideals* about interdependence than any *real* qualities of their environment.

This raises the question of why Aboriginal societies took such pains to ensure that their land-based traditions were not only pluralistic but also that each land and its people were interrelated with and interdependent upon other land-groups. Such queries are inevitably elusive, but we can at least suggest one prominent result of such an arrangement which seems to be readily appreciated by non-Aboriginal people. In all the records of Aboriginal history there are but two known instances of territorial warfare between Aboriginal communities, and both of those belong to contexts where colonization was clearly a contributing factor. This is not to say violence was not a prominent feature of traditional Aboriginal societies, but there seem to have been no attempts to conquer the lands or the powers derived from lands of another people. One ready explanation for this fact is that not only did Aboriginal ideologies stress the immutable rights of specific people to their lands, they furthermore – through the principles of structural ritual interdependence we have discussed – ensured that to overthrow others was not to add to oneself. Instead this would have meant losing access to parts of one's subsistence environment which those others, and they alone, could regulate through cosmic balance ritual.

THE EMERGENCE OF LIFE FROM LAND

We have seen already that Aboriginal ritual practice is predominantly a process of regulating facets of the cosmos by ensuring the continual balanced abundance of those life-essences deposited by the Events of Ancestors in the land. The rites performed to regulate other species were also performed to control the population of human babies. As Aboriginal people will say: 'We are born from the country'.

This is a radical claim when it is realized that it implies humans are not derived from their fathers or even from their mothers. While it is of course not denied that mothers carry their children, they are not said to contribute to their essential nature. Rather, they carry a life-potentiality from a site. Precisely how that life-essence enters them varies in detail from region to region, and the essence itself may take the form of a fish or a mischievous child-like creature, or be transported by some intermediatory agent. Again, its all-important place of origin might variously be identified by recalling the place where pangs of pregnancy were first felt, or the revelations of a dream, or by associating a foodstuff (which itself has a site) with the occurrence of the pregnancy. The details, however, do not alter the fundamental principle that the life which enters the human mother is that of a place which is imbued with an Ancestral presence. Indeed, in some Aboriginal languages the same word is used for Ancestral marks upon the landscape and the human spirit.

While it is a rather negative question, and one which has been the subject of tedious debate spanning almost a full century, it is here perhaps worth briefly resurrecting once more the matter of whether Aboriginal people did in fact have some understanding of the relationship between sexual intercourse and procreation. As far as we are concerned, the answer is unquestionably affirmative for northern Australia, and fairly certainly so for the rest of the continent. The northern data itself has regional variations. Donald Thomson investigated the issue among the Koko Ya'o and their neighbours of Cape York and he believed Aboriginal concerns to identify similarities in appearance between fathers and their children were a clear statement of the recognition of paternal physiological contributions, while with the Wik Mungkan he found myths referring explicitly to semen as a fertility symbol.

As for Arnhem Land, it is evident in myths of the All-Mothers (see chapter 2) that ('incestuous') intercourse precedes, as something of a prerequisite, their giving life from their uteri. In these regions, furthermore, people acknowledge the preparatory significance of coitus, although they do not allow it sufficient or exclusive capacity to produce life. In desert regions such associations are less explicit, but symbolism of various forms of mating can be detected in association with the fecundity of cosmic balance rituals, and a people could hardly fail to generalize from there to human reproduction.

Here we need not pursue this controversial issue, however. Lloyd Warner's words from his investigations among the Yolngu are both candid and highly illuminating. Caught up in the debate over the alleged ignorance of physiological paternity and maternity, his investigations led only to his embarrassment:

> An occasion arose in which I could inquire of certain old men just what the semen did when it entered the uterus of a woman. They all looked at me with much contempt for my ignorance and informed me that 'that was what made babies'. I had not been able to obtain this information earlier because the [Yolngu person] is far more interested in the child's spiritual conception ... than he is in the physiological mechanism of conception.[5]

We can, perhaps, go even further than Warner and say that Aboriginal people, despite their accurate powers of observation of natural rhythms which could not have failed to realize the relationship between sexual intercourse and pregnancy, actually downplayed, even suppressed, such interpretations of the origins of life insofar as they were at odds with their understanding that life was due to the fertile powers of land alone.

If not biological, what then is the significance of motherhood and fatherhood in Aboriginal Australia? This too is a contested matter, but one factor which is of focal importance is that while all Aborigines assert they are born from land, in some areas (in fact those same regions where there is more explicit recognition of sexual reproduction) there is also a somewhat contradictory insistence that ritual and territorial identities are transmitted from fathers to their children (i.e. patrilineally). Among central desert peoples like the Aranda and Pintupi, a person belongs to the land from which his or her spirit emerges, and this is the place for which he or she must perform cosmic balance rituals. Insofar as there is a tendency to reside in the husband's land there is a skewing towards children containing the same Ancestral spirit as their father, but this is no more than a tendency. In other regions, however, such as in Cape York Peninsula, this tendency has become almost exclusively patrilineal, although in the final analysis it is insisted that, if the child entered the mother from outside the father's spirit-land, then the child will belong to a different place to his or her father. Arnhem Landers go further than this, and allow patrilines actually to dominate over territorial principles. The Yolngu wish to ensure a child's spirit comes from the same waterhole as that of its father, but if it is evident it did not the child still belongs to the father's land and ritual group, although he or she also retains some privileges and responsibilities for his or her conception place.[6]

Scholars who have considered the tension between geographical (the spirit site) and social (the father) recruitment to one's ritual land throughout Australia agree (although there is no absolute proof) that place determination is the more fundamental and ancient of the two, with the patriline developing more recently out of a concern to ensure a control over inheritance within the family. A. P. Elkin feels this may have only occurred since colonization. Warren Shapiro gives it a slightly older date, while Annette Hamilton sees in it a move towards male hegemony within Aboriginal societies which was still in flux at the time White investigators observed these societies. An absolute date is impossible, but we too consider strict patrilineality to be relatively recent and, as it is more prominent in coastal regions, perhaps due to contacts with Melanesians, Indonesians and, finally, Europeans, which we will document later.

Despite widespread tendencies towards recognizing shared spiritual essence with one's father, there are indeed few instances of children having the same Ancestral spirit as their mother (the tendencies towards this are confined to far northern Cape York, Bathurst and Melville Islands and some sections of Arnhem Land). This is not to say there are no matrilineal transmissions of ritual and territorial rights, but children do not share the Ancestral *essence* with their mothers as they do with their fathers.

Some have interpreted this as evincing men manipulating society to give them a dominant position, but it does not really explain why belonging to one's father's ritual group gives a man generally more hegemony than if the child is recruited to some other man's ritual domain, nor does it explain why a mother contributes to her own alleged downfall by 'finding' her baby in her husband's spiritual domain. An alternative explanation might be that the increased significance of the lineage arose out of the need to bolster continuity and order in areas where sites alone were insufficient organizational principles (for example, where outsiders had disrupted or threatened land affiliations), but fatherhood was chosen, as it were, by default insofar as it did not directly counter the doctrine that people were born from land. If a child were to share its essence with its mother this would be tantamount to recognizing the autonomy of the body over land, and this would indeed be threatening to the entire Aboriginal world-order. One can share one's father's spiritual identity without suggesting at all that one is in fact born from one's father. Clearly motherhood and fatherhood have quite distinct symbolic attributes, which leads us to the related issue of the respective religious lives of Aboriginal women and men.

WOMEN AND LAND

One of the most controversial issues in Aboriginal Studies of late has concerned the position of women within traditional life generally, and traditional religious life specifically. The initial anthropological dogma, reflecting more of the stereotypes of researchers than any reality of Aboriginal understanding, was that while men were believed to progress through a sacred realm during their lifetimes, women's lot was exclusively profane. Even those such as the psychoanalytic ethnographer Geza Róheim, who with his wife's assistance specifically set out to consider women's traditions, could conclude that Aboriginal women's cosmoi consisted of but a fear of demons which could hardly be compared with the genuinely religious doctrines of the men.

That this was an androcentric interpretation is now universally conceded, but developing a more adequate interpretation has not been without its complications. The initial first step was for women themselves to conduct research into Aboriginal women's religious life, for there is little in this domain that traditional women would comfortably disclose to a man. Besides pioneers such as Katherine Parker and Daisy Bates, it was Phyllis Kaberry who, in her important book *Aboriginal Woman: Sacred and Profane* (1939), first sought to redress the balance. Although she provides incontestable evidence that Kimberley women in fact maintain a sacred world, however, she really does little more than argue that, like men, women are in need of some psychic safeguard against fate and misfortune. In other words, she does not specifically consider and develop what might be unique to a woman's religious domain in contrast to that of men.

Those who have attempted to ascertain what might define the unique qualities of Aboriginal women's traditions have invariably, if on occasion indirectly, appealed to the body; to the facts that Aboriginal women give birth, raise children, collect the vast majority of all foodstuffs consumed and invariably have a lifestyle which, while mobile, is for much of their life less so than that of men. Some, such as Nancy Munn, argue that women's traditions are camp-centred while men's are concerned with Ancestral mobility – a view echoed by Fred Myers, who considers Pintupi women's rites to be more localized than the more territorial expansive men's cults. Others, such as Diane Bell, would strongly resist the image of different cosmic structures, arguing instead for different functions, women being more nurturing, men more procreative.

The question these interpretations each raise in different ways is the significance of the body in determining women's religiosity. To begin we must note that menstruation and childbirth themselves do have religious dimensions in Aboriginal life, and invariably have their sanction in the Events of Dreaming. A girl's first period to some extent announces (with far more biological precision than any male equivalent) a coming of age, and at this time girls undergo an 'initiation', however modest it may appear in contrast to the rites for the making of young men. Girls' menstrual blood may be used in the ritual context; and a further introduction to their Ancestral identity through icon and song typically forms an integral part of the proceedings during which the girl is taken to a separate ritual camp and later reintroduced to the community in terms of her new status.

Again, at a later junction, childbirth is likewise a ritual moment, although like menstruation it does not mark a major ceremonial occasion. Nonetheless, there are Ancestral songs to make for an easy birth and prevent complications, as well as food tabus, incantations and medicines designed to ensure a trouble-free labour. Birth, furthermore, is a moment of extreme power, and while there is usually no notion of pollution associated with it (or with menstruation), the process of giving birth and the remaining placenta are things from which men must be guarded.

Given this information, some theorists have been tempted to postulate that the womb and birth are the quintessential features of women's, and in a covert manner even men's, religiosity. In some parts of Australia, this thesis has some solid support. For instance, the central-northern All-Mother cults make explicit reference to the emergence of all life from the Mother's womb and, while the men control the fertility ceremonies, they assert that Dreaming men in fact stole these from women. More explicitly, one woman stated of one form of these rituals: 'That's men's rubbish. Men make *Kunapipi*... Women make babies.'[7] This is unambiguous enough, but throughout most of the rest of the continent the womb is not explicitly acknowledged as such, nor do Ancestors use 'normal' bodily functions to spread their essence. In these, the majority of cases, the most that could feasibly be said, to quote Bell, is 'the physical acts of giving birth and of lactation are important but are considered to be one individual moment in a much larger design ... of nurturance ... modelled on the Dreamtime experience.'[8]

While women's birth-giving powers are an undeniable reality in general they are not elaborately celebrated in themselves. (The exceptions are the regions of the All-Mother cults, to which we return in chapter 2.) The reason for this should be evident from the preceding section, when we noted Aboriginal spiritual thought stressed that life emerges from land, not the womb. Indeed, there is a tension between the two principles of bringing life into being which is perhaps most clearly expressed by men appropriating women's birth-giving abilities at a symbolic level. In men's secret initiation ceremonies the inmates are reborn in a fashion recognizing that they are derived not from their mothers but from their spirit-lands. Of this we will say more in a moment, but it is worth noting that even women's birth rituals in some areas seem to acknowledge the priority of land, for as soon as a child is born it is placed in a small depression in the ground and is reborn from the country.

Is this, then, to suggest Aboriginal women's construction as mothers in fact lessens their spiritual status insofar as it conflicts with a philosophy giving absolute priority to land fecundity? This is possibly a partial truth, but it must not be allowed to lapse back into the blatantly false doctrine that women are therefore profane. Aboriginal women do have their own secret and sacred ceremonies; these, like men's, can give rise to cosmic balance, harm and heal, and celebrate the activities of the Ancestors. And yet, all this not-withstanding, it seems to us, and now increasingly to women anthro-pological writers (feminists included), that the 'separate and equal' model of men's–women's sacred life is both romantic and simplistic and that male-structural hegemony in some aspects of Aboriginal socio-religious life cannot be ignored. In a philosophical world of place, women's biological powers are often either appropriated or denied. As Jane Goodale has said of the Tiwi: 'Women are not expected to be innovators or creators – they do not even create "life"![9]

While it is partly true that men and women have separate religious worlds, those of women, we feel, are less autonomous. Male-controlled rituals are generally larger in scale, and where men and women join together in rituals men invariably have more (though not necessarily total) control. Furthermore, there are restrictions on women *vis-à-vis* men which are not reciprocated: a woman whose husband dies, for instance, has in many areas long speech tabus, and men are in a position in many parts of Aboriginal Australia to perform ritual operations on pubescent girls (tearing or cutting their vaginas, deflowering with hard-wood penis-shaped sticks, compulsory sex with the initiating men) which are totally closed to women in the case of equivalent young boys. And, of course, Aboriginal men could marry many wives, while the inverse never occurred. Finally, and perhaps most tellingly, Aboriginal women's own secret or semi-secret rituals have far more focus on (human) men that men's do on women. Now we do not mean to revert to the dated notion that women's ceremonies are purely 'love magic', but while their songs do have Ancestral and land themes, no researcher has denied that the songs can and are used to attract lovers, especially by younger women. This, furthermore, is an integral, not incidental, part of the songs. Songs are explicit; for example, translating as:

> Long one penis penis vulva.
> Labia opens sees clitoris.
> Copulate boy goes dizzy.
> Coitus vulva semen.[10]

It must again be emphasized that Miriwun Yirbindji songs, such as these, do not only focus on attracting men. They can harm and heal and also maintain cosmic order. Yet while the broader emphasis might be on nurturing the world, the structural presence of men as men (in contrast to male Ancestors) cannot be ignored. As one woman from the Victoria River area said of their Djarada ceremonies:

> When we sing about chickenhawk eggs and snake eggs, they like that, we want that chickenhawk, that snake, to have plenty of eggs, plenty of young, and women too, plenty of babies. But some want to sing for sweethearts, they can sing. But some want to sing for Dreaming, well, they can sing for Dreaming. Some of us

don't want to sing for sweethearts all the time, we like to sing for Dreaming.[11]

Clearly, women's ceremonies are land-based and can serve the same role as men's cosmic balance rites. Here there is undeniable and essential sacredness. But we cannot ignore the fact that these very same ceremonies are used (especially by the young) to attract, and have a content clearly orientated towards, men. While men also have a class of 'love magic' techniques, their major rituals are quite separate from these and significantly do not focus at all upon (human) women. Again, this seems to signify greater autonomy in men's spiritual domains.

Despite a *relative* separateness of men's and women's sacred life, therefore, we cannot ignore the reality that men's traditions have greater autonomy and are believed to have more power to bring existence into being. As Diane Bell writes, 'Men stress their creative power, women their role as nurturer.'[12] This may reflect a universal male quest for dominance (and, despite some recent disclaimers male dominance *is* a *structured* reality of Aboriginal society), yet intertwined with this is also the Aboriginal understanding that human life does *not* come from women but from land. Women's powers to give birth, if elevated to a religiously primal position, could indeed threaten the order of their place-bound world. This is perhaps nowhere clearer than in men's own rituals, especially the giving 'birth' to young men, when women's bodily symbolism is appropriated by men to the cause of elevating the dominance of land.

MAKING MEN

One of the first things Western observers noticed with regard to Aboriginal ritual life was the presence of an initiatory ordeal. The bodily manifestations were quite conspicuous, so that, for example, in 1814 Matthew Flinders noted with wonder that 'the most remarkable circumstance ... [among the northern Aborigines was that] the whole of them appear to have undergone the Jewish and Mahomedtan rite of circumcision.'[13] Circumcision is a widespread practice but not universal – it is not practised in the south-east, Cape York, the south-west coast and the north-western corner of the Northern Territory, as is the largely coterminous higher initiatory practice of cutting open the urethra or subincision, more colloquially known as 'whistlecock'. Other bodily signs of initiation include the removal of a tooth, the scarring of the body, the plucking of bodily hair and so on. As the conspicuous initiatory manifestations on neophytes' bodies were invariably made during a time of major communal ceremonial life, it is not surprising that initiation readily came to the attention of non-Aboriginal observers. In fact, descriptions of the public aspects of such rites are available from the eighteenth-century reports written only a decade after colonization. The significance of such rites, however, has not been at all adequately explored.

The first thing to note is that the context of initiatory ceremony varies significantly throughout the continent. In some regions the making of men is a part of broader ritual complexes such as the All-Mother and All-Father traditions, which will be discussed fully in the next chapter. In eastern Arnhem Land male initiation employs sequences from the Djunggawon, Kunapipi, Ngurlmag and the respective Narra rites of the two moieties. The first three of these are sustained by the famous myth of the Wawalag sisters, whose menstrual and birth blood attracts a Rock Python Yulunggur, who swallows the sisters as the monsoonal rain begins to fall. While Yulunggur is sometimes female (or at least androgynous), he is understood to be associated with men (he has a rather phallic and sometimes erect form) and the myth has a theme of the male subsuming the female. This is highlighted in initiations, as boys are made to bleed from arm-veins and this, like the sisters' blood, attracts the Python, who devours and later regurgitates the boys. In western Arnhem Land, in partial contrast, the female qualities of the serpent are emphasized, the swallowing culminating in a re-emergence from her womb. In both instances, however, men control the symbolic manifestations of Ancestral Events, and even where womb-like symbols are used they are employed in order to deny the powers of women's actual procreative powers. Life does *not* come from their wombs but, so to speak, from men's ritual wombs which give birth to a new life. Here, again, is a familiar theme: we are not born of our mothers' bodies but of land, which is the truth the lads are being introduced to through the ceremonies.

While it is only in the central-north of Australia that we find such explicit emphasis on the womb, it is nonetheless a recurrent theme at a less overt level. Although Aboriginal men do not labour the interpretation, it is a reasonable observation that subincision is at least partly a means of men symbolically obtaining women's physiological powers. Subincised penises not only look more like a woman's genitals, but following the operation men must squat to urinate and the periodic reopening of the incision in ritual contexts produces something symbolically very akin to menstrual blood. Even more generally, there is an underlying theme in the making of men's rites that the boys undergo a death which is followed by a rebirth – a process which inevitably entails the use of symbols of women's actual birth-giving.

Dealing with the symbolic passages in turn, it would seem that, at one level at least, each of the conspicuous bodily operations noted earlier is considered to be an indicator that the neophyte has died. In the south-east initiations associated with Bora rites, lads are said to have originally been cut to pieces or swallowed by the All-Father or an associate of his; they are then re-formed, but with an incisor missing. As in Arnhem Land, there is again a theme of the existing boys being destroyed; in this case their return without a tooth is a sign that they had indeed died. The Warlpiri of the Central Desert maintain circumcision is a form of death, while in east Arnhem Land the loss of the foreskin is an indicator of re-emerging from the All-Mother. Practices such as the removal of bodily hair and the ritual use of blood on the neophyte each have at least some significance as a sign of death.

The death, however, is of importance only as a prelude to a rebirth. And yet we must bear in mind Ronald Berndt's words: 'Generally, however, initiation is *not* so much a ritual death or a ritual rebirth. The focus is on life, on sacredness, and on a greater identification with the mythic beings.'[14] While it is undeniable that death and birth are important symbols of the initiatory process, we miss the mark if, as some scholars (psychoanalysts, feminists and others) have done, we elevate these to a position of defining the essential focus of the ceremonies. In fact, to emphasize once again what we have noted before, Aborigines' references to expressions of birth from women's bodies serve more to take power *away* from biological birth than actually to celebrate it.

To put the matter summarily, the making of young men seems to strip boys of their self-developed status since their actual birth, and to give them a new birth which is regulated and symbolically realized in secret by men. While men control the process, however, it should not therefore be interpreted merely as a case of men taking over women's power and women's birth-giving abilities. This is to miss the point. What is being asserted is *not* that youths are born to men but rather that they are born from Ancestral powers residing in land. Once again, it is a matter of removing authority from the temporal body and locating it instead in Abiding places. This, as

Berndt says, is a true focus on the fundamental basis of life rather than simply a death and rebirth.

It has been argued, without overly extending the truth, that Aboriginal initiations might be compared with the Platonic notion of anamnesis – not an instillation of a new identity but rather a bringing to consciousness of an unrealized part of one's essential self. Insofar as the neophytes *are* the Ancestors and *are* the land, the focal revelations of ceremonies, embodied in designs and song, in dance and story, are a means of opening boys to an awareness of their eternal being. At one level they 'die' and are 'reborn', but at another what is being celebrated knows no death and is antithetical to the notion that life can be born from human bodies. Like Aboriginal notions of coming into being, those of initiation rest on a vision of existence which has no room for any authority save that of land.

FROM LIFE TO DEATH

If, as we have maintained, Aboriginal people defined life, human and other, exclusively as a transformation of the Ancestral powers within lands, then it might be asked: to what extent do they consider death to be undesirable?

The answer, it would seem, depends upon the details of the death. Certainly, it is incontestable that Aboriginal people believe that each life should be full and culminate in the prestige of old age, and yet, inevitably, many people die untimely deaths. This, by Aboriginal standards, while a feature of existence, should not be considered as one of its essential qualities. It need not be – it is not part of life's plan – and results only from wrongful behaviour and malicious intent. Each serious sickness or death thus leads to investigation and accusations of sorcery. In the days or weeks following an 'unnatural' death a formal 'inquest' is held; through various means, the deceased communicates to the 'coroners' which individual or group was responsible for the sorcery, and revenge is extracted. The significant feature of these elaborate procedures is that they clearly imply the death resulted from human intent and therefore need not have been 'natural'.

Insofar as serious illness, like early death, is not a fundamental part of the Ancestral life-order, healing is not an occasion for major religious celebration. Certainly, the 'clever-men' who often perform curative acts have especially close associations with certain Ancestral Beings – indeed, they have often been killed by them and then been remade with new vital organs of extraordinary power – but they are rather personal specialists, who are not essential to religious life. There are areas in Aboriginal Australia which either permanently or temporarily lack such people, but this does not unduly disturb the ongoing sacred order of those regions. Sorcery and healing are indeed conspicuous aspects of Aboriginal life, and they do draw on Ancestral powers, but they are not *requisites* of the world and they need not and, from an Aboriginal vantage, ideally should not be.

What, however, of death at the end of a full life? There is some significant discord in the literature, but on the whole it seems Aboriginal people do not resist the finality of death, nor do they have regrets that, for instance, except for some Ancestral mistake life might have been otherwise. On the contrary, death is for the most part simply accepted as the culminative conclusion to the process of life and is marked and commemorated by appropriate, socially encompassing and extensive ceremonial procedures.

The fate of the spirit is a prime concern of mortuary ritual. This, as we will see in chapter 2, is a matter readily transformed when outsiders intrude into Aboriginal domains, but a widespread underlying and seemingly once universal understanding is that the spirit should return to the place from which it emerged – to restore the powers of a site. In a sense, and from an Ancestral perspective, it is but a case of a life-essence returning to its rightful abode. Much of the mortuary ceremony is therefore taken up with singing a spirit to its place. Insofar as it is invariable that the spirit's powers return unchanged to the land, there is no retribution for life's actions, no rewards or punishments for past deeds and, in fact, little room at all for any features of individual personalities to endure.

For the living, of course, there are grief, mourning and even bodily ordeals to express one's loss. The rites of separation, furthermore, are extensive, frequently entailing stages (which might involve platform exposures of the corpse, desiccation, burial, cremation, ochreing skeletons and so on) spread out over several years. None deny that death causes a major disruption to life, but because life is understood as a temporary billowing, in human form, of the powers of land, death cannot be resented for returning a spirit to its place of origin.

The exceptions to this rule are not spectacular and belong mainly to coastal areas of northern and eastern Australia – areas where alien contacts have a substantial history. In these areas there are mythical references to a longing for eternal life. What is significant about these cases is that they emerge in association with symbols which focus on women and bodily birth rather than sites and birth from land. Here, then, is again that tension between principles of existence that was noted in our discussion of conception, the respective religiosity of men and women and the making of young men. The All-Mother traditions of central-northern Australia attribute death to the Mothers. It was Stanner who first emphasized this point, when he detailed how the Murinbata felt that, had not Mutinga swallowed several children, who were subsequently freed by cutting open her womb (not her stomach), life would not have been flawed by the presence of death. The Mothers' menstrual and birth blood led to the instigation of death. 'If they had not menstruated in . . . [the python's waterhole] this would not have happened. Everyone would have stayed single.'[15] It is significant that copulation is seen as significant to birth-giving in this area, and inversely birth from women's bodies, like birth from the Wawalak, introduces death.

The Ancestor who is most often portrayed as wishing to escape death is Moon. Among the Yolngu, Moon announces to Dugong, his sister, that he refuses to die:

> 'I'm not going to die like other people,' the Moon answers. 'Why then do you want to do that?' asked the Dugong. 'I want to die and come back alive again,' he told her. 'All right, but when I die, I won't come back . . .' 'Well, I'm different,' the Moon said, 'When I die, I'm coming back.'[16]

In Cape York Peninsula we find a similar story. Here the Koko-Yalunyu Moon, although killed, keeps on springing back to life saying, 'I'm not dead.' What has most importantly been observed here, as in Arnhem Land, is that moon myths are very closely linked to women's bodies and also to an increased emphasis on physiological paternity and maternity. The anthropologist Ursula McConnel was quite convinced the Koko-Yalunyu myth reflected a correspondence between women's periods and the moon's phases. (At least one other researcher into Aboriginal myths has noted that menstruation can become phase-locked to lunar cycles.) In Cape York the moon is believed to control women's menstrual and child-bearing functions; to the north, in the Torres Strait, Moon actually deflowers girls to cause their first menstruation. In the south-east the link between Moon and women is equally clear. The Yuahli see the moon as a patron of women, while, as one Gambayngirr man said, 'It's the moon that works the women . . . so if there's no moon, they'll all be dead.'[17]

There are two noteworthy things in these notions of the moon. The first is that in refusing to die he is shown to be aberrant. This is evident in the Yolngu case where his sister, Dugong, like other Ancestors, seems rather unimpressed by the rebellion. Moon is not a saviour (although in recent times moon stories have tended to be conflated with stories of Christ's resurrection) but a restless being refusing to accept what he ought to. Such myths do not promise life everlasting but rather warn of the aberrant and harmful quality of such cravings. Death should be final for individuals.

The second point that seems to emerge is that it is overemphasis on the body which leads to a longing for freedom from death. But the dominant Aboriginal understanding is that ultimately we are not humans born of other humans, we are beings derived from land. Our fathers, and even more surprisingly our mothers, do not bring us into being. In initiation that first birth is both symbolically appropriated and reversed by men to reveal the land's true land-self. And again, finally, upon death, despite some nostalgia in a few regions, the Aboriginal belief that spirits must return to become once more a fragment of the power of their country is a dominant theme which leaves no room for the eternal life of the embodied self or the individual personality.

We have come to the end of our exposition of the basic principles of Aboriginal religion and in the next chapter we will go on to consider how various forms of outsider intrusion into Aboriginal lands gave rise to cults which made important ritual and mythic changes to this fundamental plan of life. Before we discuss these, however, and to conclude this chapter, we will look briefly at the Melanesian (or possibly Polynesian) influences on Aboriginal traditions at the northern tip of the Australian continent. Here, while there was religious innovation there was no real territorial infringement, and above all the cults of this region serve to underscore the differences between Aboriginal and Pacific islander worldviews. The final section of this chapter, therefore, forms a bridge between Aboriginal traditions and the traditions from elsewhere in Oceania, which we outline in chapter 4.

THE AUSTRALIAN/PACIFIC ISLAND DIVIDE

There is considerable uncertainty as to exactly who the Aborigines' northern neighbours originally were and how long they had been there. The Torres Strait islanders, it has long been assumed, were people who took refuge on high lands which became islands as the land-bridge between Australia and New Guinea was submerged about 6,000 years ago. For this there is no evidence, however, and except for Sabai, just off the Papuan coast, no archaeological evidence has been found of human occupation of the islands exceeding 1,000 BP. Indeed, the islanders' own traditions seem to suggest they arrived only about two centuries ago, and some scholars feel genealogical data supports this date. Nonetheless, the first Western historical records from the *Rijder*, captained by Gonzal in 1756, reveals that the island of Muralag was then populated.

The derivation of the Torres Strait islanders is equally uncertain. The assumption has been that they were Melanesians, but their own stories of their immigrations possibly point to an original home in Polynesia. Be this as it may, in historic times they certainly shared a predominantly Melanesian culture and cosmology.

Despite these uncertainties, it is at least clear that the Aborigines at the tip of Cape York were in contact with a people very different from themselves long before any ethnographic records were made of their way of life or worldview. It is also clear that Aborigines and islanders avoided allowing their traditions to fuse. While earlier scholars suggested, for instance, that Australia was simply unsuitable for agricultural pursuits, it is now clear Aborigines could have cultivated certain vegetable species in Cape York and that, through islanders, they had the knowledge of how this might be achieved. And yet, even though their myths tell of how islander agricultural ways were originally derived from Australia, they themselves did not follow this way of life.

This was not merely an economic decision. In both Australian and Pacific island cultures subsistence is an integral part of a broader cosmic Law. It should be recalled that Aboriginal people generally insisted that all life emerged purely from the Ancestral power of sites. Humans, even parents, contributed nothing to this except insofar as they too were life emanations from a land and could thus help ritually to release the powers of fertility from their spiritual home. They could not, however, achieve anything not already established through land-ties.

In agriculturalist communities, in contrast, including those of Melanesia, Micronesia and Polynesia, people worked the land in a way in which they achieved some human ascendancy over place. The Torres Strait islander use of agricultural rituals employing symbols of sexual procreation indicated a shift from ceremonies focusing on place to ones which recognized the power of the individual human body; procreation in the islands (and even to an above-average extent in Cape York) was attributed to biological processes rather than land-essences.

One of the intriguing features of the Torres Strait islands is that we can actually observe a continuum extending from Australian land–spirit traditions to those recognizing the autonomy of human endeavours over land. In the western, and culturally most Aboriginal of the islands, land was largely (but not quite exclusively) inherited in terms of an eternal spiritual link with estates. This was also true for *coastal* areas in the eastern islands, but inland, where gardens were cultivated, rights to land were determined by those who worked them; these lands could in principle be passed on to whomever one wished. In other words, it seems agriculture allows for an individual's dominion over land and a weakening of eternal land–people links. With this there emerges in Pacific island traditions something we have seen to be alien to Aboriginal Australia – boundary disputes.

The implications of allowing the absolute equation of people with sites to be relaxed is indeed far-reaching. For if there is not an eternally fixed spirit association between a defined group and their place, why is it not possible to appropriate their land and/or their spirit-power? The Pacific islander response is that it is indeed possible. The clearest expression of this is the fact that although there is ritual cannibalism in Australia where specified kin consume parts of the corpse, in other Oceanic cultures cannibalism, especially headhunting, allowed people to consume the power and essence of their *enemies*. While Westerners have invariably squirmed at the very idea of eating human flesh, in cultures where this is taken for granted the real matter of etiquette is not whether or not one is eaten, but by whom one is consumed! The resolution of this issue will determine whether your power is to return to your own group and land or will be appropriated by others.

That the understanding of the spiritual relationship between people and land is transformed beyond the northern tip of Australia as we enter the Torres Strait islands is apparent in myths from this region. In Cape York, there are the so-called Hero cult traditions which are not found in other Aboriginal cultures but which are shared to some extent with islander and Papuan peoples. Yet while telling myths that are specifically stated to be the same as those of northerners – the Aborigine Dick Luff of Mapoon said, 'Shiveri . . . that's our lingo; the Islanders call him Kuiam'[18] – Aborigines nonetheless introduce changes which radically alter the significance of the beliefs.

The two main Heroes of Cape York are Shiveri and Iwai, who are associated with the western and eastern parts of Cape York respectively. While their stories do not at all overlap, they have very similar structures. The Heroes emerge from their land as great ceremonial singers and innovators of ritual. They establish some Melanesian cultural objects (e.g. drums, bows and arrows, double-outrigger canoes or cultivated foods) and then, due to a sexual infringement, are forced to flee the mainland. As they travel they give shape and meaning to the islands until they reach their new homes, which are almost exactly halfway to New Guinea (Mabuiag in the west and Mer in the east).

These myths, in their full form, are clearly concerned with the power of ritual song (which for Aborigines provides a manifestation of a person's link to their Abiding place) to regulate associations with outsiders, through the Heroes' expansion of the known world. In the islander versions of the story of Shiveri, however, the Hero Kuiam is not a singer who puts sacred power into land but a head-hunter who, to 'payback' his own murder of his mother, goes on a rampage throughout the islands, massacring whole populations and taking their heads. Kuiam is an ambivalent figure, full of the uncanny power from his taking over of others' being, but 'wild' and a failure as a gardener. As his father was an Aborigine and as he used Aboriginal weapons, it seems the myth contains an islander image of Aborigines (a people who do not use violence in terms of islander 'rules' of headhunting and so, from their perspective, are 'wild').

There is much that is shared by both Australian and Pacific islander traditions – a concern with reciprocity and revenge, an awareness of the spirit-consciousness of all that exists, and so on – but even where they share a common cult the differences are also evident. That difference as expressed in the Hero cults might be characterized as one between the supremacy of song (in the Aboriginal sense of the world) and headhunting. In the former case what is paramount – at the expense of other ways of life and philosophies – is maintaining an absolute link between all life-forms and their sites. Fertility is land; human life is land. In such a worldview, it is problematic to recognize the autonomy of the human form; either as an entity, for instance, springing from other bodies, or as some-thing which might produce fertility in land. To some extent at least, the Aboriginal understanding of land is responsible for their 'denial' of physiological paternity and maternity, and their 'lack' of agri-culture.

Melanesian, Micronesian and Polynesian traditions, like the islan-ders' Hero, do not concede that people and other life-forms are totally and only derived from land. In their cultures the body and spirit have more autonomy from place, but this also opens the way for territorial disputes and organized warfare. Indeed, warfare and practices like headhunting can come to the fore as underlying principles of religious life in which one's own group's ongoing life, rather than drawing exclusively from land, draws off and appropriates the powers of others. This is a theme developed in more detail in chapter 4. In that chapter we also consider other factors of Pacific islander religious life which should be noted as contrasting with those of Australia: the prominence of sky gods, the hierarchical structure of cults with their chiefs and 'big-men', and the partial shift in focus of sacred places from sites to architecture in the form of temples, shrines and club houses.

NOTES AND REFERENCES

1 T. G. H. Strehlow, *Songs of Central Australia*, Sydney, 1971, pp. 706ff.
2 Untitled circulated leaflet, sighted in 1986.
3 M. Harvey, 'The Dreaming', foreword in J. Bradley, *Yanyuwa Country: the Yanyuwa People of Booroloola Tell of Their Land*, Richmond, 1988, p. xi.
4 W. B. Spencer and F. J. Gillen, *The Native Tribes of Central Australia*, New York, 1968 [1899], pp. 184–5.
5 W. L. Warner, *A Black Civilization: a Social Study of an Australian Tribe*, New York, 1958, pp. 23–4.
6 We await important work from Pattel-Gray, Djungadjunga Yunupingu and others, however, to show that this pattern did always apply, and that there are also female elements of belongingness requiring further investigation.
7 A. Hamilton, quoted by L. R. Hiatt, 'Secret Pseudo-Procreation Rites among the Australian Aborigines', in L. R. Hiatt and C. Jayawardena (eds), *Anthropology in Oceania: Essays Presented to Ian Hogbin*, Sydney, 1971, p. 88, n. 18.
8 D. Bell, 'Aboriginal Women and the Religious Experience', in W. H. Edwards (ed.), *Traditional Aboriginal Society: a Reader*, Melbourne, 1987, pp. 240–2.
9 J. G. Goodale, 'Tiwi World Views and Values', in M. Charlesworth *et al.* (eds), *Religion in Aboriginal Australia: an Anthology*, Brisbane, 1984, p. 379.
10 P. Kaberry, *Aboriginal Woman: Sacred and Profane*, London, 1939, pp. 262–3.
11 R. M. and C. H. Berndt, *The World of the First Australians*, Sydney, 1977, pp. 269–70.
12 Bell, 'Aboriginal Women', p. 243.
13 M. Flinders, *A Voyage to Terra Australia . . .* , London, 1814, vol. 2, p. 212.
14 R. M. Berndt, *Australian Aboriginal Religion*, Leiden, 1974, Fascicle 2, p. 11.

15 Warner, *A Black Civilization*, p. 297.
16 R. M. Berndt, 'A "Wonguri-' Manjika Song Cycle of the Moon-Bone', *Oceania* 19 (1948): 16–50, esp. p. 20.
17 H. Buchanan, typescript of interview at Nambucca Heads, original source unknown.
18 W. Laade, 'Further Material on Kuiam, Legendary Hero of Mabuiag, Torres Strait Islands', *Ethos* 1–4 (1967): 70–96, esp. p. 71.

2 Cults of intrusion

Having offered an overview of traditional religious life in Australia in the preceding chapter, it is now necessary to begin to consider the religious innovations that developed in response to invasion and to colonial life. If we are honest, we must admit that there are very few accounts of communities that were written before Western society had played havoc with 'tradition' – although, until recently, most ethnographers downplayed, even ignored altogether, the colonial realities of their research environment.

The colonial experience in Australia has differed from elsewhere in Oceania. In contrast to those in the Pacific islands, Aboriginal notions of spirit and land did not sit comfortably with many forms of employment and enterprise. Aborigines were able and fast-learning workers, but for the most part were not seen to be relied on to bring *long-term* gains into a cheap colonial labour pool. In fact, they were seldom employed until pastoral expansion began to open up northern Australia.

If the White Australian reluctance to employ or exploit Aborigines (other Oceanian peoples, especially the Kanakas, were brought in instead) is one feature distinguishing Australia from other Oceanian colonial environments, the Aboriginal response to the motivation behind labour was another. Because Aborigines define themselves as place-beings, there is little room to gain prestige save by developing and learning one's spiritual identity. In contrast to Melanesia, Micronesia and Polynesia (see chapter 4), there are no Aboriginal 'big-men' who are raised above others by the giving of gifts. Commodity wealth in Australia has no traditional value, either as something one possesses or as something one gives away.

Given both the reluctance to bring Aborigines into the world of wages and labour, and the Aboriginal attitude towards 'wealth', it is hardly surprising so-called cargo cults are less marked in Australia than elsewhere in Oceania. They do exist, nonetheless, as we will see towards the end of this chapter, but on the whole we need to seek more subtle expressions of religious transformation in Australia than scholars are accustomed to investigating.

From an Aboriginal perspective, the history of intrusion in Australia begins before the First Fleet arrived in 1788. As it eventuated, their lands were not invaded before that date, but in the north of Australia the Indonesian presence at least posed the threat that this might occur, and the cults which developed in response clearly focus on the matter of legitimate rights to land. We begin this chapter, therefore, in the coastal areas of central-northern Australia.

THE MACASSANS

In 1803, when Sir Matthew Flinders was off the coast of Arnhem Land, he was surprised by evidence that there were almost as many 'Malay Mahometans' in the area as Aborigines. Their 'chief', named Pobassoo, informed him they came in their praus to collect trepang (*bêche de mer*) and had been doing so for only about twenty years.

This account needs clarification. First, these 'Malays' were mainly from Sulawesi (Celebes), and while more recently referred to as 'Macassans', which they predominantly were, the ships were also sailed by Bugis and Toraja from Sulawesi, and even by other Indonesian peoples. Second, although Macassar had by then been an Islamic kingdom for over a century, the seamen – traders in gin and drinkers of port – seemed to hold to traditional Indonesian beliefs and practices as much as, if not more than, Islam. Third, while Pobassoo's claim that the industry had begun only twenty years earlier may be true for his wave of expeditions, there is historical evidence from Sulawesi that the voyages were being undertaken at the beginning of the eighteenth century, while archaeologists suspect (but cannot at all prove) that the journeys may have begun many centuries earlier.

The relationship between Aborigines and the Macassans was well regulated and yet ambiguous. Certainly, Aboriginal people today recall the annual Macassan visitors fondly, stating that (in comparison with White Australians generally) they were their friends to whom they allocated classificatory kinship status and with whom they traded – iron tools, cloth, alcohol, pipes, tobacco and rice in exchange for tortoise shells, pearls, pearl shell and, temporarily, women. At the same time, however, conflict and violence were involved in these associations; they were directed towards ensuring the trade-based reciprocal relationships were equitably upheld. In particular, it seems that violence erupted in what Aborigines would have seen as Macassan failure to reciprocate by not offering goods or by having sexual relations with Aboriginal women without proper consent and due exchange.

While at times violent, relationships with Macassans, mediated through trade, were on the whole workable and 'moral'. Indeed, the elaborate forms of ceremonial exchange evident in central-northern Australia certainly seems to have emerged in the wake of the Indonesian contacts – the northern sector of the Yolngu exchange cycle, for instance, being expressed by a generic term for all goods obtained from Macassans. Trade, especially in ritual form, gave it a certain cosmological and morally sanctioned significance. The problem, however, was that the new relationship, unlike those within the Aboriginal world, lacked a foundation in known *places*. Aboriginal exchanges, including marriage, were, at least at one level, a means of interrelating people who were manifestations of lands. This could not be so with Macassans, and in fact reciprocal marriage of any kind was impossible – as Indonesian women did not travel on board the praus.

Insofar as Indonesians were not a part of the Australian land-spirit, and, further (unlike Melanesian/Aboriginal contacts), their own homes were distant and largely unknown lands, their presence, while not an invasion *per se*, at least raised the threat of invasion. Here were a new people, travelling at will throughout central-northern Australia and seemingly oblivious to Aboriginal notions of rights to land. What, this appears to ask, gives one legitimate associations with a place? Is it an eternal spiritual link? Or is it simply the desire and power to be there? Indonesians were not trying to take Aboriginal lands, but in myth and song we can see Aborigines were concerned that the logic of their arrival contained the principles of invasiveness.

There are in central-northern Australia many myths dealing with the problem of the Macassans. Most of them have a common underlying structure, in which the separateness of the two ethnic groups was initially non-existent but then a physical racial difference emerges and the two peoples are allocated their respective cultural items and lands. The stories stress that the two groups are fundamentally different yet also related. Nonetheless they warn that, no matter how friendly, they can never be one and Indonesians cannot belong in, or have a right to, Aboriginal places. In the following myth,

Barwal the dingo-man rejects all offers from the undeniably friendly Macassan, Yoortjing, to join together as 'one company':

> Yoortjing asked: 'Do you want to come inside my house?' 'No,' answered Barwal. 'We are going to sleep in the grass.' 'But there is a big rain coming on,' said Yoortjing. 'No matter,' said Barwal. 'You see that rock and that ant-bed? That is where I and my wife will sleep. This is my country. It is better that you go back to your country. You see that fire a long way off in the country Yoormanga? That is your country. It is better that you load up your Miteetjang, your boat, with all your things. Pull down this house and take everything back along your country.'
>
> Yoortjing talked: 'You are angry with me, Barwal. I will give you blankets and tucker. Are you still angry?' 'Yes, I am still angry,' said Barwal. Then Yoortjing said: 'Look, Barwal, you and I can sit down as one company. We can be one company.' 'No,' answered Barwal, 'this is my country. It is better that you go back to your own country. You and I are different colours.'[1]

The concern of the story is clear enough. Macassans, no matter how friendly, no matter how generous their gifts, cannot belong to the same land. At one level the reason is because their skin is of another colour, but the difference surely goes deeper to a diverging way of relating to the world.

Other traditions dealing with outsiders help us refine our interpretation. It is possibly true that the Timorese were in association with Kimberley Aborigines for some time, and among other things helped inspire the Wandjina beliefs and iconography of that region. Coastal Aborigines in the north-west locate their land of the dead across the western sea, and Timor is the closest land in that direction, but the truth is we lack any historical data which would provide solid evidence on such matters.

In Arnhem Land, there is also another group of strangers, the Baijini, who were said to precede the Macassans, but, again, Western history and prehistory can discover nothing of them. We are here better off, however, than in the case of the Timorese, as the Yolngu at least have their own stories about these people. They were light-skinned, built stone houses in Arnhem Land, brought their families and established a rice-based agriculture, but like Macassans were primarily there for the trepang (since the Macassan trepang was for Chinese markets, and since there is some, admittedly imperfect, evidence of a Chinese presence in central-northern Australia, some have entertained the notion that these Baijini were Chinese). In the

All-Mother songs, the Baijini are said to have been in Australia even before these Ancestors. As the Mothers and their brother come to the mainland they say:

> Listen is that the sound of the Baijini talking?
> Are those their words that drift from the roofs of their huts, from the young Baijini playing?
> Yes! That is the shine of their light skin! They are standing about, and working the trepang . . .
> What can we do, how can we make them move?
> We, waridji, shall quietly chase them away, they can't stop there! . . .
> We ourselves are making the country, putting a sandhill there, putting our footprints.
> We hear the roar of the sea, and the spray wets us. Waridj Djanggawul, we are putting our footprints here . . .
> This is for us, waridj, this trepang ladle left by the Baijini . . .
> Ourselves we are putting the country, hiding the ladle beneath our arm.
> It is sacred![2]

This is a revealing song. It states clearly that these people cannot stay where they are, *not* because they are not well established or lack priority of occupation, but because the Mothers made the land *sacred*. They were putting spiritual essence into the land, and this was the more fundamental principle of land-association.

In all the central-northern reflections upon outsiders there appears to be an underlying concern with the arrival of people lacking spiritual links to land and an assertion that while these trepangers might travel the land (and pose the possibility of invasion), the only true right to a country is to share its spiritual essence.

Given this predicament, we might anticipate that central-northern Aborigines would attempt to relate at a deeper level with Indonesians and to seek some means of moral regulation of association which went beyond the merely economic side of trade networks. This expectation is fulfilled. As we have seen in the song extract, even the Ancestors took something of the Baijini to make it a sacred emblem. Now the Mothers belonged to the *dhuwa* moiety while the Baijini were *yiritja*, and this offers a clue to some intriguing religious innovations in Arnhem Land.

It is well recognized that of the two moieties (which classify all existence, not just the social order, into a binary system), the *yiritja* traditions are preoccupied with outsiders. Their great song-cycle trilogy focuses on the Baijini, the Macassans and the people of Badu (an island in the Torres Strait to which Arnhem Land Aborigines travelled on Macassan ships), although more recently Europeans and Japanese have been added to this repertoire. Furthermore, even sacred objects marking the link between people and land are frequently of Indonesian provenance, not only in conspicuous cases of gin-bottle *rangga* or funerary posts said to represent Dutch custom officials in Macassar, but arguably in the entire spectrum of Arnhem Land sculpture – which is quite unique in Australia and bears clear similarities to Indonesian styles. Be this as it may, the fact is that including outsiders in symbolic association with the entire *yiritja* moiety means that each marriage between the exogamous moieties brings aliens into a symbolically spiritual and quasi-land-based alliance.

The Arnhem Land innovations go further than this, however, for they actually establish spirit links between Australia and outside lands. As we argued in chapter 1, in Aboriginal thought generally, the deceased's spirit must return to the site from which it emanated. This holds also for the central-north where the *birrimbirr* returns to its waterhole. Yet, paradoxically, the same spirit, the *birrimbirr*, also travels to a Land of the Dead, and in the *yiritja* case this is Badu (or, sometimes, Suluwesi itself), a land these Aborigines only learned of through Macassans. Were this not clear enough, the ceremony to usher the deceased to Badu is one modelled on the raising of masts on praus. The chants are in pidgin Macassan and a Macassan 'prayer' is recited for a safe voyage.

Thus, in the final analysis, and despite the *threat* of invasion, the central-northern Aborigines extended the reciprocity of trade to a reciprocity of spirit which linked their lands to a virtually unknown land and its alien people. This is not the end of this story, however, for the most conspicuous feature of Indonesian influence has yet to be considered: the cult of the All-Mother.

THE ALL-MOTHER CULT

While the Indonesians' presence created religious innovations directed towards containing the association with outsiders, they also brought another problem – how would Aborigines in central-northern Australia relate to one another? According to G. E. Earl, an eye-witness in the first half of the nineteenth century, northern Australia was not only a place with visitors representing at least half a dozen Indonesian regions, but there were also Aborigines from a dozen different language groups. Some of these Aborigines sailed to Macassar each season and a few even became Muslims, but, more importantly, they were generally proficient in the Macassan language used throughout coastal parts of the Northern Territory. Some scholars consider the widespread Yolngu language itself to be a post-Macassan phenomenon. The effect of this *lingua franca* was to bring Aboriginal communities together and partly to dissolve smaller communities into a wider socio-political body.

It was in the context of this new sense of pan-Aboriginality that we observe one of only two classes of truly transcendent beings in Aboriginal Australia – the All-Mother. By 'transcendent' it is meant that, unlike other Ancestors who stand in a specific relationship, mediated by land, with specified individuals, the Mothers are Beings said to stand in a single relationship with all Aboriginal people in the area. In fact, according to the testimony of Gunwinggu women, the matter goes further than that, for they say: 'She is our mother. All of us everywhere, dark skin or light skin, people of every place and of different languages . . . We all call her mother, our true mother.'[3]

The Mother has different manifestations throughout the area, but a common theme is her transcendence as the Mother of All. The Djanggawul sisters of eastern Arnhem Land, for instance, arrive by sea with their conical uteri mats and phallic sacred poles and, following an incestuous relationship with their brother, they travel creating the waterholes containing spirit-essences and bringing out the first children from their wombs. In western Arnhem Land, Waramurang-gundji fulfils a similar role and after she copulates with her husband she gives birth to all people of the region so that, no matter what their relationship to one another, they all call her 'Mother' (or 'mother's mother'). In the Roper River region the Mother is Kadjeri, and at the places where she stops to camp she brings forth children from her womb.

The All-Mothers are *not*, as some have overhastily suggested, considered to be Earth Mothers, but, unlike the only other class of transcendental Being in Australia, the All-Fathers of the south-east (see below), neither are they divorced from the earth. Like most Aboriginal Ancestral Beings, they end their sojourns by transforming into particular sites and their travels are always related to the land. This geographical immanence tempers the Mothers' social transcendence, but nonetheless the powers they have focused upon themselves are considerable. For instance, the cosmic balance and initiatory rites for the area are tied to each Mother's traditions.

They are certainly Mothers ensuring the fertility of the world generally, and in the making of young men the ceremonial ground is the
Mother's womb from which the neophytes are ritually born.

The broad compass of the Mother's domain, and her position as
the single Being who gives rise to all life and to whom all people
relate in an undifferentiated manner, clearly provide a sense of
cosmic unity capable of stepping beyond the localized traditions
typically found elsewhere in Australia. It seems reasonable to
enquire whether this pan-Aboriginal development can be shown
to have emerged in consequence to the sense of unity which
developed as a result of association with Indonesians.

There has been, in fact, a long-standing anthropological suspicion
that the All-Mother cults were derived from Macassans. Arthur
Capell, A. P. Elkin and Ronald Berndt, among others, have entertained this thesis without actually investigating it. Their position is
that insofar as these cults are found in this area alone, and as they
clearly seem to have been superimposed upon the 'normal' form of
Aboriginal religious life, it is reasonable to suspect some external
influence. Their main appeal, however, was to the fact that the
Mother's stories themselves say she came from a northern land
across the Timor and Arafura seas to Australia.

The Djanggawul song-cycle begins:

> Although I leave Bralgu, I am close to it.
> I, Djanggawul, am paddling,
> Paddling with all the paddles, with their flattened tapered
>   ends.
> Close I am coming.[4]

Although the song-cycle begins with Bralgu (suggested to be some-
where in the Gulf of Carpentaria), which is the place of the *dhuwa*
Land of the Dead, the Beings are said to come initially from another
land even further away. As they come closer, they smell the Baijini
on the mainland, intriguingly suggesting these Ancestors arrived
after the first wave of trepangers.

Further to the west, the Gunwinggu Mother traditions are more
specific: 'She came underground from "Macassar", to Madabir, near
Cooper's Creek, bringing people inside her – people who later made
more people.'[5] Again, although less specific in its reference, the
Roper River people assert Kadjeri came from across the seas, their
songs saying enigmatically:

Tidal water flowing, white foam on the waves.
Fresh water from the rain flows into the river,
There are the paperbark trees: the soft bark falls into the
   water,
Rain falls from the clouds
Waters of the river are swirling
She emerges and walks on dry land.[6]

This is far less specific than the Gunwinggu case, but Berndt nonetheless felt it was an attractive thesis that this suggested an external
influence on the cult he was considering.

The next question to be asked would be: is there an Indonesian
cult similar to that found among Aborigines, indicating direct bor-
rowing? To this, we suspect the answer is no, for the All-Mother
cults are too neatly grafted on to more ancient beliefs and practices
for us to entertain any ideas of wholesale appropriation of foreign
ideas. As we have seen, furthermore, the logic of the All-Mother
cult fits the new Aboriginal social world too neatly to be considered
merely an import. Nevertheless there still remains the possibility
that something in Indonesian traditions supplied some religious
inspiration for Aborigines to remodel their own cosmologies, and
for this at least we have adequate evidence.

To begin with, it should be noted that one of the main things that
Aborigines associated with trepangers was rice. This was a food
which was traded and welcomed by Aborigines during monsoonal
seasons. It was also something the Baijini were said to have planted
in Australia and which is conspicuous in *yiritja* song-cycles: 'Cooking
rice in the fire: pouring it into a pot from a bag/Pouring rice from
a bag: rice, rice, for food,'[7] and so on.

Given the focal position of rice in association with Macassans and
Baijini, it is significant to observe that one of the most important
Beings in the cosmologies of southern Sulawesi is the Rice Mother
who, like the All-Mothers of Australia, is responsible for all worldly
fecundity. The cults of the Rice Mothers are conspicuous and prominent; they continued beyond the Islamic period and indeed still
flourish among the Bugis today. It seems a reasonable possibility,
therefore, that the Indonesian Rice Mothers were the inspiration
behind Aborigines fashioning their own Mother cult that, despite
similarities, was nonetheless in the final analysis a truly Aboriginal
cult that addressed their new social order and their emergent pan-
Aboriginal understanding of themselves.

Finally, it must be emphasized once more that the Mothers, while unifying much of the Aboriginal world, were not in any sense Supreme Beings. They did not, for instance, create the cosmos but rather supplied a pre-existent world with the first people and ensured ongoing fertility. Furthermore, since Aborigines do not share the same land-spirit as their mothers, although the Mother is the Mother of All this common parenthood does not negate the old order of local spiritual ties for people, as those who emerge from the Mother can nonetheless each have a different spiritual link with places. In fact, in the Mothers' wanderings, they seem themselves to ensure this plurality is not undermined as they establish localized spirit sites and take care to change languages as they go, to segregate communities. There is, then, nothing imperialist in the Mother's symbolism of unity. Rather, she allows a means of bolstering solidarity without undermining the spiritual boundaries of the world. In this sense, she perfectly mirrors the reality of the Indonesian presence which, though *threatening* lands and demanding a new sense of Aboriginal collective identity, did not unduly reshape the Aboriginal order.

What, however, might have happened with a true invasion? This of course is something we need not speculate upon, for some time after the Indonesians arrived the invasion did occur, in the southeast of the continent.

INVASION

The First Fleet arrived in Australia in 1788. Precisely what form of religious life was practised in the Sydney area, and in the south-east generally, before colonization we can never know. It was the best part of a century later that amateur ethnographers began to make a concerted effort to piece together a picture of Aboriginal cultures in this region, but by then the changes had been immense. True, as early as the 1830s missionaries and explorers had provided some early scraps of information about Aboriginal beliefs. True again, David Collins had described the public aspects of an initiation ceremony as early as 1798. But even this was too late.

Invasion had instant and devastating effects in the areas surrounding the point of contact. In the very first year after colonization an epidemic of smallpox – which was possibly deliberately released as a form of germ-warfare – wiped out two-thirds of the estimated 250,000 people in the south-east. By 1850, 96 per cent of the population was gone.

Disease alone did not take this toll, however. In the areas immediately surrounding Sydney it was a major factor, but further afield pastoral practices, using mainly convict labour, often included wholesale murder as a means of 'pacifying' the areas. Those few Aborigines who survived were forced to take refuge on the occasional benign station or, more often than not, on newly established missions. It was here that ethnographers gleaned their data.

Considering that Aboriginal religious life is inseparable from land and social life, it is unthinkable that such titanic disruptions would not have radically changed their traditions. The standard assumption was that Aboriginal people were a broken remnant and all that was left were memories of the old ways, but the argument that mere recollections of bygone eras was all that endured can no longer be entertained. Rather, it is evident that their religious life survived as a living, continuous and rapidly adapting tradition. Our enquiry, therefore, is into what changes were wrought by such a momentous impact as invasion.

It is possible to see several phases in the responses in the initial period of invasion. The first was widely reported but rarely understood. Here are the explorer E. J. Eyre's words:

> It is a general belief amongst almost all the Aborigines, that Europeans, or white people, are resuscitated natives, who have changed their colour, and who are supposed to return to the same localities they had inhabited as black people. The most puzzling point, however, with this theory, appears to be that they cannot make out how it is that the returned natives do not know their former friends and relations. I have often been asked, with seriousness and earnestness, who, among the Europeans, were their fathers, their mothers, and their other relations.[8]

This well-known phenomenon was something which delighted the colonial wits, and which even in modern scholarship is seen as a quaint instance of the inability of Aborigines to be able to 'see' things so strange to their ways. Such attitudes miss the point.

Perhaps Aborigines in the first moment of Whites landing were confused (as were Whites themselves, who reported Aborigines seemed like 'monsters'), but the deceased kinsfolk interpretation persisted well beyond such moments of initial confusion. Furthermore, it came to supplant other recorded first impressions (e.g. that they were malevolent spirits, etc.), and therefore must have appealed as a *concept* to Aborigines. For if these people were their kinsfolk it was possible to establish moral contacts with them and relate them both to their fellows and to their lands. This is something clearly present behind Eyre's words.

Inevitably, Whites failed to comprehend the moral significance of Aboriginal overtures, and even had they understood this would not have dissuaded them from their colonial need for land. Unlike Indonesian contacts, there was here no room for strangers to use land and yet simultaneously leave the Aboriginal world in order. Violence and warfare were inevitable at both the mundane and spiritual level. There are instances of ceremonies for ridding wayward ghosts being employed on the unruly 'returned kin'. As such means failed, there arose a number of anti-White rituals designed to rid the land of all the newcomers.

This was already evident in the first decade in the Sydney region. An Aboriginal woman living in a clergyman's house warned that Whites would meet great misfortune because of a portent from a falling star. A similar case was reported by Eyre, who observed a comet in 1843 and was told that it signalled the overthrow of Europeans and the destruction of their houses and town. This was to be achieved by the 'clever-men' who could control stellar activity.

There are other instances of this kind. Some were fairly open and public, re-enacting in ceremonial form the White murder of Aborigines and then a retaliation which defeated the Whites. More ominous was the calling of the serpent Mindi using a ritual in which men and women danced single-file with tufts of feathers which they used to touch engravings of the snake. Mindi, who was associated with introduced epidemic diseases, was said to be going to destroy all Whites in south-eastern Victoria; in a fine application of retributive justice, they would be exterminated by an outbreak of smallpox.

In the final event, however, both attempts to locate Whites as kin or to eradicate them failed. A new kind of human without land-spirit ties had arrived to conquer Aboriginal lands. They were an amoral people by Aboriginal standards, who, unlike Melanesians and Indonesians, were unreachable even by equitable trade exchanges. There was no relationship, only the presence of a conquistador.

In such a context, it is hardly surprising that the spirits of the lands were threatened. People were wrenched from their countries (or killed outright) and lost touch with their places. It is in response to such a situation that we can understand something quite unusual in the ethnographies of the south-east. While there is evidence of earth-based powers and cosmic balance rites in the region, these have been pushed to the background by another doctrine which does not so much complement as contradict this view. For in the south-east by the time of our ethnographic reports, Aborigines were saying that the locus of spiritual authority was *not* their lands but some unknown world beyond the clouds. It was a utopia, a heaven. It was better, they said, than this world and was full of game and water. When they died, their spirits would not, as was the case elsewhere in Australia, return to their lands but would travel to this heavenly realm – a future which some were said to anticipate with great fondness.

Insofar as there is evidence to indicate the existence of the 'normal' Aboriginal beliefs of spirits emerging from, and returning to, their lands and the release of the powers of earthly fertility, we can guess that the removal of spiritual authority to the sky world was a response to the devastation of their countries and a breaking of their bonds with their sites. Our suspicions are deepened when we turn to the most conspicuous innovation in this region, the cult of the All-Father.

THE ALL-FATHER CULT

Religious life in south-eastern Australia was dominated by the All-Father, known variously as Baiami, Daramulan, Bunjil, Brewin, Mungan-ngaur and so on. What they have common is that they are the creators (not just the fathers) of all, that they reside in the land beyond the clouds and that they have drawn all the powers of the cosmos into themselves. As R. M. Berndt has noted, 'All power, whether religious or magical, emanates from Baiami.'[9]

In earlier texts, the features of the All-Father, or High God, indicates he is truly a Supreme Being. The Reverend James Günther, who first reported the Wiradjuri belief in Baiami, said he was believed to be eternal, omnipotent and entirely benevolent. He had created the world and then left for his heavenly domain. In later times another Wiradjuri man put it intriguingly: 'He was always amongst the people long ago ... When the White people came to Australia, Baiami heard that they were coming. He then got "frightened", and cleared away.'[10]

With such statements we find ourselves asking, as scholars have done for over a century, whether the All-Father tradition only developed in the wake of invasion. Certainly, some early accounts offer some anachronistic details, with the Father's son descending so that his spirit spreads from 'Sydney to England', and the god's domain being complete with ladders, steps and thrones of pillars.

Possibly such accounts are idiosyncratic (or reveal the weakness of early ethnography), but in the context of the spectrum of information we have they are certainly not beyond credibility.

The debate over Christian influence on All-Father beliefs is long and tedious. Those who maintained the doctrine was indigenous (and in doing so tried to nurture their own Eurocentric faith that the notion of a Supreme Being was somehow a fundamental creed) tried to prove it was present prior to the arrival of missionaries. This was not the case, however. The All-Father cult was first reported by Archdeacon Günther at the Wellington Valley mission, in the mid-northern highlands of New South Wales, and he said the inmates had themselves only just learned the ceremonies from other Aborigines who were spreading the cult. It seems quite possible, therefore, that this was a new and rapidly disseminated religious movement that covered the whole region where the early invasion spread.

If we venture back into the archaeological records, we cannot be certain whether there are specific icons of an All-Father. A few scholars have believed they have uncovered such figures, but, intriguingly, these are not at all ancient, as we can tell by their association with representations of sailing ships or even by the presence of horns on the 'All-Father' figure (there are, it should be noted, no indigenous horned animals in Australia).

Returning to the ethnographic records, there are enough passing references to the effect that Aboriginal people had admitted their views were partly derived from Whites, or alternatively descriptions with give-away details, to make us consider seriously the likelihood that the All-Father's was a new, post-invasion, religious movement. Even Alfred Howitt, a staunch defender of the position that the beliefs were ancient, was told by his main informants that their High God Brewin was none other than Jesus Christ – a doctrine Howitt received by instantly demanding they reconsider their views. In later years, as the debate stormed, he happily let this evidence, along with his recording of the view that the All-Father had a herd of cattle, slip his mind!

The evidence for religious innovation is not only that the High God's aloof dwelling beyond the clouds is totally at odds with Aboriginal opinion elsewhere in the continent. It also involves an entire spectrum of features which in concert add up to a coherent picture of a total reworking of south-eastern cosmologies emerging as people were forced from their lands and entire communities were decimated. In particular, the notions of evil and that the world would soon end, are quite remarkable by Aboriginal standards.

From our discussion in chapter 1, it is evident that elsewhere in Aboriginal Australia, 'evil' is absent as a religious concept. Certainly, things are said to be wrong or bad, and both humans and Ancestors perform immoral acts. To be 'evil', however, is to be intrinsically unLawful and incapable of redemption, leaving open only the option of purging the world of the evil being's existence. Traditional beliefs, in contrast, stress a perpetual maintenance of all that exists, with spirits emerging from the land and, whether good or bad in life, returning to the place from which they emanated.

By contrast, in the south-east it is evident that the cosmos had admitted evil, although it is not always clear exactly where this resides. In some accounts, it is an adversary of the all-good High God who is the source of evil. He is in some versions the God's brother, who causes wild and devastating events, such as smallpox epidemics, for trivial reasons. In other instances, the All-Father himself seems to take on this unprovoked fury – a contradiction not so foreign to Western minds once we recall that Aborigines were often told, even by the most sympathetic missionaries, that their peoples' death was 'the will of God'.

The most substantial indicator that 'evil' has emerged as a cosmic notion is seen in attitudes towards after-life and eschatology. It is again an aberration for this region alone that we read of the spirits of the dead not only travelling to a heaven, but being tested and, if failing, destroyed. Rewards and punishments, let alone eternal damnation, are entirely at odds with the understanding that land-spirits must always retain their identity as an emanation from a site imbued with an Ancestral essence. With spirits departing for the sky and being tested and perhaps destroyed, we witness a total inversion of the notion that spiritual authority forever resides in countries.

Such cosmic instability, one might suggest, seems almost to herald the collapse of the world-order, and it is thus not surprising to discover that, while it has been an anthropological truism that Aborigines do not entertain eschatological ideas, in the south-east there was indeed a threat of a world-end.

South-eastern eschatological beliefs were widely reported, and in some respects have an uncanny parallel with those from the Kimberley Kuranggara traditions on the opposite side of the continent (see below). In one account, it was reported that Aborigines had been stealing European axes, saws, ropes and dray wheels which were being passed from community to community. Their ultimate destiny was the 'old man' (the High God?) dwelling in a distant place to the west. The European goods were needed literally to hold the cosmos together, for the poles holding the sky above were collapsing and if not propped up the heavens would fall, causing disastrous flooding.

In Kamilaroi stories of this era the old man at the world's end is Baiaimi himself, even though he is also a Sky God (in both cases his home is beyond known sites, which is the important factor). It was said Baiami and his brother had a rift when the latter prophesied the end of the Aboriginal world. Again, in other accounts Baiami is said to be sleeping, but when he awakens a flood – akin to that in the preceding story – would wipe out the current order of existence.

Considering these scattered references to an imminent eschaton, we would expect to be able to discover some major cultic manifestation to ward off such a disastrous end. The cult anticipated in fact seems to be a reformed version of the initiatory ceremonies for the region, usually referred to in the literature as Bora. Thus, the Yualyai clever-men, who were said (again, atypically) to have visions of the future, saw that their people would grow paler and 'White devils' would ultimately be all that remained. At this point, Baiami would stir, bringing the end. The only way to defuse this situation, they said, was to hold fast to their Law and, in particular, to perform their Bora rites diligently.

Unfortunately, we will never be able to uncover the full significance of the transformed versions of the Bora cults. While we have numerous accounts describing their ritual grounds, designs and bodily movements, we have virtually no details explaining the significance or meaning of these. This was simply beyond the ethnographic agendas of the period. We do know that the ceremonies were controlled by clever-men, were said to mediate between the earth and the All-Fathers' sky domain, and that the ritual grounds were said to represent the High God's camp on earth when he created existence.

Given these bare facts, a little detective work pays some dividends. In the only existing photographs of Bora, introduced species such as pigs and cattle represented in the sand sculptures are being ritually speared; the place of cattle in these cults is mentioned in several accounts. Cattle, of course, were the *raison d'être* for the colonial presence in most of south-east Australia.

Our fullest descriptions of the ceremonial grounds are provided by the trained surveyor, R. H. Mathews. His more detailed articles are fascinating. Represented on the All-Father's ground were bullocks, horses, parts of a horse-drawn vehicle, Aborigines clad and wearing 'king plates' and even Whites. Here is one of his more telling accounts:

> The imitative faculties of the natives were displayed in a few drawings, copied from scenes in the life of the white men, which were intermixed with the others. At one place an attempt had been made to represent a railway train, the carriages with their windows, the numerous wheels, and the two rails on which they were running. At another place a native artist had drawn a chain like those used when working bullocks in a dray. The links of the chain were on a colossal scale, being four feet nine inches long, and one foot three inches wide. The chain was close to the raised figure of the bullock previously described. Another draftsman, apparently a poker player, had succeeded in representing the four aces. Four rectangular spaces, about two feet long and eighteen inches wide, were first made side by side to indicate four cards, and on the middle of each of them one of the aces was delineated.[11]

In summary, we can conclude that the All-Father traditions were of recent derivation and were in the process of being disseminated at the time of our earliest accounts. They were, furthermore, a complex of beliefs and practices radically different from those discussed in the first chapter of this book, which, instead of drawing on the Abiding powers of land, focused on a distant spiritual force in an unknown world and on the future as a time which would bring either the millennium or a disastrous end. When we observe European doctrines and cultural items associated with the All-Father it comes as no surprise, for the logic of the cult really reflects the effects of invasion and the life of people who have been wrenched from their spirit-places. In such contexts, religious authority would of necessity be removed from their sites, while the emphasis on the future was the promise or threat of a cosmos which had lost its enduring balance.

In the south-east in later periods, land-powers to some extent did become re-established, but that is a story centuries away. We must now follow the history of invasion's changing face as it swept to the north and into remote pastoral regions.

MULUNGA AND THE MILLENNIUM

While there were some recorded expectations of the destruction of all Whites in the south-east, the most widespread millennial movement was in fact never observed in that area. Rather, it swept all around it, beginning in central-northern Queensland before it was transmitted westwards, then southwards, until we lose sight of it just as it was about to reach the opposite side of the continent. The name of the cult was the Mulunga.

Mulunga, all our sources agree, was a new ceremonial complex which had immense appeal and was diffused with great speed. Yet, for the most part, descriptions of this movement are totally silent as to what its meaning was. It is informative to trace it through the ethnographic records.

Mulunga is first reported by Walter Roth, who saw it performed in 1883 and 1886. He says that in Queensland there are many new ceremonies which have been discovered by the clever-men, including some representing Aborigines spearing cattle and subsequently being tracked and killed by Whites. It is the Mulunga, however, which had truly captivated the people of the area. They said it began with the Woagaia people on the Georgina headwaters, and was then transmitted to the communities near present-day Camooweal and Lake Nash until it reached Carandotta, where Roth saw it in 1883. It was then still on the move, spreading simultaneously to the south, west and east.

Roth describes the ceremony in great detail but is at a loss as to how to interpret what it represents. It seems to him to deal with a 'devil' who can only be seen by the clever-men. The vengeful Mulunga is skilled at covering his tracks from enemies and in areas where his cult is not performed he rapes all the women. The hero of the complex is manifest on the fifth and final night by a dancer decorated in ochre and feathers and holding a long, feather-tipped spear. This dancer rushes the people as if to spear them on several occasions as the climax of the ceremony is reached.

Baldwin Spencer can add little to this frustratingly incomplete interpretation when he in turn witnesses the Mulunga (his informants refer to it as Tjitjingalla) among the Aranda several years later. Spencer's account confirms key ritual ingredients of the cult – the bodily designs and, in particular, the use of a large stick shaped like a tuning fork – but he can only guess that the performance celebrates a man renowned for his wisdom and strength whom the others are trying to obstruct from returning to his home so that he will join their party. The main thing that strikes Spencer is that in comparison with Aboriginal ritual generally, which he finds to be profoundly dull, this is an exciting performance.

We next hear of the Mulunga reaching the Lake Eyre district at the turn of the century. There it is observed by J. W. Gregory, who has no idea at all as to its significance, and Otto Siebert, who provides the *only* explanation available to us. We will return to his all-important account in a moment, but first let us trace the fate of the cult.

Daisy Bates later notes its arrival at Penong on Australia's south coast in 1915. Only three years later it reaches Eucla, which lies on the state border between South and Western Australia. As Bates did not actually see the ceremony she can add nothing regarding its content or significance, but she does help us calculate the speed of its transmission. She suggests it has taken eleven years to spread from central-northern Queensland to the south coast of Australia, but in fact mistakes the date of the publication of Roth's book for the date when he saw the ceremony. In fact, it took a maximum of twenty-two years to span the distance of about 1,600 kilometres, and even then it is still vital and on the move. Bates last sees it heading towards the north-west, and she believes it will ultimately reach the Kimberley via the west coast. This seems reasonable, as this is a well-documented trade route skirting desert regions. What is significant for us, however, is that this also represents a great circle of remote pastoral frontiers which came to surround the arid desert. The speed of diffusion almost certainly owes something to pastoral life and we even have documentation of the cult being transmitted along the stock routes by Aboriginal station-workers.

If we consider the Mulunga, which spanned the best part of Australia, to be a ritual complex associated with the spread of pastoral frontiers, then when we return to Siebert's account, his words are less unexpected. He writes:

> According to the information given to me, the Múlunga Dance originated as follows: In the far north, white men had shot down a number of natives, and the magic dance was therefore an act of revenge carried out on all whites. This serves also to explain the otherwise incomprehensible belief, that all those who do not see the dance will be bewitched; otherwise all natives, whether heathen or Christians, are expected, indeed compelled to be present at the performance of the Múlunga Dance. The main theme of the performance is to depict how the blacks were shot down.

Roth's Figures 294 and 296 represent riflemen, and the forked objects they are carrying represent rifles. . . .

At the end of the dance the *Kánini*, represented by a man, appears 'out of the water', that is, behind the above-mentioned hut, and mimes the killing of all white men. The *Kánini* is a water-spirit; perhaps the leader's water-test, in which he proves his ability to remain under water for a whole day, is connected with the fact that the 'Grandmother' is a water-spirit.[12]

Siebert, in other words, considers Mulunga to be a clever-man-controlled complex focusing on a Water Mother who emerges to kill the rifle-carrying performers. Kanini has the power to destroy the Whites of the pastoral world. Insofar as other accounts do not offer any alternative explanations, and nor do their descriptions of overt behaviour contradict Siebert's understanding, it is at least possible that this interpretation would fit all our accounts.

What, however, of the cult's alleged origin in the White shooting of Aborigines? First, we must consider where to begin our historical research. Several scholars (A. P. Elkin among them) have taken Aboriginal statements that Mulunga began in the far north to refer to Arnhem Land. This, however, has no foundation. Earlier accounts agree Mulunga emerged in the Gulf of Carpentaria; Roth, our earliest source, specifies the Woagaia. If he is correct, then we require evidence of a skirmish in that general region before 1893.

As it turns out the evidence is precisely located, and the event was arguably the most monumental war to erupt between Whites and Aborigines. Even today the site still bears the name Battle Mountain, and White Australian military officials (whose standards are grudgingly stringent) recognize this as one of the few occasions when Aborigines have faced Whites in open battle.

In September 1884, it is estimated that as many as 600 Kalkatungu men gathered on Battle Mountain. They had regrouped there after the failure of their drawn-out guerrilla resistance. Their territories had been invaded by pastoralists in the 1870s, and in response they had killed cattle and settlers alike. Among the pioneer Whites, the most doggedly persevering was Alexander Kennedy, who had managed to quell the first wave of Kalkatungu protest. He was warned, however, by his Aboriginal worker that a new 'corroboree' was being performed. The admittedly infelicitous translation is that the song stated: 'We kill many-legged animal/The White man brings the strange beast to our land.' The ceremonial focus then shifted to: 'Our water is taken by the cattle/Kill the White man/Kill the White man.'[13] This is not the Mulunga cult *per se*, but it is at least the Mulunga mood. Photographs of the Kalkatungu from this period reveal ritual designs comparable (but not identical) with those of Mulunga, and there are even photographs with dancers wearing leather straps in precisely the manner of the native mounted police troopers sent against them.

The use of sacred powers to resist invasion continued. Kennedy's partner was discovered in the burning heat, his head doubled under his body, disembowelled and his kidney fat stolen (kidney fat is used in Aboriginal sorcery). It was also said that clever-men were about to bring storms and lightning which would drive the Whites out. It was as this sense of supernatural retaliation gathered that mounted police were called and the retreat to Battle Mountain occurred.

The Kalkatungu were poised to win, until they employed a mystifying tactic. They formed into ranks like disciplined soldiers and, advancing in formation, marched into the path of the firing carbines.

This surely was an event worthy of the Mulunga traditions which went on to spread through pastoral frontiers throughout Australia. Pastoralism, however, was something not destined to be repelled by Aboriginal resistances in either the physical or the sacred domain. The millennial hopes of Mulunga were for a speedy return to the traditions and the lands still strongly embedded in Aboriginal minds. With time, however, different responses would be required to confront prolonged colonial pressures and an entrenched pastoral presence.

CULTS FROM THE PASTORAL WORLD

As pastoralism spread across Australia, the stories from the frontiers repeated the same themes: invasion, guerrilla resistance, 'pacification'. For many, the Mulunga cult addressed their experiences. The one region where we might have expected this new ceremony to flourish, the Kimberley, turns out, however, to be an area where Mulunga was suspiciously absent. Perhaps, as Bates suggests, it reached the area from the northward sweep along the west coast, but for this we have no evidence. On the other hand, it is also possible that the Kimberley people responded with the innovation of their own new ceremonies and beliefs suited to their more specific experiences. For this, we have evidence aplenty.

The Kimberley pastoral world was rich with (human) Heroes. One of them, Djandamarra, better known as Pigeon, was a rebel who very much echoed the Mulunga mood. Among the earliest of men brought into the pastoral world, he developed many settler skills before rebelling to establish a guerrilla band and launching an offensive against Whites, ultimately hoping to take over the town of Derby itself. Whether there were millennial expectations associated with this movement is unknown, but today Bunaba people recall Djandamarra for his supernatural rather than mundanely military skills:

> Pigeon's body could not be destroyed. It was already riddled with bullet holes from his many encounters with police. Any man would have died, but not Pigeon. He was indestructible, almost immortal, for his life was seated, securely tucked away, in the fold between thumb and finger of his left hand. Only when the police were wise enough to bring in an Aboriginal witchdoctor from the Pilbara, could the tide be turned against him. The clever doctor, suspecting the truth about Pigeon's seeming immortality, shot Pigeon first in the right hand – without success. Then tying the left hand and aiming his magical weapon, a death pointer, carefully at the specific spot, the desired result occurred. Pigeon died instantly. However, shortly afterwards the assassin was himself killed by lightning.[14]

Djandamarra's resistance, like the Mulunga, suited a period of ritual invasion. As pastoralism set in, however, new Heroes emerged – none greater than Boxer, who even today lives in Kimberley legend.

Intriguingly, although Boxer spent his life as a worker for the famous Durack pastoral dynasty, his roots lay in Queensland with none other than the Kalkatungu, and it was said his own powers came from this area, transmitted by uncanny means. By White station standards, Boxer was without peer. He was a self-assured, introspective and reliable leader. By all accounts he was enigmatic, but for Aborigines he is remembered as the most remarkable of clever-men and the dreamer of new ceremonies. His skills included the ability to transform into an emu, heal or bring down storms. And he could open his own intestines. Bulla recalls: 'I nearly died of fright. This boy old Boxer pulled his guts out and they fell on the ground by Christ. He was very dangerous.'[15] For a now unknown reason he was gaoled at Wyndham, but needless to say no prison could contain him. Nonetheless, he did not try to flee, realizing his powers, the police simply freed him. Just prior to the Japanese bombing in Wyndham in 1942, Boxer returned to Queensland, died and was finally buried in Darwin – or so it was thought. Years later, he was seen by a White friend in north Queensland, and when the man returned to Darwin to seek out his grave, the earth was seen to have split open.

While Boxer's life and powers were spectacular, he is even more significant for being the man who was said to have single-handedly revolutionized Kimberley ceremonial life. This almost certainly exaggerates the truth, and one suspects diverse innovations have been posthumously attributed to the great clever-man. Nonetheless, the cults, if they are not all his innovations, are the type of ceremony very much in character with someone like Boxer. Many of them have mythic tracks going to the Kalkatungu area, and some were sung in Aboriginal English.

The bulk of the traditions accredited to Boxer passed into disuse without leaving any trace in the ethnographic records, but central to them all was the Being known as Djanba. Like Mulunga, Djanba was a dangerous figure who would travel secretively, obliterating his tracks by tying up his toes. Djanba's most conspicuous skill, however, was his ability to infuse himself into pre-existent cults. In this there seems to have been no limits to his power. It is recalled that on one occasion the Catholic missionary in the area tried to add some indigenous flavour to mass by having traditional songs accompany a service. On that occasion Djanba entered Holy Communion, so that he now even has power over Whites.

We are fortunate in that the German Frobenius expedition of 1938 arrived at a time when Boxer was active in the Kimberley, for their anthropological findings give us another vantage point from which to view Djanba. Andreas Lommel and Helmut Petri reported Djanba ceremonies were indeed in pidgin English, but their observations went further than this. This trickster Hero seems to have drawn the whole European world into his symbolic realm. He was said to live in a house made of corrugated iron. Behind the house he grew poisonous plants with which he could impart the introduced diseases of leprosy and syphilis. Djanba hunted with a rifle, used iron tools and, while disseminating the sacred boards used in his ceremonies, travelled by car, steamer and aeroplane. In return for the boards, he demanded European food (tea, sugar, bread), which were therefore a part of his cult. So too were a range of ritual workers who had names derived from European forms of employment – 'clerks' to care for sacred objects, 'mailmen' to regulate groups, 'police-boys' to oversee the Law and 'bosses' who were the custodians of the complex.

As we have said, it would be taking oral sources somewhat too literally to imagine that Boxer introduced all these innovations unaided, but the figure of Djanba – spanning two symbolic worlds – reflects the experiences of people in a life situation akin to that of Boxer – a man who had brought two worlds together. Djanba was pre-eminently a mediator, a part of the moral order of rations and wages which regulated pastoral life, yet someone who could reach those still belonging to the bush. Against all odds, he seems to have been someone who had held on to the sacred powers of the now distant land from which he had sprung, yet equally he was capable of manipulating the White code of being.

While his Ancestors who died on Battle Mountain may have given their lives to inspire the Mulunga complex which was something of a millennial cosmic revolution, Boxer, of a later generation, had found a permanent place within the world of wages, work and rations. This was more than a new mode of subsistence. No matter how hierarchical and oppressive, it was a way of sharing a moral order with White Australians. It went beyond the experience of the Lawless invader to a new kind of relationship which was controlled and defined by Whites and encoded in commodities, money and labour. At a cosmological level, this was perfectly symbolized by Djanba, who himself possessed White cultural items, infusing himself into all the pre-existing cultic order.

Yet we are not witnessing a simple exchange of one understanding of life for another. For while Djanba subverted cults to his cause, we can by no means suggest these Aborigines had therefore sought a new salvation through the acquisition of 'cargo' – although this was something soon to occur. Rather, there seems to have been a co-joining of two Laws in such a way as to reinforce the now dangerously distended link between peoples and their lands with a White moral Law of rations and wages.

The alliance was unstable at best. This brings us to the most noted of all of Djanba's ceremonies, and the one that has been reasonably well documented. Known as Kuranggara, it began in southern Arnhem Land as a segment of the All-Mother cults. The pan-Aboriginal focus of the original seems to have been retained, but beyond that it is hardly recognizable as belonging to the Kunapipi. Indeed, its underlying theme seems to have had far more in common with the All-Father traditions from the very opposite side of the continent.

For an older generation, Kuranggara was troubling. They felt it would undermine their locative religious order and the association between spirits and sites – in brief, as cosmic balance would not be constantly maintained they saw their entire world collapsing. For them, the invading Djanbas (for Djanba the one could be Djanba the many) were place-destructive, sucking the land dry as they travelled. The elders, like their fellows in the south-east in an earlier era, were pessimistic, envisaging a land denuded of spirit and, ultimately, the literal end of the universe as the poles separating earth and sky collapsed.

But for a new generation who had become a part of the station world, Kuranggara was a dynamic revival, containing not only the great Djanba with his partly White lifestyle, but also songs telling, among other things, of Aborigines flying in aeroplanes and even an Ancestor travelling by train. It was a ceremonial complex which forged the foundations of a new moral cosmos in which Whites and White ways were recognized as part of the order. And it paved the way for cargoism.

THE WAR AND CARGOISM

Colonial history of Australia has three distinct phases which are significant in understanding Aboriginal religious responses to the White presence. In the initial phase, there was almost inevitably brutal and relentless invasion. People were massacred or otherwise 'pacified' as land was taken. From an Aboriginal perspective, this was the period of the Lawless aliens with whom no relation was manageable. It was associated with cosmic millennial revolts, as we have witnessed in the south-east and the Mulunga. In the second period, however, after land was secured, it was realized in the remote pastoral regions that Aborigines were fine station workers, and they were thus brought in to the White order of wages and labour, sometimes at gunpoint but more often by subtler forms of enticement. In this phase, Aboriginal cults seemed particularly to express the interrelation between Whites and traditional worlds (as we have seen with Djanba), but the moral order was one which was hierarchical, or even feudalistic.

The third distinct phase, which is still with us, is one in which Aboriginal people were and are demanding equality in a cosmology that now embraces White people. This might take the form of a return of separate autonomy, which is linked with the somewhat millennial expectations of land-rights movements, or of working through Western symbolic forms, which is discussed more fully in chapter 3. Another alternative, discussed in the remainder of this chapter, is to seek parity by bringing the symbolic order of wages, commodities and labour into the Aboriginal religious domain, and seeking equality in this realm. This is cargoism, and while it is infrequently reported in Australia, it is clearly present from World War II onwards.

The rise of Aboriginal cargoism seems to be linked particularly with the activities of a White man named Donald McLeod. McLeod was a card-carrying Marxist, passionately drawn to the defence of Aboriginal rights; while his critics saw him as a self-proclaimed messiah, he saw himself merely as a martyr. In keeping with his communist ideals, he advocated at the very least a form of secular utopianism, but some have said his ideals were millennarian, and even cargoistic in his promises of equality in the White labour world. For the moment, however, it is necessary only to note that he was instrumental in organizing the first Aboriginal strike for equal wages.

The strike was postponed due to the outbreak of war when, it should be recalled, northern and north-western Australia was under threat from Japanese forces. Allied forces, including American reinforcements, were also stationed towards the interior of the continent. The first signs of cargoism appeared at this time, when Aborigines found themselves working side-by-side and equitably with Whites, but were also offered decisive proof of the vulnerability of White hegemony. In central Australia, it was reported that the American soldiers were cast by Aborigines as the new, egalitarian redemptive Whites (and Blacks). At the end of the war, it was recorded at Angus Downs central Australia, they would return with a large number of trucks laden with tea, sugar and flour. Indeed, they would have made these gifts immediately the war ended, except for the fact that White Australians deceived the Americans and stole their goods. But the future would see the promise fulfilled, and it has been tentatively suggested that a possible ritual of pushing tin-cans connected to a wire to form a wheel would hasten their return (today, these are used as children's toys in central Australia).

Some of the central Australian information rests upon ethnographic speculation but, returning to the north-west, where McLeod was beginning his activities, the reports are echoed. There, in 1942, it was reported that Aborigines believed the Japanese were coming to liberate them. They would teach the first Australians to read and write, provide them with necessary food and even form marriage alliances with them. White Australians, in turn, would then be placed in a servile role to Aborigines. From the scattered data we have on these beliefs, it seems clear that the prophecy was founded on the divination of knowledgeable Aboriginal people.

While the reference to expectations of the Allied American saviours was no doubt considered quaint and hence, for the most part, left little historical trace in colonial history, the longing for the Japanese was clearly more distasteful to the military mind. The degree of Aboriginal enthusiasm for the Japanese can be measured by the fact that those proclaiming the virtues of the enemy were arrested, and a mobile force was organized to round up all unemployed Aboriginal people in certain regions, so as to restrict the movement of these 'potential enemies'. In one zone, the order had been given that in the event of invasion the first strategic response was to be to shoot all local Aborigines.

Immediately after the Japanese threat abated, the strike which McLeod was instrumental in organizing came into operation. It brought the Pilbara wool industry virtually to a halt. The demand for equal recognition in terms of White Law was relentlessly pursued, and the strike continued for years. The 'McLeod Mob', meanwhile, moved into its own mining ventures and used its initial profits to purchase its own pastoral stations, the most famous being Yandyerra (we will meet its Aboriginal manager, Peter Coppin, presently).

While McLeod's Mob was active in political and economic domains, and while the Mob's influence was spreading to the Kimberley, the Kuranggara cult was also spreading to the area, forming a new focus of religious vitality. Some time later, following the collapse of the Mob's companies, the Kuranggara had developed into a messianic and millennarian 'cargo cult', centred on the La Grange area and focused on the Hero known as Djinimin.

Stanner had some time earlier recorded the myth of Djinimin among the Murinbata, particularly noting how it appealed to the troubled mood of the people and how it opposed the more reconciliatory adjustments realized through the All-Mother cults. At this stage, Djinimin had no rituals, however. Stanner sensed a millennial and prophetic quality to Djinimin, and suggested that in other places, such as Melanesia, these qualities would certainly have been given ceremonial form, but he was not surprised Aborigines did not pursue this option.

A few years later, nonetheless, Djinimin had his cult. This was the Woagaia, which is closely related to the Kuranggara. It is said that Djinimin descended from heaven to a large inter-tribal gathering, revealing himself not only as the flying fox Ancestor but also as identical with Jesus Christ. He had both dark and light skin, and although the people were afraid of the revelation they claimed to have taken photographs of the event. It was the teachings of Djinimin/Jesus that were significant, however. He told the gathered people – who, after reflecting, said they had always believed in Jesus, even prior to the coming of the missionaries – to be steadfast in their traditions, and in this way the difference between Aborigines and Whites would disappear and all would share the land equally.

There was more, for Djinimin also promised cargo. The missionaries, it seems, had lied to Aborigines in order to conceal their redemptive supply of wealth. For Noah's Ark had not come to rest in another land, but rather was lying in the Great Sandy Desert – the spectacular discolouration of Geikie Gorge was evidence enough of the Great Flood having occurred in the Kimberley. The Ark has a dual soteriological value to Aborigines. On the one hand it will lift them to safety when a second deluge of holy water comes to purge the world of Whites. On the other, it is laden with gold, crystals and other items of wealth which will provide Aborigines with funds to assure their well-being in the world of European cargo.

Having made this proclamation, Djinimin/Jesus returned to heaven, but rather than giving Aborigines a new ceremony he took theirs, which was none other than the Woagaia; a practice somewhat akin to Djanba's practice of taking over another's cults.

Helmut Petri and Gisela Petri-Odermann, who have recorded these beliefs, draw parallels between Djinimin's promise and that of McLeod. Both sought a new future in which Whites and Aborigines would be equal (at the least) and both, while not denying traditional Law, conceived this new parity in terms of equal access to and control of the world of commodities and wealth. Yet the authors can provide no absolute link between the strikes and the cult, and some have considered the whole event something of an aberration in the literature. In reality, however, the Djinimin theme still endures and even now retains solid links with the Pilbara and the activities of McLeod's Mob.

One of the key factors of the Djinimin traditions was the belief that the Dreaming Ancestors were leaving their localities to congregate at a cosmic centre called Dingari, and this is a theme carried on today by the movement known as Djulurru, which emerged at much the same time and place as the Djinimin/Jesus cult. The precise details are not known, but the evidence all points to Djulurru beginning in the late 1950s or early 1960s, with La Grange or even Nullagine or Port Hedland in the Pilbara as its original place of inception. Significantly, this is the precise place of the seat of the activities of McLeod's mob. An even more explicit correspondence, however, is provided by the well-known Aboriginal storyteller, Paddy Roe, who maintains that Djulurru was a ceremony first 'dreamt' by 'Coffin', who seems likely to be Peter Coppin (often transcribed as Peter Coffin), McLeod's successor and manager of Yandyerra.

As it is told, Coppin was visited by the spirits of 'Malays' who had drowned with the sinking of the steamer *Koombana*. They gave him their ceremonies (with Islamic themes, some say) to pass on to Aboriginal people, and from there the movement spread across the southern Kimberley into the Central Desert. Be this as it may, it is equally evident that the Djulurru is related to the Kuranggara traditions and is in fact the name of one segment of the latter (which, in turn, was a segment of the Kunapipi).

The focus on Dingari, the relationship to Kuranggara and the link with 'the Mob' all suggest a kinship between Djulurru and Djinimin. The most substantial evidence, however, belongs to the beliefs themselves, which share both the appropriation of the Christian godhead and the cargoistic vision.

The Hero of the complex, Djulurru himself, is said by some to be both Black and White (or a 'half-caste'), yet by others to be none other than the Christian God. But he is also a charismatic cowboy (an image of Jesus used by missionaries in this area) with white clothes and hat, six-guns, horses and motorbikes. In that he is invariably drunk, he is associated with Catholic rather than Protestant missionaries.

The details of Djulurru's ceremonies need not detain us. It is sufficient to note they are overseen by 'bosses' and symbolic representations of White people, and induct novices known as 'prisoners' who are released into the new and highly conscriptive Law. The mediators of that Law are the 'table-men' – a rather felicitous term conjuring something of Aboriginal experiences of White Law – both clerical and judicial, which is always based on books resting authoritatively upon tables.

The dances certainly are *not entirely* innovative, and much of their form and meaning relate to the older Kuranggara strata. However, the brightly coloured wool used in bodily decorations and references to aeroplane battles and to ship-fires certainly suffice to indicate the novel themes entailed. The climax is a twin revelation: on the one hand the manifestation of the three captains of the *Koombana* (possibly including 'Coffin' himself), and on the other the arrival of a massive iconographic aeroplane which embodies a promise of 'tea, flour and sugar'.

Clearly, Djulurru extends the mood of Djinimin, symbolically appropriating White Law so that equality may be achieved in terms of that new Law. This, it seems, is the message of 'cargoism' in Aboriginal Australia. It is by no means the only response to invasion – indeed, it is relatively rare among Aborigines and, as land-right legislation develops, seems to be increasingly on the wane.

Aboriginal cargoism, nonetheless, is significant and must be acknowledged in any history of their religions. That it has been relatively inconspicuous in Australian history is due to the fact that traditionally Aborigines do not define themselves in terms of material wealth (either as possessions or as gifts), and that White Australians have mostly been reluctant to usher Aborigines into their world of commodities, labour and wages. Where Aborigines do enter this White way of life (voluntarily or involuntarily), and further, where they in their own ritual world demand equality in terms of White Law and its symbolic forms, then cargoism seems to have emerged. These preconditions stand out more clearly when we turn in chapter 5 to the Oceanian regions of the north of Australia, where cargoism was spectacularly developed. For now, however, we continue to trace the history of Aboriginal religion in the world of missions and urban environments.

NOTES AND REFERENCES

1 R. Robinson, *The Feathered Serpent*, Sydney, 1956, pp. 53–4.
2 In R. M. Berndt, *Djanggawul: an Aboriginal Religious Cult of North-Eastern Arnhem Land*, London, 1952, pp. 101–2.
3 R. M. and C. H. Berndt, *Man, Land and Myth in North Australia: the Gunwinggu People*, Sydney, 1970, p. 121.
4 In Berndt, *Djanggawul*, p. 63.
5 Berndt and Berndt, *Man, Land and Myth*, pp. 117–18.
6 In R. M. Berndt, *Kunapipi: a Study of an Australian Aboriginal Religious Cult*, Melbourne, 1951, pp. 188–9.
7 In R. M. and C. H. Berndt, 'The Discovery of Pottery in North-Eastern Arnhem Land', *Journal of the Royal Anthropological Institute* 77 (1947): 135.
8 E. J. Eyre, *Journals of Expeditions of Discovery into Central Australia*, London, 1845, vol. 2, pp. 366–7.
9 R. M. Berndt, 'Wuradjeri Magic and "Clever Men" ', *Oceania* 17 (1947): 334, n. 16.
10 ibid.
11 R. H. Mathews, 'The Bora of the Kamilaroi Tribes', *Proceedings of the Royal Society of Victoria* 9 (1897): 146.
12 Translation by E. J. Sharpe from O. Siebert, 'Sagen und Sitten der Dieri

und Nachbarstämme in Zendral-Australien', *Globus* 97 (1910): 45–50 and 53–9.

13 H. Fysh, *Taming the North*, Sydney, 1933, pp. 123–4.
14 E. Kolig, *The Noonkanbah Story*, Dunedin, 1987, p. 27.
15 In B. Shaw, *Countrymen: the Life Histories of Four Aboriginal Men as Told to Bruce Shaw*, Canberra, 1986, p. 181.

3 Missions, Christianity and modernity[1]

In the preceding chapter we considered some Aboriginal religious responses to invasion and colonization. No matter how innovative those cults may have been, they still remained firmly embedded in distinctly Aboriginal ceremonial forms; so much so that many ethnographers failed to appreciate the dynamic nature of the rituals they observed. This, however, was not the only type of religious transformation wrought by the arrival of outsiders. For many Aboriginal people, the old ways of expressing religious ideals became increasingly difficult to maintain. In this chapter, we consider two domains in which this was particularly true. The first was the mission institution. The second, which came into its own in a later era, was Aboriginal life in predominantly White towns and cities.

MISSIONS AND MISSIONARIES IN AUSTRALIA

The story of missions to Aborigines for the south-west Pacific as a whole is a massive and not infrequently tangled tale. The conversion of Aborigines to Christianity was not an initial priority on colonial agendas, and it was not until 1821, a third of a century after the arrival of the First Fleet, that the Wesleyan Missionary Society appointed William Walker as the first missionary to Aborigines. This is not to say that prior to then Christian thought was entirely inaccessible to Aboriginal people. There are records of Aborigines attending settler churches in the eighteenth century, and Governor Macquarie's school for Aboriginal children had an ex-missionary headmaster and a substantial prozelytization function. Furthermore, there were freelance missionaries, such as the Catholic priest John Joseph Therry, who on one occasion was observed arriving to preface an Aboriginal ceremony with a baptism. Nevertheless, it remains true that missionary societies were sluggish in their recognition of the first Australians.

In the decade after 1821, the missionary presence began to spread until ultimately, by the mid-thirteenth century, it had all but covered the continent. By all standards, including that of the missionaries themselves, the early period was one of repeated failures. The first land grant for a mission was made to the London Missionary Society in 1825, but by 1837 the Reverend Lancelot Threlkeld was forced to close an institution in which only three inmates survived. The second station, formed by the Church Missionary Society at Wellington Valley in 1932, closed barely a decade later, seemingly without success although, as we have seen in chapter 2, it did play a significant role in the spread of the All-Father cults.

The subsequent flood of mission activity was so vast as to make a detailed summary too cumbersome to present here. Most historians, faced with the sheer bulk of data, have chosen to focus on the lives of heroes, and, less frequently, villains of the mission saga. The danger in this approach lies in the fact that these individuals are noteworthy precisely because they stand out from the monochromatic norm. There is also the problem of interpretation. Catholic mission history for example, includes in its canon of heroes the pioneers Rosendo Salvado and Duncan McNab and the missionary anthropologist Ernest Ailred Worms. Detractors, on the other hand, portray Salvado as a land-hungry power-broker, Worms as a sometimes patronizing and frequently unreliable scholar, while McNab, some Aborigines indicated in their parodies of him, was to them simply an interfering buffoon. Were Lutherans such as the famed Carl Strehlow great appreciators of Aboriginal culture, or were they rather sophisticated tyrants of total institutions? Were the oft-eulogized John and Ernest Gribble truly seeking to establish Yarrabah as a humanitarian community, or was their vision, as one Aborigine raised on that reserve once said, just that of 'the Gribbles' stud farm'? Clearly, the heroes-and-villains approach is fraught with interpretative hazards.

Given the ambiguity of the evidence, and the high passions involved in the subject, it is not surprising that overall evaluations of missions in Australia have been heavily divided. The historian D. J. Mulvaney, for instance, has popularized the opinion that 'missionary organizations stressed the abomination of savage society and spared no thought for investigating its past or recording its present',[2] a view endorsed by the Aboriginal writer Jack Davis, who says:

The attack by Christianity on the spiritual life of Aborigines was disastrous. Initiation ceremonies were regarded as barbaric; the giving of young girls to older men was forbidden . . . Christ's unhappy face loomed on the horizon and gradually eclipsed the Aboriginal's existence.[3]

Alternatively, the anthropological sympathizer Kennelm Burridge reminds us that 'it is often convenient to forget that had it not been for the work of the Christian missionaries, it is doubtful whether Australian Aborigines would have survived into the present',[4] and the Aborigine Phillip Pepper concurs: 'Only for the missionaries there wouldn't be so many Aborigines walking around today.'[5]

If, however, we take these seemingly opposed statements as points of consideration, rather than as excuses either to honour or to condemn missionaries, we can come closer to appreciating the significance of early missions to Aborigines. For we can concede, with Burridge and Pepper, that missionaries were frequently outspoken in the defence of Aborigines, not only to save their lives but also to argue for their right to be recognized as being fully human in their intellectual ability. This is almost self-evidently true, for if there were not a people awaiting and intellectually capable of receiving the Gospel, then there was no logic to establishing a mission. Equally self-evidently, missionaries, even if not always saying outright that traditional Aboriginal life was entirely 'abominable', were at least seeking vigorously to change it – this, after all, was the missionaries' *raison d'être*.

Broadly speaking, therefore, missionaries sought to save Aboriginal lives, but at the same time they strove to transform the very lives they had protected. This leads to an interesting comparison. It has been shown that in the early nineteenth century, at the same time as missions to Aborigines were being established, European legal systems shifted their focus from the ritual of public torture of the body to using 'the body . . . as an instrument or intermediary' to lay hold of and recreate the 'soul'.[6] This shift was manifest in the birth of the modern prison system, and the comparison between prisons and other disciplinary institutions such as missions are these days well recognized.

In both prisons and missions, the means of manipulating the soul was the regulation of the bodies whose lives had been spared or saved. In both cases, this was achieved by the use of timetables to control the inmates' waking life, and enforced segregation when not gainfully employed. An example will make our point clear. The list of mission rules for the Church of England mission at Poonindie, South Australia (1850–95) was as follows:

> At 6 am the station-bell rings. The natives ... feed and water their horses.
> At 7 am the chapel-bell is rung for morning prayer, when all the inmates of the Institution are expected to attend.
> At 7.30 am breakfast.
> At 8 am the station work-bell is rung and the workmen go to their different employments.
> At 9–11 am all the children who need to be instructed ... and [again at] 2–3 pm are assembled in the schoolroom. A sewing class assembles at the same time.
> At 12 md the dinner-bell rings for the whole establishment.
> At 1 pm work is resumed on the bell being rung.
> At 5 pm winter and 6 pm summer the labours of the day cease.
> At 6.30–7.30 pm in the evening there is school for adults and boys.
> At 7.30 pm evening prayer is read by the Superintendent, with a lesson from Scripture, and two hymns are sung.
> At 9 pm the single boys and girls are mustered at the Mission House, and then retire to their respective dormitories.[7]

While some mission regimes were more benign (and some much worse), the timetable and dormitory segregation were tools commonly employed on early missions. More recently, it might be argued, mission attention turned towards the more socially acceptable regimented institution – the mission school.

Missions, as protective total institutions established to transform Aboriginal souls, peppered the continent of Australia. In remote regions, there developed an informal denominational division. Catholics dominated the Kimberly and the western coast of the 'Top End'. What now constitutes the Uniting Church occupied northern Arnhem Land through to the northern Gulf of Carpentaria (as well as the Presbyterian mission in central Australia), while the Anglicans took a slice just to the south of those longitudes. The Lutherans pushed up from the south as far as Central Australia, leaving the Baptists to take over the area to the adjacent north. Large 'gaps' in western and central south-eastern Australia were then filled by the non-denominational United Aborigines Mission and Aborigines Island Mission.

Obviously, such a diverse spectrum cannot be embraced by a single model without there being exceptions, but in the period up until World War II missions could in the main be characterized as regimes designed to recreate the Aboriginal vision of life and their place in it. What that vision entailed and how it compared with preexistent beliefs is something we must now consider.

MISSION WORLDVIEWS AND ABORIGINAL RESISTANCE

What most markedly distinguished the missionary worldview from traditional Aboriginal worldviews was the concept of 'oneness'. At a cosmological level this, of course, was the notion of a single Supreme Godhead. This was equally reflected as a social ideal in which all people were 'one in Christ'; a common missionary phrase, now echoed by the title of John Harris' book telling the story of those missionaries: *One Blood*. Third, missionaries operated from an understanding of the oneness of a world created solely by their Supreme God. One God, one people, one world. These were the foundations of missionary ideology and were in turn manifest in two key life ideals which they exhorted Aboriginal people to follow. These were love and work.

All cultures, naturally, have expressions for love, but the mission doctrine was of a special kind of love embedded in 'oneness'. It was a love of a single God which radiated universally to the entire world, and it was a love which people should in turn give freely to *all* people as one. The Biblical foundations of such beliefs are secure. The Gospels state God's love falls to the just and unjust alike (Matt. 5:44ff.) and is neither deserved nor a right of an exclusive group. Because none have earned God's love, we too should love universally, forgiving trespassers (Mark 11:15) and loving even one's enemies (Matt. 5:43ff.). Aborigines received this message from the outset. The oldest documented Aboriginal sermon was written and then delivered by Thomas Brune on 19 February 1838. He began:

> And now my friends let us love the Lord thy God with all thy hearts and all thy souls and with all thy strength and with all thy might and with all thy mind. Love thy neighbour as thyself. And now my friends we ought to keep these things because these are things that we must be to them that love God.[8]

If we strip such statements of their familiar theological terms, which often obscure their structure, what is asserted is that a single source of sacred power and authority penetrates humanity and the world as a whole, universally. There are, so to speak, no fundamental channels or paths which confine religious energy to specific places or people. In Protestant thought, the only requisite mediators are the Word and the sacrament, which can and ideally will be made available throughout the world.

In Aboriginal traditions, on the other hand, there is no single ultimate religious principle which transcends human society and the world. Rather, as we saw in chapter 1, sacred knowledge and power are embedded in specific sites and the people, who themselves are emanations from these places. This is not a universal creed but a multitude of locative faiths in which wisdom and rights are decidedly *not* open to all people. The tension between oneness and plurality, between the universal and locative, was the heart of the conflict between traditional Aboriginal and mission worldviews. As one Aboriginal critic expressed it: 'Everything come up out of the ground – language, emus, kangaroos, grass. The missionary just trying to bust everything up. They fuck it up right through. Before, everything been good ... No missionary.'[9]

Prior to the period of World War II (although in some circles this approach still continues), a great deal of missionary effort, aided by the manipulative tools of timetables and dormitories, was directed towards breaking Aboriginal ties with the sacred immanence of their lands. Such beliefs about the land were considered variously the work of the Devil, superstitious, or the design of cunning elders bent on keeping women and youths under their control. Conversion would thus entail a liberation from tradition which would open people to God's love radiating indiscriminately to all people.

Missionaries saw 'oneness in love' as being more than a cosmic principle, however. It was a social plan. Many missionaries, themselves marginalized within Western society, sought to establish among Aborigines small utopian communities united in Christian love. In their quest they confronted two main obstacles which once again reflected the Aboriginal concern to maintain boundaries between religious/land domains. The first problem was violence. Rather than being 'united in love', Aborigines frequently used violence as part of a process of maintaining demarcation between land-based social groups. The second matter which offended missionaries was equally related to principles of a land-based spirituality: marriage.

Arranged marriages provide an opportunity to strengthen the fabric formed by interweaving lands and their peoples in alliances. The missionaries, however, believed these threads should be untangled and pairing be guided by love alone. Again, they sought a single God-given universal principle to replace one which was land-locked. Thus, wrote the mostly sympathetic missionary Joseph Shaw in 1868:

> A young man cannot always select a wife for himself, much less a young woman select her own husband ... the question is decided by a council consisting of the elderly men ... Love on [the wife's] part is entirely out of the question.[10]

On the other hand, we clearly recall talking at dusk with a senior Warlpiri man who looked out over his community, reflected for a moment and then concluded that all of the many problems then being encountered were due to the fact that his people now married – and he spat these words in disgust – for love. He saw clearly that such marriages were loosening the very foundations of his cosmos.

While the concept of oneness, expressed as universal love, is quite evident as a cosmological and social principle, it was equally, if not more, intrusive upon Aboriginal domains as an economic ideal. Whether this is something truly embedded within Christian ideology, or whether it is instead a bastardized adjunct which was taken on board during the Reformation only to accompany imperialist expansion thereafter, is open to question. Be that as it may, it is indisputable that the Gospel the missionaries brought was equally one of Christianization *and* of civilization; of love *and* of work. Those utopian missionary communities were modelled not only upon the ideal of unity in God, but also of toiling in the deity's love.

The logic of work followed that of the oneness of God and his creation. There was but one world which belonged eternally to him. God might allocate lands to a people (as he had to the Jews), but there was no absolute connection between specific peoples and specific lands. By the time of the Enlightenment, it had become accepted that, since the world was thus unified and unownable, the only right to land was that land with which people had dug in their spirit through the ritual of work. This was in fact the legal principle which allowed Captain Cook to claim Australia for George III as being 'unoccupied', but it was equally evident as a Christian ideal. Thus the Lutheran missionary Johann Flierl could say, without requiring any connecting argument, not only that 'the main point of all Mission work is to Christianize the heathen – so consequently they become good civilized [*sic*] too', but further that it was a Christian duty to teach Aborigines to work to ensure a 'permanent food supply in return for the labour of their hands and the sweat of their brow'.[11]

In sum, the missionary message of oneness worked from an understanding that a single Godhead who created this world as his own radiates his sacred presence as love equally to all of his creatures. People in turn should love universally, while the world, ultimately unownable by any save God himself, becomes something humans transitorily mix with their spirit through work. This, from our reading, was quintessentially the missionary message in Australia, at least until the time of World War II, and this was the transformation of the soul that they sought to achieve through the employment of the timetable and dormitory within their total institutions.

Inasmuch as a frontal attack on their worldview was presented, the Aboriginal response was invariably one of determined resistance. The records show that many entered the mission world, became able workers and understood the new message, and then, having understood, chose not to accept. There were of course exceptions, and converts to Christianity *and* civilization were made, but for much of the early period missionaries were left to lament that their inmates had reverted to their economic 'wildness', their social 'tyranny' (or, alternatively, 'promiscuity') and their cosmological 'paganism'. Yet if missionaries were sluggish in their beginnings they made up for this with their persistence, and inevitably accommodations were made.

TWO LAWS OR ONE?

Short of a prolonged downright resistance to mission ideology or alternatively succumbing to it and being totally converted, what options were open to Aborigines who could not avoid the encounter with the prozelytisers? A range of possibilities was explored, which we will consider in the following sections. They include so-called fusions or syncretisms, the maintenance of parallel traditions or 'Two Laws', adjustment or alliance movements, and indigenization.

For many Aboriginal people, the solution to the contradiction between their own traditions and mission doctrine was simply to affirm their acceptance of contradiction. They *both* declared they were Christian (in the mission sense) *and* held on to the pre-existent faith, which in itself was a radical departure from the either/or choice they were being asked to make. From the perspective of Aristotelian logic, this might seem an unsatisfactory resolution, but we should not see Aborigines as cosmological schizophrenics so much as appreciate that theirs was an intellectual heritage which did not shy away from paradox. Indeed, it might be asked whether anything but antinomy could adequately express the colonial world in which they found themselves.

What might be called parallel worldviews or dual cosmologies is expressed more succinctly by Aborigines who say they have 'Two Laws'. Two-Law thought has a particularly wide distribution and enduring history in Aboriginal Australia, although in its pure form it is perhaps currently on the wane. It was a means whereby Aborigines could accept doctrines that were forced upon them and which also expressed the logic of White Australian attitudes to the world, while simultaneously holding on to their previous understanding of existence. What defines the Two-Law orientation is a total disinclination to allow any interaction between the two traditions. It is characterized by the conspicuous absence of syncretisms; something many scholars have come to consider the norm in inter-religious contacts.

An example will make this clear. The Warlpiri with whom we worked had been missionized by Baptists for about four decades and in that time they had learned to relate Christian stories in a Biblically accurate fashion and with few errors in detail. From time to time people would enquire as to how such stories might equate with their own. We were asked whether Moses had travelled in the Tanami Desert; if the drowned Egyptians had turned into dugongs off the coast of Arnhem Land; whether Moses' act of striking a rock and hence producing water was the same as a site-specific Warlpiri rain-making ritual; and if the Dreaming serpent depicted in their church window was also the serpent of Eden. When in each case we replied that this was not the usual White person's interpretation, the Warlpiri did not push the matter but instead let the two stories in question remain distinct.

We might anticipate however, that this would cause more serious consideration if the myths in question suggested some contradiction. Did one God create the world and did a multitude of Ancestors transform it? Does sacred authority reside in heaven or in sites? When a person dies, does his or her soul travel to God or return to its land? We asked questions very much like these and the answer, invariably, depended upon context. If the query was interpreted as being cast in terms of a Christian discourse, then we received a Christian answer, and vice versa. The contradictions are managed by ensuring the borders between the Two Laws are shored up and that the appropriate Law is applied to interpreting a particular situation.

The value in accepting Christian beliefs in this fashion is that, without intruding upon tradition, it allows people to confront the reality that theirs is now a world which goes beyond traditional parameters. Dreaming Law adequately accounts for and indicates responses to death by spear or sorcery, but what of social disruption caused by drunkenness or the effects of sniffing petrol? Church Law is invariably directed towards regulating phenomena associated with the White world. And again, ambiguity is not a serious problem. In one day, we accompanied a man who was sick, but who was not certain of the cause, as he sought the healing powers of the hospital, the church and the traditional 'doctor'.

At the other extreme of Two-Laws thought are syncretisms which fuse two traditions so that their separate origins are no longer discernible. This is in the main a response conspicuously absent in Aboriginal Australia, and even the exceptions to this rule mostly indicate a desire to demarcate divisions rather than to produce a single unified cosmos. For while we sometimes encounter myths conflating Biblical and Dreaming figures and themes, these stories frequently do so only in order to explain how the European and Aboriginal worlds became separate. While this is a response documented at least as early as the mid-nineteenth century, the following myth recorded among the Otati of the far north of Cape York Peninsula in the early 1900s is a clear example of the use of syncretism to underscore separation:

Long ago all men were white; they lived in houses and food was abundant and easily obtained. Their chief was wise and powerful, and told them what was good to eat and what to avoid. One fruit, a berry growing in clusters and called *unmoi*, he particularly told them not to touch. One day, some men and women saw this fruit and said, 'why should the chief prevent our eating this; it looks good, let us try it; he will never know we have eaten it.' So they plucked some and ate it and found its taste good. But a man saw them and went to the chief saying, 'Look at these people; they have plucked and eaten *unmoi*.' Then the chief got very angry and calling the culprits said, 'you bad men, did I not give you plenty of fruit to eat, was there not plenty of white fruit and green fruit growing on the trees? Now, because you have not obeyed me but have eaten black fruit (*unmoi* = black) you and your children shall have black skins; you shall have no more houses and no more clothes, you shall walk about naked and you shall have hard work to find your food, which, since you like dirty food you shall find in the ground. But I and the people who have obeyed me will go to another place.'[12]

In another story, from the Yir-Yiront, a people further to the south of the peninsula, God had initially taught all people the White Law but Aborigines protested it was too hard. And so God said, 'You give me back all those pencils and letters. You keep your spears but give me back those guns you have been using.'[13] Again, by splicing God into a Dreaming story, the distinction between Aboriginal and White worlds is reinforced rather than blurred.

While most of Aboriginal Australia is well represented by our generalization thus far, the south-east requires further consideration. In that region of prolonged and intensive contact, there have been noted attempts to align the old Law with the new; which is perhaps, as we have argued in chapter 2, fitting insofar as the 'old' Law had itself been remodelled by its association with Whites. Examples of the equation of the two Laws are plentiful enough in the south-east. In the late 1950s at Wilcannia, George Dutton saw parallels between Catholicism and traditional myths of eaglehawk and crow and so, he said, 'I squared it up.' In the same region Walter Newton spoke in the same vein of 'Holy Eaglehawk', 'Holy Crow' and 'Holy Devil'.[14] For him the Rainbow Serpent was equated with the snake in Eden. In southern Queensland, Jesus was identified with a Being in traditional rituals and is said to have been killed by the Woagaia people. As one man explained, 'I learned about Jesus and He seemed very kind ... I can't believe He would object to ... the Rule.'[15] Indeed, he was a part of it.

The most famous example of an Aboriginal Jesus is usually cited as being intrinsically linked to Pentecostalism. While it is a story that was told by Bandjalang Pentecostal Christians, it has a wide distribution and a long history which entirely transcends contexts. It is perhaps worth tracing this intriguing syncretistic myth.

The first to record the emerging narrative was A. P. Elkin, who was told by Kaatung men initiated before 1900 of a remarkable grassless circle near Southwest Rocks, associated with Gulambra, 'our Saviour', who had a 'virgin' mother and was killed by a spear in his side. While Elkin does not comment upon any possible fusions, the Kaatung have more recently identified Gulambra and Jesus. He was the first agriculturalist (planting a sycamore seed) and later, when in battle, he hid his loincloth in a tree, saying if it bled it would signify his death. He was eventually speared in the chest and buried in Cape Hawke:

And they buried him there, buried him there, and the third day he rose. He rose in the air and he said to his tribe, he says, 'I will put two spots [stars of the Southern Cross] in the sky, and when they miss, and when they were missing, I am coming, I am coming again.' The grave is there today, at Hawke's Head, the Saviour's grave, and the twelve men, his twelve disciples, sat around and where they sat . . . the grass don't grow on it.[16]

Among the Gumbaynggir, further to the north on coastal New South Wales, the All-Father was known as Yuludara. He created all that existed, say our late-nineteenth-century sources, and had dominion over all spirits. Yuludara is also known by the name Birugan, literally 'handsome'. Again, he lives with his mother, is engaged in a battle, hangs a portent (this time a bag of ochre) in a tree and is killed. In the Gumbaynggir version, his burial site is that recorded by Elkin, a ringed place near Southwest Rocks.

There are various published and unpublished Gumbaynggir/Jesus narratives. John Flanders says Birugan was one of the two sons of 'God', the other one going to the far side of the world. 'Birroogun is our Jesus', says Flanders, and an additional intriguing element is that the place of his death was where a racecourse (now a golf course) once stood (the ring with no grass Elkin describes?).[17]

Harry Buchanan, initiated in the 1920s, was a well-known spokesperson for Gumbaynggir beliefs. Buchanan not only interpreted dendroglyphs as representing the spear thrust in 'Christ's' side, but made the following comments on Birugan:

Birugan – that's Christ. And the lord himself, they call him Baba. Baba means Father . . . those places – they not let anybody see them see. Even women, see. That's all men's secrets and women got their own secrets . . . there's no women allowed to go there to look at that [diamond tree] . . . they go blind – or do something. You see, that's the blackfellow's bible – he needs that just the same as he's reading the Bible out to you. All those diamonds [on carved initiation trees] – that's all lines for him, see. You know the lines where you read – you read all about Christ and all about God – they can read it out to you there – right around the tree.[18]

Buchanan also linked the Gumbaynggir tradition with those of the Bandjalang to the north (using a 'Noah's Ark' mytheme), but what is clear is that this story is by no means tied only to the Bandjalang Pentecostal Revival.

ADJUSTMENT AND ALLIANCE

Despite a few spectacular exceptions, broadly speaking, until the post-war period Aboriginal people seeking to hold on to their old world-order did so either by flatly rejecting Christian life, or alternatively by accepting it as a parallel tradition in the maintenance of Two Laws. As we have seen, even syncretistic stories, where they were told, more often than not sought to highlight the disjunction between the Aboriginal and the White cosmos.

The late 1950s, however, saw a new development which went beyond extreme compartmentalism, yet which equally avoided conflation. Ronald Berndt calls the best known example of such movements an 'adjustment', but we might equally consider it an 'alliance'. Says Badangga of Elcho Island:

> I believe in both ways – our own and the Christian. If we had taken both ways and thought of them separately, we would have become confused. We believe in the old Law and we want to keep it: and we believe in the Bible too. So we have selected the good laws from both and put them together.[19]

Clearly, this is not an expression of a desire for fusion, for while the Laws in question are being dovetailed together, they nonetheless keep their separate identity. Equally clearly, it is not a case of two entirely discrete laws, as Bandagga feels such an approach would in the long term be disorienting. What is being articulated in the above quotation is the concern to shape and span the Two Laws so that while they are still in fact *two* they adjust to one another's form and therefore form a mutually sustaining alliance.

First, however, we should consider the context of Bandagga's words. He is referring to the logic behind an event in which previously secret carved and painted poles (rangga) were publicly and permanently displayed. The icons mostly referred to the Laindjung-Banaidja myth-cycle (which belongs to the conspicuously innovated yiritja moiety discussed in chapter 2) but at the apex of one of the fifteen rangga was a cross. The entire display, furthermore, was located upon a concrete base built adjacent to the Elcho Island church. This juxtaposition states explicitly: 'He keep this mareiin, but the Bible is there too. He would like to keep both Laws.'[20]

The Elcho Island memorial nicely augments a type of innovation concerned with accommodation and alliance. There is no merging but there is a bringing together: the rangga beside the church; the cross aloft the traditional icons. The concern to achieve a *rapproche-*

ment which does not necessitate blending is quite evident, but what, we should ask, does this signify? Berndt sees its relevance as having two levels. Internally, the public display of restricted sacred objects will undermine the autonomy of the clan, providing a momentum which will lead towards a wider socio-political base, that can be used as a united front with which to negotiate with Whites. Externally, Berndt believes it offers Europeans an exchange. In return for the knowledge of the rangga, the Yolngu, he says, anticipate economic and educational services. If this is so then it seems they were indeed naïve.

There is, however, another interpretation. More recently, Howard Morphy has profitably argued that besides their value as sacred 'wealth', rangga must be considered as articulating the relationship between clans and their lands. Thus, said the famous artist Narritjin, when displaying his paintings in Australia's capital city:

> All [paintings] got meaning, their own story. Everything has been done here in order to teach the Europeans in Canberra, so that they can understand the way we are travelling and why we are carrying on the way and why we are living.[21]

Feasibly, the memorial is an attempt to make a statement concerning the fundamental relationship between the Aboriginal links to their lands and the White understanding of the order of the world. It seeks a mutual accommodation between the missionaries' message of one God, one people, one world, and the traditional principles governing Yolngu society.

This interpretation becomes more credible when we consider other occasions in which Aboriginal peoples have juxtaposed their iconography in a Christian context. In 1962–3, several years after the memorial was made and on the adjacent mainland at Yirrkala, the Yolngu again displayed their designs in a church. This time, two large panels, from the dhuwa (mainly representing the Djankawul) and yiritja (predominantly of Laindjung and Banaidja) moieties respectively, were placed behind the altar. Among the artists was Narritjin, whose views on art as education have just been quoted. What is most illuminating in the Yirrkala case is that the drive to produce the paintings arose immediately after an announcement was made by the Prime Minister that mining would be allowed on Gove Peninsula. Western legislation, encoded on paper, was met by a reciprocal revelation of 'deeds' to land embedded in sacred designs. The resident missionary clearly saw that 'the art boards represented a statement of land claims'[22] at a time when these were under threat. Using similar reasoning to tackle the secular face of White Law, the same people a little later sent the Australian government the famed 'Bark Petition', which set traditional designs and White legal arguments side-by-side, in order to protest at the aforementioned mining excision and to announce a prior right embodied in Yolngu Law.

As the Yolngu protest is a focal point in the emergence of the land-rights movement, it seems feasible to view the concept of adjustment or accommodation between the Two Laws as a phenomenon linked to the rise of relative Aboriginal autonomy and the weakening of missions as regimes for the transformation of the Aboriginal spirit. Freed from such constraints, Aborigines have thus sought a *rapprochement* between the Laws which is nonetheless true to their diverse forms.

Since the 1960s, the use of traditional icons in church contexts has been widespread in remote Aboriginal communities, although insofar as this is a seemingly simple action it has rarely been investigated. Among the Warlpiri people at Yuendumu, however, we detected largely the same motivation for their display of their icons in their church. It should be stressed, however, that they presented this not as an alliance between Aborigines and Whites so much as one between White and Aboriginal Laws.

As early as 1967, the Warlpiri had made an exchange presentation by giving God land for his (they believe the Christian God to be male) church. Old Wiliaraba Jabaldjari had said, 'This land he gives to us. You all hear? We give it to him, this one up high. He gives this to us and we give it to him, the land.' Darby Jampidjinpa then confirmed: 'This land to our Father we give it, to our Father, all of us know him, we give this land to our Father.' Almost a decade later, in 1975, elders then consented to display painted shields in their church, 'giving' them to God, while later still they allowed their designs to be incorporated into a stained glass window with a central crucifix. The graphic representation was indeed close to that of the Arnhem Land memorial. Darby Jampidjinpa said while pointing to the panels, 'We give it for Wapirra [Father], that's why we been give it. We been give it this one too. We been give it whole lot. Well, Wapirra know 'im now. He can talk Warlpiri.'

Just as Narritjin saw paintings as educational, so too Jampidjinpa argues for a teaching process, but in this case God himself has been taught to 'talk Warlpiri'. We should not consider the presentation of traditional iconography as a sacrifice of the old to the new, but rather as a reciprocal and balanced exchange or alliance between two worldviews which have been allowed to inform one another. Basic to these worldviews is their understanding of the sacred relationship between people and land. Occurring as it did at a time when they were beginning a struggle to have Western legal codes recognize their entitlement to their lands, the Warlpiri adjustment, like that of Arnhem Land, sought to relate, but not conflate, the one God, one-world ideology of colonial Christendom to their own understanding of their eternal affinity with a multitude of lands.

Other instances of 'adjustments' could be cited. In Cape York Peninsula, for example, Bora and church ceremonial lives have been intimately juxtaposed without their separate identity being compromised. Body designs from Bora rituals have been left in place as people attend Communion, and have even been displayed at the ordination of deacons. Enough has been said, however, to indicate the basic concerns of such movements. It is now necessary to move on to consider another variation of this orientation.

THE MEDIUM AND THE MESSAGE

Like 'adjustments', indigenization also falls between the extremes of syncretism and separate Two-Laws outlook. The key to understanding indigenization lies in recognizing a tension between different levels of meaning. There is, of course, the overt significance of the narrative being communicated, but at another level there is also a message encoded in the medium of expression itself. For the most part, indigenization in Aboriginal Australia has not entailed a radical alteration of Biblical myth. There are, in this respect, few syncretisms or even errors. However, in some places, these myths are now told not through Bible readings or sermons but by using traditional Aboriginal modes of communication – iconography, dance, song, etc.

Anyone who has seen Aboriginal people rubbed in ochre and pipe-clay and adorned with ritual paraphernalia, dancing to traditional melodies with a high-stepping, stamping gait, might be forgiven for failing to realize that the story enacted could be of Biblical derivation. Once realized, however, there can be no doubt in the observer's mind that the transformation of narrative form has equally entailed a refashioning of its meaning. What the meaning of the medium is, however, is a difficult question to answer.

A clue is provided by considering an early instance of indigenization among the people instructed at the Daly River Mission, which was founded in 1887 and abandoned twelve years later. Half a century after the institution's closure, descendants of the old regime were still telling the Bible stories they had learned. One or two syncretistic elements had been added, but the most conspicuous change was that the stories now took the form of an Aboriginal myth-cycle.

The cycle had five segments which were invariably related in the same order. The first told of the miraculous birth of Jesus. The second had God (Baijang, literally Father) making Adam and 'Riva' (Eve). Here there occurs a familiar mythic fusion to underscore the separation of the Two Laws (see above). Adam and Eve were Black, like Aborigines, because they ate a forbidden fruit and so they too had to live as hunters and gatherers, unlike Jesus the gardener. Section three told of Jesus' escape from the soldiers. The fourth segment related the story of the Last Supper, while taking up once more the theme of racial separation. Here God said:

> 'All this is [food] for White men. They will have iron, houses, and everything.' Thus the Baijang put motor cars, aeroplanes, horses, houses and so on for all White people; he also made rifles, guns, panikans, and knives; and Baijang spoke to Christ, 'that is the Dreaming for all you lot.'
> 'Jesus Christ was on the side of the White people – he gave all that food to them.'
> 'Adam had only native food, for Adam and Riva were Aborigines.'[23]

Here the myth obviously stepped beyond orthodoxy. The fifth and final section told of the crucifixion.

Without denying the significance of this cycle in accounting for the divide between two people and Two Laws, it is also true that, this aside, the departures from the Biblical accounts are not particularly glaring. The names (Adam, Eve, Jesus, Magdalene, Michael, etc.) are all easily identifiable, as are the events related. What, however, of the form? The factor which emerges clearly in Biblical history represented as Aboriginal myth-cycle is that they entail a different understanding of *time*. As the recorder of the cycle noted, Aboriginal people considered all of the activities of the cycle to have occurred simultaneously as Dreaming Events, and hence they were understood to have a narrative order entirely divorced from historical chronology.

In central Australia, among the Warlpiri, we found an identical attitude towards time in Biblical stories. When we asked several old men who out of Abraham, Moses and Jesus had lived first, they were clearly quite puzzled and replied assuring us that they had all lived on the 'same day'. It was this statement which gave us some hint as to the deeper significance of the process of indigenization.

To say, as we have, that Aboriginal interpretative forms lack a concept of temporality is perhaps to place the emphasis on a negative side of indigenization. Put positively, what all Aboriginal art forms share, be they story-cycles, song, designs or performances, is a focus on land and sites. If the Book, the quintessential mediator between God and humanity in Western Christendom, is essentially a portable religious medium which links individuals *qua* individuals with another transcendent world, then the Aboriginal indigenization of Christianity transposes this into forms which are geared towards fixed places and a collective experience of the immanence of sacred powers. This will become clear if we consider some further examples.

These days it is becoming quite common to see Biblical stories represented in Aboriginal iconic forms. Rather than collating instances of this, it seems more profitable to explore in more depth a case with which we are particularly familiar. Warlpiri Christian paintings have been executed using a typical highly abstracted desert 'dot and circle' style. The Passion is thus depicted as a series of concentric circles, indicating 'camps' or places where events occurred, and interconnecting 'tracks'. What is significant in this is that we are not presented with a frozen moment in time as we are in Western artistic traditions, but rather an extended period has been portrayed simultaneously by rendering events in time in terms of an arrangement of places. Even at a linguistic level we can see the intrinsic relationship between iconography and geography. The Warlpiri word for a design, including church art, is the same word used to refer to marks on the landscape revealing the activities of the Ancestors. To repeat what has already been said when referring to adjustment movements, art works constitute 'maps' of the country. While Christian designs actually lack a place in Aboriginal lands, the forms of communication through indigenization at least announce the religious concern with place.

The same is true of song and dance. The Warlpiri are noted as the people who have preeminently explored the use of Christian 'Law songs' and (public) ceremonies. But again, their word for song, yirdiyi, has a spatial significance. It literally means 'track', referring once more to the paths the Ancestors took through their country. When people sing a song-cycle they actually visualize each site the Ancestor visits, using such visualizations as mnemonic aids.

It must be stressed that although there are some noteworthy

exceptions, in the main Aboriginal people do *not* actually insist that Biblical events occurred in their country. There is, however, very much tension between the medium and the message in the process of indigenization, for while the form is entirely land-locked, the actual story transcends Aboriginal conceptions of place. In this regard, indigenization probes, in a somewhat different manner, the same issues which are focal to adjustment movements, but instead of juxtaposing and aligning both the myth and mode of expression from two traditions, the story of one is conjoined with the communicative medium (which in itself has meaning) of the other.

To summarize our account so far: we can see that Aboriginal people have been reluctant to endorse without qualification the one God-people-world ideology of missionaries, although they equally see it as expressing much of the logic behind colonial life. Besides uncompromising resistance, they have pursued various ways of accepting Christian notions without abandoning their earlier worldviews. In particular, this has taken the form of a Two-Law existence in which Christian and old Laws stand as entirely separate domains. More recently, as autonomy has increased for Aboriginal communities and as they have sought political *rapprochement* between their land-Law and Western legislation, the Two Laws have been brought together in accommodating ways which do *not* attempt syncretistically to fuse the old and new. Both 'adjustments' and indigenization, as we have seen, explore this concern in their differing ways.

From the point of view of a staunch traditionalist, and with the benefit of hindsight, there were dangers in allowing the Two Laws even limited interactions, for in areas where this occurred, and indeed in most of Aboriginal Australia, there has developed since the 1980s a strong enthusiasm for a Christian life which, despite all disclaimers, is closely akin in both its medium and message to White Australian evangelical Christianity.

EVANGELICAL REVIVALS AND THE MOVE TOWARDS AN INDIGENOUS CHURCH

The massive acceptance of evangelical Christian life among Aborigines has a history which we can pick up by considering, ironically, the failure of the missionary vision. Mainstream denominational missions rarely succeed in going beyond envisaging themselves as total institutions; and in the post-war period, when many Aboriginal people found themselves living in predominantly White towns and cities, the denominational churches were at best ill-prepared to accommodate the inmates now freed from the regimes of their mission societies. It was the specifically Aboriginal (non-denominational) missions, such as the United Aborigines Mission (UAM) and the Aborigines' Inland Mission (AIM), who could in such situations best serve Aboriginal needs, and yet even there Aboriginal people were readily convinced that Whites would never allow them to control the organizations. And so it was that apparently without conferring, a UAM meeting at Wattle Grove, Western Australia (in December 1967), and another on the other side of Australia sponsored by the AIM at Cherbourg, Queensland (in January 1968), led to the formation of two groups with identical names: the Aboriginal Evangelical Fellowship (AEF). They merged, and their first national conference was held in 1970.

The AEF was established to promote Aborigines proclaiming the Gospel to Aborigines. While it initially operated in tandem with mainstream churches, by 1973 its focus had shifted to establishing local Aboriginal evangelical churches. The doctrine and ritual of the AEF contain little that is distinctly Aboriginal – indeed, in its early years the AEF attitude towards traditional culture was essentially that of its White missionary critics. This condemnation has since softened, but while there is now tolerance of the old way, it is clearly inessential to AEF Christianity. Services include the well-worn evangelical techniques of altar call, dedications, preaching, Bible readings, healing, song and communion. The religious experience tends towards the Pentecostal, with vocal 'amens' and an enthusiastic lifting of hands.

That this type of religious life appeals to many urban Aborigines is perhaps not surprising, but more unexpected is its favour in remote Australia. Among those Pitjantjatjara, for example, who were first missionized by the UAM and then by the Lutherans, evangelical Christianity sponsored and supported by the AEF has in recent years marked their first real enthusiasm for Christianity. The revival is actively promoted, and requires a substantial commitment in terms of time and effort. The rituals are essentially those of dedication and evangelical song, and the hope is of a salvation which resolves the social problems that these people currently encounter. What is most significant in such cases is that despite the fact that the movement is perpetuated entirely by Aborigines, the worldview being promoted is derived from Western Christendom. This is not a Two-Law approach, but rather the watch-words are praise for God's 'one strong Law'.[24]

Evangelical and Pentecostal Christianity are now sweeping much of Aboriginal Australia, and the centres of revival are not confined to cities. One area worthy of note is Yarrabah, a reserve in Cape York Peninsula, and a key personality there is Arthur Malcolm. Malcolm was mission-raised and travelled to New South Wales and Victoria in ministry before returning home. In the following year, 1975, he was ordained a deacon, and then a priest, and in 1985 he became Australia's first Aboriginal bishop. Since his return, Yarrabah has been noted for its visionary experiences – a tradition going back to Malcolm's uncle, James Noble, the first Aboriginal deacon. The visions of the 1980s are of a different order, however, with the best known being a child's 'butterfly' painting which was said to have been opened to reveal the 'head of Christ'. Some time later it was further discovered that the 'beard' of 'Christ' contained within it a 'bishop' which was interpreted as signifying the ordination of Malcolm. Other visions have been manifest in tree formations, clouds and the scorch marks made on paper by an iron. Common exegesis refers not only to the revelation of God's concern for Yarrabah Aborigines but, further, to the wider overcoming of resistance to Aboriginal leadership in church structures. It is said that Yarrabah has been revealed as the heart of a new Aboriginal church; given the presence of Yarrabah-trained priests in areas such as Palm Island, Oenpelli and Oombulgurrie, as well as Malcolm's own travelling ministry (e.g. to Groote Eylandt, where his visit coincided with another local revival), this may indeed prove to be a prophecy containing some truth.

Yarrabah evangelism, like so much of contemporary Aboriginal Christianity, has a strong emphasis on social and individual healing. In this regard, Malcolm's 'exorcism' of a watch-house where several prisoners had committed suicide has perhaps received the widest public attention. Malcolm also makes strong use of deliverance prayers, sometimes accompanied by glossolalia, and Yarrabah Christians frequently proclaim their salvation from a life dependent upon alcohol and drugs. The evangelical style once again reveals little which is distinctly Aboriginal, and Malcolm himself, while not opposed to traditional belief and practice, is more concerned to advocate a Biblical life for Aborigines than a specifically Aboriginal theology.

Parallel to the Yarrabah-based revival is that of Arnhem Land, with its heart at Elcho Island. Its most prestigious evangelist is the Reverend Djiniyini Gondarra, who, like Malcolm, is believed to have been chosen to spread the Aboriginal experience of God. After a traditional initiation, Gondarra travelled as a theologian to Papua New Guinea and was then ordained in 1976. In the year Malcolm became a bishop, Gondarra was appointed Moderator of the northern synod of the Uniting Church.

Arnhem Land revivalists cite 14 March 1979 as the day of the Aboriginal Pentecost. Having returned from holiday, Gondarra met friends concerned to see the growth of Christian life in Northern Australia. He writes:

> Suddenly we began to feel God's Spirit moving in our hearts and the whole form of prayer life suddenly changed and everybody began to pray in Spirit and in harmony. And there was a great noise going on in the room and we began to ask one another what was going on. Some of us said that God had now visited us and once again established His Kingdom among His people who have been bound for so long by the power of evil. Now the Lord is setting His church free and bringing them into the freedom of happiness and into reconciliation and to restoration.[25]

This event was galvanized by the arrival of a White evangelical Christian named Dan Armstrong in May 1979. At his services about half of the entire population of Galiwinku, or 800 people, were converted. Glossolalia, healing and deliverance were focal to that religious experience. Armstrong then travelled to Warburton in Western Australia with a team from Galiwinku, and so the Arnhem Land revival spread to the Western Desert and towns such as Mt Margaret, Wiluna, Kalgoorlie and Jigalong.

Clearly, these evangelical Christian movements are reaching beyond local boundaries to embrace all Aboriginal people. The vision of a truly pan-Aboriginal Christian organization freed from White control and constraints was brought closer to realization by an Aboriginal man from north Queensland who had been raised in a Pentecostal family and had been involved in Aboriginal revivals in Brisbane. Later, when Reverend Charles Harris was in New Zealand, where he was inspired by Maori church leaders, he conceived the idea of establishing a new body in Aboriginal Christendom. This vision, together with the Arnhem Land revival, led to the formation of the Aboriginal and Islander Christian Congress, which is noted for its strong emphasis on ecumenism as well as on social justice for Aborigines and the end of racial oppression within Australia.

What characterizes each of these Aboriginal evangelical developments is their transcendence of local identity in the formation of a continent-wide united Aboriginal Christian front. While none of them – save the very early AEF – would deny the legitimacy of traditional land-based life (and all proclaim the justice of land rights), both Aboriginal and White critics have argued that, insofar as such movements do not specifically contribute to tradition, the new vanguard of revivalists have in effect stepped in as Aboriginal neo-colonists to fulfil the missionaries' dreams. These criticisms are not entirely without substance, as is evident in a comparison between the Arnhem Land adjustment movement and the more recent revival. For while the spirit of specific lands as embodied in rangga was intrinsic and essential to the adjustment, they are neither necessary nor conspicuous in the revival. The revival leaders, themselves the sons of those instigating the construction of the memorial, have sought to claim their predecessors as having first announced 'we will worship only the true god of heaven',[26] but we have seen that this was hardly their forebears' true intent. As we noted however, there was a danger in accommodations and alliances of the 'adjustment' kind, and this recent reinterpretation of apparently ambiguous symbolism highlights precisely this point.

We are of course not decrying Aboriginal evangelical Christianity. It is a faith which many thousands of Aborigines hold dear and which they firmly assert has given them personal strength as well as healing their wider community. What cannot be ignored, however, is that this latest development does not really nurture Two Laws, but rather feeds one while allowing the other to remain relatively undernourished. The focus of this new revival is the supremacy of the Godhead and, if not the unity of all people in a single world, then at least the ideal of a single united Aboriginal community. Again, while not denying specific people's rights to their lands, there is an ever-decreasing emphasis on that ritual life establishing spiritual identity with places in terms of the old Law.

Were the new breed of revivalists abandoning the old as an ideal, as the early members of the AEF had done, then the logic of their conversion might be more self-evident. This they are not doing however. They claim that the old order was God-given and has its place, even though they have largely ousted it as an arena of religious celebration and now proclaim principles seemingly at odds with it. How can such variance between ideology and practice be overlooked? The answer, it seems, is that it is in fact not overlooked. Rather, the issue has been defined by a reinterpretation of what in fact constitutes the old Law. When Aboriginal Christians avow a faith in the Gospel and the old ways, what is obscured is the reality that 'the old' has often been reconstructed after the acceptance of the new. It is therefore necessary to consider just what, in the late twentieth century, Aboriginal people consider to be the essence of Aboriginal spirituality.

REINVENTING THE ETERNAL

Today, while some 70 per cent of Aboriginal people describe themselves on census forms as Christians, few in settled Australia would separate this from the broader image of their spirituality. What it means to be a Christian and what it means spiritually to be an Aborigine have been so thoroughly integrated as often to seem inseparable. This is once again not a case of fusion or syncretism, but rather a remodelling of tradition so that in many cases it now perfectly follows the contours of a new Christian creed.

The sources on which those creative Aboriginal people – artists, novelists, poets, storytellers, songwriters, dancers, musicians and the like – who have expressed contemporary Aboriginal spirituality can draw, are indeed as wide as the world. They include not only Christian tradition but also the images of pop culture, ecology, the New Age and so on.

Consider, for instance, the influences in the life – and previous lives! – of Australia's first Aboriginal novelist, Colin Johnson (now Mudrooroo Nyoongah). Raised in a non-'bush' Aboriginal family, he was taken to a regimented Christian Brothers orphanage/high school and then to gaol before coming into contact with the Aboriginal Advancement League (a predominantly Protestant Aboriginal organization). Soon afterwards he wrote *Wild Cat Falling* (1965), a book that also reveals a smattering of French existentialist thought. Having heard of the Buddha in jail, he then travelled to South-East Asia, India and Pakistan, learned some Sanskrit and Pali and became a Buddhist monk for three years, before returning to Australia to write *Long Live Sandawarra* in 1979 (Sandawarra is the 'Pigeon' of our chapter 2), *Doctor Wooreddy's Prescription for Enduring the End of the World* (1983) and most recently, *Master of the Ghost Dreaming* (1991). Each of his novels has had a great impact on Aboriginal literature and thought, and while Johnson has recently argued all authentic Aboriginal literature must refer to that reality encapsulated by the word Dreaming, we are left considering precisely what that term might now entail. After all, Johnson himself had previously insisted that 'All existence is Dukkha – suffering . . .

Thus to be an Aborigine ... is to suffer ... it is your *karma* to be an Aborigine.'[27]

Other Aboriginal reworkings of spiritual ideals are even more eclectic. New Age and religio-environmentalist outlooks, for example, are evident in a Bandjalang person's description of 'cosmic energy around the planet',[28] which is focused on Nimbin; or in Gaboo Ted Thomas' rally to gather Aborigines, Maoris, Native Americans and environmentalists together at *Uluru* (Ayers Rock) in order to 'rebirth the earth'.[29] When we hear Aborigines saying 'in our tribal legend, we came here, not by land, not by water, but by spaceship',[30] we realize there really is no limit to possible sources of inspiration behind the reshaping of 'traditional' Aboriginal beliefs.

Given the diversity of sources for ideas, it is a sign of Aborigines' strong sense of shared identity that there is nonetheless a discernible form to a new all-Aboriginal macro-myth, which we will attempt to articulate in the following pages. It is a myth which, for all its emphasis on being ancient, sits comfortably enough with new Christian Aboriginal lives.

The first thing to note about the new myth of the old Law is that it is heavily temporalized, even dated. The period of the Dreaming seems to be equated with the time before colonization and is somewhat synonymous with traditional life. This era is mostly spoken of as beginning 40,000 years ago (some now use other dates, reflecting more recent archaeological opinion) and ending, abruptly, in 1788. Not only does the myth seem to share a Judaeo-Christian concern with temporality and historicity, it also reveals a part of its cosmogonic pattern. For the pre-colonial period is invariably depicted as an idyllic eco-Eden, while 1788 surely marks what can only be termed the Fall.

The first illustrations of the new myth are taken from the well-known poet and essayist Kevin Gilbert. He writes: 'Our Beginning, our Dreamtime, or creation occurred in this land. Our moment of creation, our "Garden of Eden" began here. We are the oldest, continuous and cohesive and developed society of mankind in the world.'

Having conflated Aboriginal existence in Australia with the Dreaming, Gilbert then goes on to elaborate on Eden:

> Our laws, given by nature, carved into the landscape, drawn upon the rocks enabled us to pass the stage of mass slaughter for lands, of murder without reciprocal response. Our laws governed the sharing of resources, caring for every member of our society,

the sanctity of ALL forms of life and the earth from whence we came and continue in sanctity as part thereof. Our people, our land, are based upon justice and universal humanity within our sovereign domain.[31]

The image of the period before the Fall of 1788 is invariably idyllic and cast in terms to contrast with the flawed world of post-colonial society. The 'Eden' era was a time without strife or conflict, war or violence, famine or ecological devastation, and was based on holistic principles of caring, sharing and community unity. The opening words of the Aboriginal Plenary to the World Council of Churches captures precisely this notion and, significantly, aligns it with Biblical thought:

> From the beginning of time, the Aboriginal people lived in peace and harmony with the land, maintaining God's integrity for the land. Our laws are as close as the Bible. We are to share everything equally; we are to love our brothers and sisters, we are not to steal; we are to care for the land, and to respect every living thing. So, in general, our people are very spiritual, loving, caring and sharing people.[32]

We are not implying at all that these things – the love and the care – were not present in traditional life, but it seems fair to note a shift so that these things are now said to *define* that lifestyle which was shattered in 1788.

The year 1788 is one of mythic significance to all Australians, but with highly contrasting connotations. In Australia's bicentenary year the White civic ritual of re-enacting the arrival of the First Fleet was a ritual in which Aborigines, *en masse* but uninvited, were determined to share. It was a ceremonial re-enactment with dual significance, and had the organizers not backed down on their plans to replant the British flag, violence may have been unavoidable, for it is quite certain Aboriginal people would not have allowed this to occur unhindered. For them, that act was a celebration of the serpent undermining their Eden.

The mythic anti-hero is not Phillip, however, who captained the First Fleet, but Captain Cook, who had claimed Australia for George III eighteen years earlier. Captain Cook is the archetypal lying and thieving White person, and his mythic significance is widespread in Aboriginal Australia, not only in urban areas but equally in regions such as Kimberley, Arnhem Land and Cape York. Representative, although particularly creative, is the Yolngu man Paddy Wainburranga's story of Captain Cook, which has been publicized widely among Aborigines in the form of a poster. Wainburranga conceived of an original Captain Cook who was a lawman who had killed Satan in Sydney. The historic James Cook, however, was one of the breed of new Captain Cooks who stole land and women from Aborigines: 'The New Captain Cooks shot the people. They killed the women, those new people. They called themselves "New Captain Cooks" . . . All the Captain Cook mob came and called themselves "welfare mob". They wanted to take all of Australia.'[33] This nicely expresses the fact that Captain Cook's mythic significance is not as a man of 1770, but as a symbol of the principle of theft which began then and has remained ever since.

In comparison with traditional localized myths which neither condemn nor praise Ancestral events, the new macro-pan-Aboriginal myth has a conspicuously Biblical structure in its temporality, its image of a utopian Eden of the past, and its conception of the Fall. But even more strikingly comparable to Christian cosmic plans is another theme of contemporary Aboriginal spirituality which was absent in the past – the ideal of worldly salvation, in this case brought into being by a people reclaiming their identity, their place in Aboriginal society and their relationship with the land.

RECLAIMING A PLACE

While contemporary images of their past emphasize an ideal world which had been denied to recent generations, there is nevertheless an immense faith in Aboriginality and a spirit of cultural revival. Jimmy Chi's musical with the rather millennial title of *Bran Nue Dae* not only draws attention to the tyranny of missions (it opens with the Pallottine Catholic mission of Lombardina) and a history of injustice and racism, but is equally rich in a sense of hope, reconciliation and the capacity for Aboriginality to survive seemingly overwhelming odds:

> There's nothing I would rather be,
> than to be an Aborigine . . .
> Now you may think I'm cheeky
> but I'd be satisfied,
> to rebuild your convict ships,
> and sail you on the tide.[34]

These words, belonging to a show which has captivated both White and Aboriginal audiences, should be read as indicating a symbolic rather than a literal reversal of the colonial process. It offers a re-emergence of the Aboriginal spirit. As one Aboriginal woman expressed it: 'There has been an amazing re-birth of Aboriginal idenity – not a re-birth, I think it's coming out from underground, and the fact that we are the oldest living culture on the planet, it just . . . it's just fantastic.'[35]

Rebirth? Re-emergence? Perhaps the well-known Aboriginal songwriter Bob Randall (who wrote the classic 'Brown Skinned Baby') chose the most apt image, saying:

> when I think about the butterfly that's in its cocoon, and then there is a rebirth, a reawakening of another animal that changed in the cocoon, into something *totally* different, *totally* beautiful and with life – that is the Aboriginal spirit to me; that was always there, still is there, and always will be there.[36]

That the spirit we document belongs truly to the first Australians is evident. That it had radically transformed itself so that, like caterpillar and butterfly, the life is all but totally new, is equally evident. Our task here is to try to specify just what that transformation has entailed.

At a national conference, 'Aboriginal Spirituality: Past-Present-Future', which the present authors were instrumental in organizing, we repeatedly noted one key aspect of the re-emergence of spiritual connection in Aboriginal Australia. This is a shift to the use of affection, intuitive knowledge or supernatural intervention to help people to find their place in the world. Traditionally, of course, such associations were learned through a lifelong education and formal initiation, but such avenues are no longer open to many Aborigines. Two examples of the new land-connection process will make the difference apparent. In the first case, an Aboriginal man who was employed to record sites in central Queensland could not find a particular old ceremonial ground clearly located on his map. So, abandoning his compass, he let his feelings guide him and was led by the sensing of sacred power in the land. He returned to this place frequently, but on one occasion when he brought with him an Aboriginal friend it was once more totally elusive. They realized this was a place significant to the first man, but not intended for his companion.

The other example involved a woman who was raised by a loving White family but who nonetheless felt torn between the culture in which she was raised and one as yet unknown to her. The sense of conflict was so strong she was admitted to a psychiatric institution.

There she was visited by two traditional doctors, whom no other person saw, and this marked her determination to re-establish her roots, which she did with profound success.

What is implicitly intriguing in these accounts, and what is declared explicitly by many Aboriginal people in urban and rural Australia, is that being an Aborigine is something in their *blood*. If they are denied a traditional education (and it must be stressed here that in establishing identity Aboriginal people traditionally placed their emphasis on culture and a learned Law rather than on blood) then they can still re-establish connection by drawing on their capacities, which are a part of being an Aborigine. Another incident, this time from the country of the Darkinung people (near Newcastle, New South Wales) illustrates our point. At one place an Aboriginal group saw the image of their old people manifest itself. The leader proclaimed that the land, unbeknown to them, was sacred, and that all present should draw on the power being offered by the past generations. The relator of the story then added:

> We've all got that spiritual contact inside us. Because of our blood; no matter what colour we are, whether we are fair or creamy or black or blue. Aboriginal people are in all colours . . . They think we've lost our spiritual contact, but we haven't; it's all inside us; it can come out of us.[37]

It is evident in several of the quotations we have given that land remains prevalent in contemporary Aboriginal discussion of their spirituality. What has changed is the relationship to land. Among a people who have lived with an enforced breach from their place, reconnection requires something which can transcend cultural continuity. This is 'blood': an instinctive sense of Aboriginality aroused by any genealogical link with other Aboriginal people of the past or present. 'Blood' is something which need not even be consciously realized, in which case the spiritual quest is something akin to Platonic anamnesis – the relearning of what is known at a non-conscious level. Sally Morgan's sense of discovery in *My Place* speaks for many Aboriginal Australians whose nagging intuitive awareness of their true (Aboriginal) selves has in time overridden their overt understanding that their forebears were so-called 'wogs' or some other immigrant people.

We will say something more of reconnecting with land when we turn in a moment to consider Mother Earth. Before we do, however, it is necessary to note that a re-established sense of place is something which can permeate all of life. Among people who, to employ their own image of rebirth, are born-again Aborigines, there is a zealous spiritual pride which institutes a vision of salvation through connection. This is evident, for example, in people's concern not only to find out which land their forebears occupied but also in their quest to trace unknown relatives. Aboriginal organizations such as Link-Up indeed have a spiritual mission.

At a national level, reclaiming a sense of community place is symbolized most notably in the concern to remove secular academic control over ancient skeletal remains and transfer it to Aborigines. The activist Michael Mansell says:

> The bottom line here is that if people tamper with the bones of the dead, so as far as Aboriginal people are concerned, they tamper with the spirits of the dead. When the spirits of the dead are disturbed it is a bloody insult to Aboriginal people.

Mansell almost certainly does not articulate the beliefs of those Aborigines who buried the bodies long ago. But before archaeologists gleefully employ this argument in their own defence (as they frequently do), it must be asked whether the significance of skeletons, and their proposed reburial, should be construed in terms of a fixed past doctrine or an ongoing, rapidly changing Aboriginal tradition. For contemporary Aborigines, Mansell speaks accurately, because the caring for bones which they claim as their own is a part of their spiritual drive to reconnect with their place.

Speaking generally, the rebirth of the Aboriginal spirit, that sense of overcoming the loss which came with the Fall of 1788 and of allowing 'blood' to reconnect Aboriginal people with place and family, is said to bring a healing from the personal and social effects of colonization. In a manner akin to that in which Christians (including Aboriginal Christians) profess to have been saved by the land from a life of self-destructive meaninglessness, so too Aborigines reclaiming their Aboriginality speak of its redemptive powers. Indeed, Redfern Aboriginal Medical Services, for example, considers connections of family and faith to be essential to Aboriginal well-being.

We have so far described contemporary Aboriginal spirituality thus: employing something of a Judaeo-Christian cosmic structure, Aboriginal people in rural and urban contexts speak of an Eden-like Dreaming which endured for 40,000 years but which was defiled in 1788. The loss and theft – symbolized quintessentially by Captain Cook – were devastating, but salvation is possible, is in fact coming, through re-establishing contacts with place in both its social and geographic sense. This link is re-established by an unforeseen avenue of continuity – 'blood' – which allows the Aboriginal spirit to rise reborn like a phoenix even though all around believe it delivered to ashes.

This appears to us a fair distillation of the most common contemporary Aboriginal spiritual voice. Were this all, however, it would contain a hollow. For while there is a great sense of spiritual awakening through affirming one's Aboriginality and asserting one's connection within the Aboriginal world, it cannot be denied that 'blood', whatever it might transmit, does not transmit those stories and ceremonies which provide the absolute link between specific people and specific places. 'Blood' might feasibly be said to give one a sense or orientation of Aboriginality, but it cannot be expected to offer details of the old Law.

It is this which has led to a most important aspect of the metamorphosis of Aboriginal spirituality, and one which has allowed it to sit comfortably with the unmodified principles of Christian thought and life. For it seems that Aborigines today increasingly define Aboriginality in terms of *how* they relate to land rather than to *which* lands they are related. Theirs is a sense of place rather than a knowledge of their specific site. This suggests that a loss of pluralism in the new pan-Aboriginal worldview is perfectly encapsulated by a new mythic image which not only speaks of *the* land to which Aborigines relate but also sits complementarily with the God of heaven of Christendom. That new image is Mother Earth.

MOTHER EARTH

Up until the early 1980s, we have no evidence of Aboriginal people referring to 'Mother Earth'. Only recently has she emerged to encapsulate the new relationship between Aborigines and land. Insofar as ecologists too appeal to Mother Earth, the concept instantly evokes the understanding that Aborigines treat the world differently to Europeans, thus placing the emphasis on the *how* rather than the *where* of land associations. On the other hand, the image is also current among feminists and others who would redress the dominance of the otherworldly male God of popular Christian thought, and so contrasts complementarily with the idea of general immanent and indigenous religious principle. In contrast to the tension between pluralism and monotheism produced by Two-Law developments and adjustment movements, Mother Earth, while clearly expressing a strong sense of a negative image of Western Christian symbolism, does not in fact counter its sense of a single world, a single people and a unified (or unified pair) Godhead. It is thus that the new Aboriginal spirituality has emerged alongside the rise of Aboriginal evangelical Christianity – indeed, as we will see, in some cases the same people are involved on both fronts.

In one of the earliest manifestation of Mother Earth, she had already revealed herself as part of a complementary pair. Kath Walker's (Oodgerro Noonuccal's) *Father Sky, Mother Earth* (1981) is a creation story in which the two beings of the title give birth to the natural world. All is well until one day high-technology-endowed humans destroy the ecological balance with guns, bulldozers and pollutants – all culminating in an image of Mother Earth's body pierced with placards erected in her defence.

In contrast to Noonuccal's children's story, the earliest unambiguous reference to an actual belief in a Mother Earth which we have encountered is a phrase used by Djiniyini Gondarra. He writes:

> The land is my mother. Like a human mother, the land gives us protection, enjoyment, and provides for our needs – economic, social and religious. We have a human relationship with the land: Mother – daughter, son . . .
>
> When the land is taken from us or destroyed, we feel hurt because we belong to the land and we are part of it. [White] church leaders have been encouraging me to write on Aboriginal theology of the land. When we become Christians, we see more clearly our relationship with the land and with God. It was God who entrusted the land to our ancestors. We were living in the land of plenty, like first creation people. We had our own technology, our own social laws, our own pattern to follow. Life was so beautiful before.
>
> I'm sorry to say it, but I picture oppressors, both yolngu [Aboriginal] and balanda [White], coming into our garden of Eden like a snake. Satan used the snake as his instrument to tempt God's people and to try to destroy God's plan for his people. The bad influence came in breaking our relationship with God, with man, and the Land. We never dreamed that one day the bulldozers would come in.[38]

Mother Earth is not referred to again. Nor is she present in the author's booklets' *Father You Gave us the Dreaming* (1988) and *Series of Reflections of Aboriginal Theology* (1986), although the latter includes a discussion of 'theology of the land' in terms of a plurality of 'totems'. It seems evident, then, that Gondarra's reference to 'the Land is my Mother' is used in a broad impressionistic sense as a way of defining Aboriginal traditions against the Christian Sky Father, who in his theology breathed life into the Dreaming, and yet who also allowed the Fall of the destructive processes of invasion. But there is, apparently, no mythic substance to his Mother Earth.

All these elements are amplified in our next example. Patrick Dodson writes:

> As the land was ring-barked and cleared so we were stripped bare of all that was precious and priceless. Life itself was being chained down.
>
> The heart was slowly being pierced and living was being substituted with existence, shame and hoplessness. The land herself, our Mother, was being despoiled and defiled – she cried in sorrow and with despair for us, her children, the Aboriginal and Islander people.[39]

Patrick Dodson, one-time Catholic priest and Director of the Central Lands Council and currently commissioner to the Royal Commission into Aboriginal Deaths in Custody, is a creative political and theological thinker. His vision embraces a region consisting of two ethnic groups – 'Aboriginal and [Torres Strait] Islander people' – the children of Mother Earth. The passage comes from an article addressed to Aboriginal Catholics specifically and to Christians generally, asking them to recognize that the bicentenary celebrations are 'grounded in the original sin of the theft of our lands'.

The ecologist's Mother Earth is evident in Dodson's thinking, but so too is the theological Mother. The only other reference to the Mother Land in his work is in the title of an article, 'The Land Our Mother, the Church Our Mother', also published in 1988. The text itself says nothing to provide any substance to the shadowy Mother, although it does state, 'when the child is born he calls that part of the country "Father" '![40]

Dodson's widely published work (the piece appeared in *Land Rights News*) and very catchy titles and phrases will do much to ensure Mother Earth becomes a deity of which most literate Aborigines are aware. What could exceed the impact of his widely distributed publications? One contender must be the Aboriginal presentation at World Expo in Brisbane in 1988, and the accompanying publication entitled *The Rainbow Serpent* by Oodgeroo Noonuccal (Kath Walker) and her son Kabul Oodgeroo Noonuccal (Vivian

Walker). Unlike the mother's earlier work, this piece celebrates a solo Mother Earth:

> I see you come into sacared place of my
> tribe to get strength of the Earth
> Mother. That Earth Mother . . .
> We are different you and me. We say the
> Earth is our mother – we cannot own
> her, she owns us.[41]

The story that follows is a pan-Aboriginal medley. We begin with 'Alcheringa', a Central Desert (Aranda) word which is equated with Dreamtime. The accompanying picture is from Arnhem Land, as are some of the references to the Rainbow Serpent on the following page. Before long we have picked up Baiami, the All-Father said here to be the sun and known throughout Australia. There are also Ancestral Beings from Queensland, and so on. The significant fact in all this is that the various elements are smoothly brought into a simple macro-myth bound together by the literally underlying Mother Earth.

A little over halfway through this glossy booklet, the machine age intervenes. The critique is gentle. Machines are not condemned, but they must not be allowed to dominate the spirit:

> I will
> always come back to this
> place to share the feeling of
> the land with all living
> things. I belong here where
> the spirit of the Earth
> Mother is strong in the land
> and in me.

At this point we are asked to allow the land-spirit to touch us all so that the way of Mother Earth may once again thrive. There is no esoteric lore here, no myths to be revealed, but rather an appeal to the affections and softly allowing the earth itself to speak.

Since Australia's bicentennial year, when Dodson and the Noonuccals made their immensely public statements, several references to Mother Earth have been made. We choose two prominent examples. The first is provided by Eve Mungwa Fesl, a descendant of the Aboriginal people of the south coast of Queensland and a linguist who currently teaches at Melbourne University. She has written what we believe to be the first statement by an Aborigine which tries to encapsulate the general tenor of Aboriginal Religion. It is called 'Religion and Ethnic Identity: a Koorie View', and already it has been republished.

The article makes the intriguing and perceptively candid statement that Aboriginal religion must be examined in relation to Aboriginal experiences of non-Aborigines, and the latter's views of the beliefs of the first Australians. The discussion which follows is a vitriolic critique of colonialists and missions, but 'despite the concerted attempts to wipe out Koorie Spirituality, it lived on. The form *of expression has changed,* but the strength of this spirituality is still strong in urban as well as rural Koories'. Acute observation and surely true.

The remainder concerns land. This is incontestably what has underpinned Aboriginal religion but in Fesl's view it has more specifically 'underpinned the land *rights* movement'. Her discussion, we think it fair to say, is both very general and very critical. Unlike Whites, Aborigines did not have wars, or develop war technology. 'In their frenzy to make money, they are destroying not only that which is sacred to us, but are killing the earth which nurtures all living things.' The strongest positive expression of faith in the article is found in two poems, and in this literary form (and *only* there) Mother Earth appears. We quote from both pieces. The first, 'Inheritance', is a positive celebration:

> Daughter of the Sea and Land am I
> – the Land my Mother, my soul.
> In my inheritance she give to me – Rights
> to care for her . . .
> A right not buyable, nor sellable
> A total commitment forever.
> My inheritance to care for her
> The sea, the Land, My life, My Mother.

The second, 'The Dying Land', closes her article and is something of a eulogy. It begins:

> As the forest giants fall throughout the world
> And the air grows hotter
> Our Mother the Earth sighs in pain

And ends:

> In firing weapons to kill his sister, his brother

> The technocrat harms his Mother, the Nurturer.
> As he marvels at his skills, the Land lies dying.[42]

What we witness here is precisely what Fesl says is also happening to non-Aboriginal traditions: 'Many world religions have begun a *re-think* about their own attitude to the planet and how their religious writings have been *interpreted in terms of caring for the planet.*'

Our final instance is provided by Anne Pattel-Gray, Executive Secretary of the Aboriginal and Islander Commission (Australian Council of Churches). It is a statement made at an international conference on Justice, Peace and the Integrity of Creation, in Seoul, 1990. Pattel-Gray begins with a mytheme of a great White spirit God who 'created the world' and established the Biblical-like laws which sustained a Paradise for 40,000 years. Then White people destroyed the Aboriginal Eden. Enter Mother Earth:

> My people become more and more distressed at the sight of the White men raping, murdering and abusing their Mother Earth through mining. We knew the price they would pay for abusing the Mother Earth. We knew there would soon be floods, drought, earthquakes and famine because Mother Earth had to retaliate in the only possible way that she knew how.

Again:

> We still fight against the destruction of our land and the abuse to our Mother Earth, and on a wider scale, we now believe the world is starting to see what their destruction has done to our Mother Earth . . . As believers in God, should we not be taking up our swords for justice, peace and the integrity of creation?[43]

God creates, Whites destroy, Mother Earth endures, Aborigines understand. Take any one of the components of this quaternity away, and the integrity of the image is lost.

Speaking generally, Mother Earth perfectly suits the needs of contemporary Aboriginal spiritual life. Unlike specific lands whose traditions are open only to those who have had the privilege of an often esoteric traditional education, Mother Earth is open to all of Aboriginal 'blood' who feel for land in an Aboriginal way. She provides a new, radically transformed spiritual continuity for those denied their place. Says Dodson: 'the land is still here, the spirit has not deserted us, we are faced with the task of helping the non-Aboriginal people to adopt the land as a mother.'

It is equally evident that Mother Earth rests comfortably with Aboriginal evangelical Christianity. Indeed, the structure of the two beliefs at times merges insofar as the love of Mother Earth, or the caring and sharing conceived of as now being the core of the old Law, virtually renders tradition (which, as we have seen, has become almost synonymous with the Dreaming) as the Eden of the Old Testament. As what is central to Aboriginality is the way of relating to land and to one another, but no longer to which lands one is related, there is no conflict with the notion of a single God whose sovereignty oversees the world.

Even this, however, is not straight-out syncretism, but perhaps it is something more revolutionary. In this chapter we have surveyed Aboriginal responses to living in domains controlled by Whites – missions, towns and cities. If the earliest Aboriginal reaction to White creed was resistance, followed by a Two-Law juxtaposition, which was brought ever closer to an accommodating relationship through adjustments and indigenization, then this most recent phase seems to indicate a transition in which the Laws, while said overtly to be discrete, have in their basic shape come to resemble one another to a remarkable degree. It is thus that contemporary Aboriginal spiritual thought, while portraying a 'tradition' with few syncretistic mythic details, has reshaped the very form of the old Law so that, like Judaeo-Christian thought, it is temporal, contains a Paradise/Fall breach, offers hope of salvation and appeals to the powers of a single immanent Godhead, Mother Earth.

As Bob Randall says, the recent change to Aboriginal spirituality has been a total metamorphosis. And yet it would be ruthless and unwarranted to deny there was a continuity, no matter how distended, with the past. While the appeal to blood and the affections is indeed a new way of establishing a sense of place, we are left to ask whether Aboriginal people, determined to reclaim whatever they could of a heritage denied them, had any option but to appeal to these means of connection. The academic cannot but note the historical transformations. The contemporary Aborigine, on the other hand, is filled instead with a sense of pride and spiritual hope in having retained some hold of their past against incredible odds. There are few Aborigines who would not feel moved by the words of the song by the Aboriginal rock group Coloured Stone:

> This land of ours still holds the secret,
> That is sacred to our people,
> The birds call out: 'Where are you now?'

We're still here
And we won't go away
For a single day.

NOTES AND REFERENCES

1 In this chapter we have drawn in part from our previously published material, including T. Swain, 'Love and Other Bullets,' *Religious Traditions* 13 (1990): 68–87; 'Reinventing the Eternal,' in N. Habel (ed.), *Religion, Multiculturalism and Education*, Adelaide, 1992; and 'Two Laws Spirituality' in *Two Laws*, Brisbane, in press.

2 D. J. Mulvaney, 'The Australian Aborigines 1606–1929: Opinion and Fieldwork', in *Historical Studies: Australia and New Zealand* compiled by J. J. Eastwood and F. B. Smith, Carlton, 1964, p. 16.

3 J. Davis, 'The First 150 Years', in R. M. and C. H. Berndt (eds), *Aborigines of the West: Their Past and Their Present*, Nedlands, 1979, p. 60.

4 K. O. L. Burridge, *Encountering Aborigines: Anthropology and the Australian Aboriginal: a Case Study*, New York, 1973, p. 207.

5 P. Pepper, *You Are What You Make Yourself to Be*, Melbourne, 1980, p. 15.

6 M. Foucault, *Discipline and Punish: the Birth of the Prison*, Harmondsworth, 1979, p. 11.

7 Bishop Short 1872, quoted in H. McDonald, ' "Two Ways": a Study of the Incorporation of European Christianity into Traditional Aboriginal Religion' (BA Hons. thesis, University of Queensland), Brisbane, 1987, p. 165.

8 Quoted in G. A. Robinson, 'Narrative of Mr. G. A. Robinson', in G. T. Lloyd, *Thirty-three Years in Tasmania and Victoria*, London, 1862, p. 256.

9 Quoted in D. B. Rose, 'Christian Identity Versus Aboriginal Identity', *Australian Aboriginal Studies*, 2 (1986): 59.

10 J. Shaw, 'Aborigines and Missionary Operations amongst Them' (unpublished MS. H17557, State Library of Victoria), Melbourne, 1868, pp. 4–5.

11 Quoted in J. and L. Haviland, 'How Much Food Will There be in Heaven?: Lutherans and Aborigines around Cooktown to 1900', *Aboriginal History* 4 (1980): 129.

12 C. G. Seligmann, 'An Australian Bible Story', *Man* 16 (1916): 43–4.

13 J. Taylor, 'Gods and Goods: a Follow-Up Study of "Steel Axes for Stone Age Australians" ', in T. Swain and D. Rose (eds), *Aboriginal Australians and Christian Missions: Ethnographic and Historical Studies*, Adelaide, 1988, p. 440.

14 J. Beckett, 'Marginal Men: a Study of Two Half Caste Aborigines', *Oceania* 29 (1958): 101ff.

15 C. T. Kelly, 'Some Aspects of Culture Contact in Eastern Australia', *Oceania* 15 (1944): 152.

16 N. M. Holmer and V. E. Holmer, *Stories from Two Native Tribes of Eastern Australia*, Uppsala, 1969, p. 35.

17 R. Robinson, *The Man Who Sold His Dreaming*, Sydney, 1965, p. 37.

18 Buchanan, typescript of interview at Nambucca Heads, source unknown (n.d.), p. 10.

19 R. M. Berndt, *An Adjustment Movement in Arnhem Land, Northern Territory of Australia*, Paris, 1962, pp. 59–60.

20 *Ibid.*, p. 60.

21 H. Morphy, ' "Now You Understand": an Analysis of the Way Yolngu have used Sacred Knowledge to Retain their Autonomy', in N. Peterson and M. Langton (eds), *Aborigines, Land and Land Rights*, Canberra, 1983, p. 110.

22 E. Wells, *Reward and Punishment in Arnhem Land 1962–1963*, Canberra, 1982, p. 61.

23 R. M. Berndt, 'Surviving Influence of Mission Contract in the Daly River, Northern Territory of Australia', *Neue Zeitschrift für Missionswissenschaft* 8 (1952): 9.

24 M. Brady and K. Palmer, 'Dependency and Assertivness: Three Waves of Christianity among the Pitjantjatjara People of Ooldea and Yalata', in Swain and Rose (eds), *Aboriginal Australians and Christian Missions*, p. 247.

25 D. Gondarra, *Series of Reflections of Aboriginal Theology*, Darwin, 1986, p. 9.

26 Quoted in Habel, *Religion, Multiculturalism and Education*.

27 U. Beier and C. Johnson, 'The Aboriginal Novelist Who Found Buddha', *Quadrant*, September 1985: 73.

28 Lorraine Mafi Williams, quoted in *Adelaide Fountain News*, May 1986, p. 8.

29 An event promoted in 1990 – we quote from the publicity brochure.

30 A statement made in an episode of 'spirituality' on the ABC television series *Blackout*, recorded 19 January 1989.

31 K. Gilbert, 'Kevin Gilbert', in D. Green and D. Headon (eds), *Imaging the Real: Australian Writing in the Nuclear Age*, Sydney, 1987, p. 83.

32 Document PL. 11.1, 'The Aboriginal Plenary', *World Council of Churches Seventh Assembly*, Canberra, 7–12 February, 1991, p. 1.

33 C. Mackinolty and P. Wainburranga, 'Too Many Captain Cooks', in Swain and Rose (eds.), *Aboriginal Australians and Christian Missions*, p. 359.

34 J. Chi, and Kuckles, *Bran Nue Dae*, Sydney, 1991, p. 15.

35 Stated on *Blackout*.

36 Stated on the 'Aboriginality' episode of the ABC radio series, *Rites of Passage*, 1990.

37 Stated on *Blackout*.

38 D. Gondarra, in I. R. Yule (ed.), *My Mother the Land*, Galiwin'ku, NT, 1980, pp. 8–9.

39 P. Dodson, 'Where are We after 200 Years of Colonisation?', *Land Rights News* 2/6 1988: 5.

40 P. Dodson, 'The Land Our Mother, the Church Our Mother', *Compass Theology Review* 22 (1988): 1.

41 O. and K. O. Noonuccal, *The Rainbow Serpent*, Canberra, 1988, no pagination.

42 E. M. D. Fesl, 'Religion and Ethnic Identity: a Koorie View', in A. Ata

(ed.), *Religion and Ethnic Identity: an Australian Study*, vol. II, Melbourne, 1989, pp. 7, 10.

43 A. Pattel-Gray, 'Aboriginal Australian Presentation on JPIC', *Justice, Peace and the Integrity of Creation: Sermons and Speeches*, 53.1 (1990): 2.

Part II
Pacific Islands

4 Tradition

The dominant motif of traditional Melanesian religions is the maintenance of collective material welfare, while in both Micronesian and Polynesian religious traditions two outstanding features are legitimations of the cosmic order and the concern for personal and group protection. As the general cultural boundaries of the three regions are relatively fluid, however, one should expect some overlapping of religious configurations. Besides, all three themes just mentioned appear basic to smaller-scale traditional societies around the world, or to the so-called 'primal', 'natural' or 'perennial' religions expressed by such societies (Australian Aboriginal groups included). No one could justly contend, in any case, that the rites of the Polynesians leave the spirit-given blessings of fertility and wealth out of focus, or that for their part Melanesian 'pragmatists' are uninterested in cosmic order. But it is as well to begin with some sense of broad tendencies, if we are to manage a brief survey of the most complex ethnographic scene on earth and of the wide scattering of peoples from New Guinea to Hawaii. We can do no more than offer a feel for what one may expect to find in various Pacific regions, and there is no better way to begin our synopsis than by considering how different peoples picture their universes.

COSMOS

It is more characteristic of Melanesian worldviews that a given group's cosmos is spatially confined and somewhat 'horizontally' conceived. A surprising majority of Melanesian cultures were actually land-locked, especially on the great island of New Guinea, and there has been a consequent tendency for the habitations of spirit agencies, along with human settlements, to be located on (and be accessible from) 'ground level'. A sense of receding ambiences, each decreasing in safety away from one's own hamlet and gardens, is surprisingly common in cultures as far apart as those of the Enga and Wahgi highlanders (5,000–7,000 metres up) and of the hinterland Orokaiva on the northern plains of Papua. If neighbouring tribes and enemies lie beyond this or that point on the horizon – often a prominence or ridge – it is also typical of Melanesian deities, spirits and 'ghost people' that they occupy uncultivated or uncontrollable places and that they come from 'out there' along a broadly horizontal plane.

Traditionally, easy reach of hamlets in one's own clan or tribal area constitutes the 'security circle', where faces are known and unexpected occurrences were minimized. Beyond known territorial boundary markers, yet in the well-tracked or cultivated districts of other tribes, there lies the danger of enemy action, unless a particular inter-tribal alliance is sure; and in the wild of the jungle, swamp or uninhabited tract, hunters or deviating war parties look out for more than savage boars, cassowaries, snakes or (near the coast) crocodiles, for 'the bush' is also a favoured dwelling area of spirit-powers. Knowing that earlier generations took the bodies of the dead into the forested heights of the mountains, for instance, a Wahgi fears ancestral displeasure – from the more powerful, 'distant' dead if a hunt takes him across old 'deposition' grounds – and lucky the fleeing game which in virtually any Melanesian terrain runs into the vicinity of stagnant, eerily still pools ('round water', or *raunwara* as the pidgin has it), because such spots are usually the lairs of dangerous, sick-bearing place-spirits (pidgin *masalai*) and hunters tried to avoid them. In the steep valleys of the Papuan highlands, crossing through mountain forests might seem to be the easiest recourse for any ambush party hoping to surprise an enemy hamlet, but the Fuyughe, among others, accept and fear the protective power of the *sila*, place-spirits which overlook each tribal zone from the heights and which are held to kill trespassers trying any circuitous route. For some peoples, when a man encounters an unknown solitary female outside the inner ambience – traditionally an opportunity for sexual aggression – her straightforward humanness is not to be taken for granted; the Lakalai of New Britain Island actually share the advice that nettles be applied to the woman's skin to ensure she is no dangerous ghost! The central highlands Gimi even 'read' the wild in terms of countervailing genders – trees as penises, the sudden flutter of birds as ejaculations, caves as wombs – the whole making up the fertile source of 'life'.

It would be hasty to conclude, however, that Melanesian religions always lack a sense of 'the vertical'. Patterns of belief about Sky Beings are known, rather significantly, in an almost unbroken arc from high Enga and Melpa country in New Guinea through the inland Gulf area of the Erave (south Kewa) down to Roku on the flat swamp plains nearest Torres Strait and Cape York. The single god of the Roku, in fact, who is both a Cosmic Serpent (called Kampel) as well as a Sky Deity, might suggest some archaic connections from a time when Sahul was one continent, but inferences of this kind can run up against problems. Although Rainbow Serpents are known all over the Australian continent, dominant sky-dwelling Beings are not important save in the south-east (see chapter 2). Besides, on both sides of the Torres Strait islands notions of spirits high above are typically more than matched by those of spirits of known and visitable locations below.

There are also Melanesian groups who deify sun and moon; to the Huli of the Papuan southern highlands they are a brother and sister, Ni and Hana, who committed incest on earth before ascending to the sky; and for the Mae Enga the sun symbolizes the great God Aitawe, who created the domain of the Sky Beings (with the moon's assistance). Even in these cases, though, it is not so much the great powers in the sky themselves which draw forth invocations or ritual responses, as the effects they bequeath to humans and their local environments. In the Huli repertory of ceremonial songs about the sun, the real reason for celebration is that Ni's movements mark them out as a chosen people:

Ni does not rise and stay
Over Abena [Mae Enga territory] at its coming
Over the Ibili [Ipili Engas] and Suguba [Bosavi groups] at its
  height
Or the Sunas [Lake Kopiago people] at its going,
But over us. We are a people!
We are the Huli!

For both the Huli and the Mae the sun's offspring are 'black eggs' – select sacred stones – and the latter people expose these objects as the focus of a special ritual (*Yainanda*) when blight or sickness threatens a tribe's very existence. At their great festivals the nearby Mendi still reveal comparable stones, digging them out from beneath the earthen floors of their long cult-houses, the entrances of which are commonly overshadowed by a large clay disc – emblematic of the sun. Such 'down-to-earth' qualities of Melanesian are indicative.

Melanesian sky gods are nonetheless conspicuous by their rare appearances. Deities one might place in the category of great or 'high' gods are conceived to be ever-present, pervasive but characteristically environal, or else they have removed themselves to some other place (beyond the horizon) after fulfilling their primordial labours. A few such deities created the cosmos, advised the first humans and then continued to monitor humanity by rewarding good behaviour and punishing delicts; such is the almost Biblical view of Yabwahine among the southern Massim of eastern Papua, although groups from the same broad culture area saw this all-seeing 'Sky Man' chiefly as a 'war god' who brought 'moments of triumph' and received all cannibal victims. In one unusual case a sky deity, the bisexual Ugatame of the Kapauka, who are highlanders from western Irian Jaya, created everything but punishes no one, for He/She is the 'predetermining scheme' (*ebijata*) or 'compulsory force' behind all human deeds.[1] In contrast, some elevated gods basically specialize in moral supervision and requital; the Huli's Datagaliwabe being a kind of all-seeing Varuna in this respect. Others are beneficient Sustainers, ensuring that the cosmos they created will not collapse, and requiring little worship or reverence, as with the Mae Enga Aitawe.

As for cases approaching *deus absconditus*, the Ngaing of the hinterland Madang speak of Parambik who 'put' the universe – 'the land, rivers, wild animals, birds and plants (including totems), gods' – yet who later had no involvement with humans and evokes no ritual from them. He only received recognition as the mythic 'plenum' (thus *parambik*) out of which all objects and events have sprung. Of the god Anut in the nearby Sengam, Som, Yam and Yabob complex of coastal Madang, one learns that he created the cosmos (or all of it which did not pre-exist him) and then produced two 'deity brothers', Kilibob and Manup, whose more interesting activities – comparable to those of various Heroes we discuss later – made Anut of less concern to humans. In these (albeit odd) instances we sense that 'high' and more abstractly conceived deities have lost hold of the imagination and have been replaced by more environmentally real pressures. The old prominence of the Lakalai Sky God Gimugaigai, to take another illustration, was more recently overshadowed by the boisterous volcano spirit Sumua, who punishes misdemeanours 'much like any powerful or benevolent ghost'.[2] This particular shift probably owes something to imported ideas, since nearby societies, such as the Mengen, see themselves as protected by mysteriously powerful volcano gods (in their case, Maglila). Volcano gods are quite common on the smaller Melanesian islands;

perhaps the most famous are Karaperamun on Tanna, southern Vanuatu, and Matshikitshi, the Hero God there, who is supposed to have piled one volcanic island upon another.

Impressive female deities are comparatively rare in Melanesia, and myths about procreativity between gods and goddesses are unusual. Actually brother Ni and sister Hana among the Huli were two of the five offspring of Honabe, the primal female deity, and her husband Timbu. Significantly, the family of gods lived on the land, which preceded their existence, and before Ni and Hana's ascent as sun and moon they engaged in their incestuous union on earth below – a serious lesson to humans because their copulation brought no results. It was only through Ni's later marriage to another female deity that the 'black eggs' were fortunately scattered through the Huli domain. In the highlands this link between stones and fertility is common, and across in Melpa and Kyaka Enga country to the east we find that a great Woman Spirit (or Enda Semangko), the object of a spreading pre-contact fertility cult, is thought to be embodied in a single rounded stone. Outside the highlands, perhaps the most famous traditional great goddess is Ia Kupia ('the Mother'), who, half-human, half-serpentine in form, is one of the dominant volcanoes overlooking Rabaul harbour. Tolai myths tell how she ordered her good son To Kabinana to kill his threatening father (now another dormant volcano), while she herself died after shedding her skin because her bad son, To Purgo, failed to keep her warm. (Myths, we note, sometimes tell how gods can die, at least temporally, and thus how the deities come to have less relevance than their descendants.)

If great female deities are few in Melanesia, however, masculine and rather mundane-looking war gods abound. As we shall soon show more fully, warriorhood was the prized role of almost all Melanesian males, and there is little wonder that spiritual powers were evoked for support against enemies – although such aids were typically lesser gods, pertaining to military activity alone or to an individual clan concerned with such. Perhaps the most successful of warriors in the whole region were the Roviana and Simbo of New Georgia (western Solomons), who had an insatiable appetite for taking heads and slaves from neighbouring islands, especially from Ysabel, the Shortlands and even from Bougainville (260 kilometres away!). A supportive Roviana spirit during raids was Liqomo, who was alleged to reveal both the position of enemies and any of their secret devices. More crucial was Musumusu, the spirit leading the war canoes, whose gruesome effigy – with vacant eyes and pendant earrings – also often stood as a warning to strangers at Roviana tribal boundaries or in glades visited only by priests; given his connection with ancestral lines it was for his benefit as well as for the dead that men hunted for skulls and made human sacrifices. Only rarely would such powers demanding blood and death become 'great gods' of the tribal cult. For Murik Lakes groups, indicatively, the war deity Karkar actually had to be constituted for each occasion of war, the priest-like Gapar rushing to procure the war clubs from the cult-house and then arranging them in a row to make the god come into effect before battle.

In 'warrior cultures' the fearsome face put upon spiritual forces could be transferred to other spheres of collective concern. A few Tauade tribes in the Papuan highlands, for instance, fed food to an awesome idol bedecked with tufts of straight (rather than Melanesian crinkly) hair, and those approaching it along a narrow ravine would deviate from the set stepping-stones at their peril. Gifts made at the statue were not for victory, however, but to prevent bad harvests. Such a power was an unusually offendable place-spirit or *masalai*, and some well-known *masalai* were indeed the objects of recurrent sacrifices. In the New Guinea highlands both Siane and Chuave tribes slaughtered pigs at the great boundary rock Elam Bari, for example, when there was too little or too much rain, in the belief that the one-armed, one-legged Being who dwelt there controlled the weather. In these cases it was anger, best known for its consequences in inter-tribal conflict but here projected on to an environal force, which was being averted.

In the more widely dispersed island complexes of both Polynesia and Micronesia there are numerous parallels to these notions of deity. In general, however, the emphases are different enough to ponder, and a great commonality of belief across these two broad regions is more obvious. The divinized sky is a major (to-be-expected) factor, for the sense of the heaven's enormity is bound to have been greater among those who sailed long distances under its expanse, and whose tiny, clustered upsprings of land are ringed by the outermost reaches of its dome. Thus among these Austronesian-speakers one must be ready for relatively more 'vertical' or heaven-ward orientations – in myth, cosmology and cultic focus. The Maori traditions (of Aotearoa/New Zealand in southern Polynesia), convey this distinctiveness most strikingly. In the secret cult of *Whare wananga* (the 'house of sacred learning' open only to the highest priestly adepts), we learn of Io dwelling in the highest of twelve heavens, like the removed, almost inaccessible Supreme Being in various

Gnostic systems. Even if it is possible that we have here some early post-contact accommodation to mission teaching, the accentuation of the vertical is characteristic, and is recognizable enough in the mythic motifs and cosmological representation of the well-known Maori 'departmental' gods, who operate in the realms of sky, earth and underworld.

Rangi (heaven) and Papa (earth) were actually conceived by the Maori as the divine Ancestral pair from whom humans derive, with their seemingly inextricable embrace over 'a vast space of time' having to be undone by the cramped progeny between them. Of their six children, only Tanemahuta, God of Forests, Birds and Insects, can raise his father up to the skies – by using his strong back and limbs, and by being 'firmly planted on his mother the earth'. Only by this *Trennung* can space be made for further divine activity and the eventual generation of humans, whose origins thus ultimately lie both above and below. Far to the north, one finds a comparable, no less famous myth of cosmic separation among the Austronesian-speaking Gilbertese. As an elder of the royal lineage of Karongoa put it, on Makin Meang atoll:

> It was called the Darkness and the Cleaving
> Together;
> The sky and the earth and the sea were within it;
> But the sky and the earth clove together,

and it is not until the young hero Naareau snares the cosmic eel Riiki that the sky is 'uprooted', 'propped' and 'split asunder' from the sinking land and the sea below. Only then can a 'Company of Spirit Fools' haul the First Land out of the depths, Naareau create sun and moon from the eyes of his father (whom he slays), and Riiki become the Milky Way when the hero flings him far overhead.[3]

In both Polynesia and Micronesia, major deities associated with biocosmic forces are usually from above. Creation myths frequently envisage the pulling up of land or island fishing from beneath the sea by sky-dwelling gods or culture heroes (and across Polynesia we find Ta'aroa/Tangaroa, usually a descendant of sky and earth, the most widespread and active of such creator figures, perhaps because of migrations or cultural influences from Tahiti). Micronesian sun cults are common and, as in Polynesia, the greater gods are almost always 'heavenly'. Micronesian cosmic creations are often from above. In the earliest of all Pacific ethnographic reports, a letter by the Jesuit Juan Cantova from the Carolines in 1728, the missionary is struck by 'the Promethean tale of the evil spirit who, after his expulsion from heaven, brought fire down to earth', while in an impressive myth from Yap in particular the habitable world originates from a rock being thrown from the sky.[4] Austronesian mythology is also generally more elaborate than in Melanesia – Marquesan specialists reeled off up to 159 divine generations! – and the narrating of genealogical relations between the deities possesses clearer implications for the ordering of ranked societies. The vertical orientation is often underscored by conceptions of an underworld. The Maori most commonly conceive the lower realm as the house of the defeated Dark God Whiro, guarded by the fearsome female spirit Hine-nui-te-po, with both beings ensuring that death must befall all. Visiting the nether region will surely bring tragedy, as when Motikitik, the Micronesian culture Hero of Yap, spies on his mother gathering food there and thus causes her death.

The vertical orientation of Austronesian cosmogenies does not have to be at the expense of spatial horizons. On Rarotonga (Cook Islands), to illustrate, the cosmos is envisaged in a major origins myth as an enormous coconut, which grows up from its base (*wadi ma takere* = 'Ancient Dirt'), rises in its encompassing 'maturity' (*pakari*), so that the wide horizons are included, and is finally and symbolically completed in the heavens (as *aratea* = 'Cosmic Noon'). Like the perennial Cosmic Egg it contains within it Araiiki, the sphere of life, and in this image we note how the Cosmic Coconut's base, though not clearly represented as a netherworld, suggests the Ancestral foundations, as part of 'the root of existence' (*matung*).[5]

As in Melanesia, prominent goddesses can be found in both the Polynesian and Micronesian regions, but are never paramount. When the 'Earth Mother' is separated from the 'Sky Father' in Maori cosmogeny, for instance, the former has less to do because the male departmental gods controlling gardening, forests and war take up the foreground in myth and ritual. But sometimes her cult is heightened. Out of the four spirit classes on Mangaia (eastern Cook Islands), Vari 'the Great Mother' is the nearest in distance to the normal world, and important for island fecundity and for descendant gods who bring forth humans. In other cases, as on Tikopia (a Polynesian outlier close to Vanuatu) women possess their own divine patroness and cult, from which men are strictly barred.

As for war gods, they were virtually endemic in Polynesia. Contrary to common conceptions, no island complex was unified at the time of contact with the first European recorders; thus tribes badly needed divine reinforcement in their altercations with proximate enemies, and in some circumstances war deities became objects of a centralized cult. If each Maori tribe had recourse to individual tribal war gods, for example, the heart of the first enemy slain in a battle was usually offered to Tumatauenga, honoured *across* tribes as 'the god and father of fierce human beings'. On Mangaia, the most victorious tribe and the one with the most temporal power (*mangaia*) was thought to be granted paramountcy through Rongo, a 'national God' of War; but Rongo's cult, dominated by two high priests, 'transcended clan borders . . . and remained neutral during war'.[6] A multitude of other deities can hardly be discussed here; suffice it to say that the full weight of Austronesian polytheism needs to be felt, and, as in Melanesia, many gods were environal – in sacred forests, stones, places of mystery and sometimes volcanoes – such as Hawaii Island's Pele, the volcano goddess of Mount Kilauea, who demanded human victims when angry.

No account of Oceanian cosmologies would be complete without attention to the mythic exploits of 'culture Heroes' and of course the place of 'the Ancestors'. These different classes of beings have comparable roles as supranormal agencies, typically possessing lesser power than deities. In Melanesia, culture Heroes are frequently groups of Beings who pass through the land in mythic times, revealing to each tribe's Ancestors the skills of warfare and food production and the technologies for building, weaving, etc. (as with the transient *tidib* of the Fuyughe), or marking the places of settlement (as did the 'white moon spirits' of Malekula in Vanuatu), before passing on to distant, unknown quarters. In other settings tales are told of individual Heroes rather than collectivities. Manarmakeri, from the Biak-Numfor region of north-western Irian, is a renowned case in point. Uncovering the secret land of Koreri (or Eternal Life) in the depths of a cave, the ordinary villager Yawi Nushado neglects his personal hygiene, becoming a scabeous old man – *Manarmakeri*. He captures the Morning Star from a tree, however, and somehow manages to impregnate a village girl with a magic coconut so as to secure a wife. After both are exiled, he visits and settles important spots in the coastal and island cosmos of the Geelfink Bay or Sorenarwa Strait area, and as a rejuvenated, transformed explorer marks the points of habitation for others to come. If Manarmakeri does not quite become a god, other comparable voyagers elsewhere are deemed to be such – for acting more as creators. Jari, goddess of the female cult among the Murik Lakes groups and other coastal Sepik cultures, was not only a great traveller. She gave form to the many places she visited – in urinating she created rivers, for example, including the great Sepik River itself; she revealed how women can avoid death in childbirth; and she introduced her 'uncultured' husband to cooked food. Narrations of such heroic journeys endow sacred significance to the boundedness of the cosmos, granting a people its sense of centrality despite the known existence of other groups further away.

Heroic achievements can also lead to tragedy. The giver of benison can be killed for his trouble, and thus become a sacrificial figure – as was the Serpent Spirit Totoima among the hinterland Orokaiva; his severance into small pieces brings *ivo* (spirit-power of fertility) to all the tribes implicated in his death (just as *ivo* is transferred from each cannibal victim to the killer). Across Polynesia by far the best known culture Hero is Maui (who has analogues in Micronesia as Motikitik and in southern Vanuatu as Matshikitshi). After first finding the abode of his mother in the spirit world, according to the Maori version of the legend, the winged Maui emerges as a mighty Hero who nets the sun to prevent it from moving too fast, pulls up a great fish to produce a portion of the earth, and by extinguishing the scorching volcanic goddess Mahu'ike he brings back fire after the world had lost it. Too reckless, however, Maui tries to destroy Hinenui-te-po, his Ancestress and goddess of death, but she devours him, and his failure 'introduces' death to all who come after him. In this legend Maui epitomizes the warrior ethos – of courage and daring exploit despite the inevitability of death – and also appears as a saviour who just eludes bringing back his best and final gift to humanity.

In most Pacific cultures the spirits of the departed are readily distinguishable from gods and culture Heroes, although in Micronesia and Polynesia, known for their high chieftainships, genealogies commonly link the chiefly lines back to the early human descendants of the gods. In Melanesia, by contrast, we find more discontinuity; the dead usually have their own separate ambience, with genealogies being preserved for an average of six generations before the name of the oldest in a remembered chain dissolves into a pool of distant Ancestors. Sometimes the deceased can be thought of as mediators between humans and the gods – among the Jaua and other Orokaiva groupings, for instance, one approaches the High God Asisi through the Ancestors – but in most cultures concern for the departed just sits alongside cultic focus on greater powers, with efforts at integration usually being left undeveloped or only symbolically suggestive. The deceased are almost always conceived as remaining part of society – which is a community of both the living and the dead – and therefore they constitute powerful and watchful participators in rites; in that sense they are usually crucial for group support, yet not confused with deities worshipped or other spirits placated.

A New Guinea highland culture will serve as exemplification. Among the Wahgi most tribes accept derivation from the eponymous Hero ancestor Mondo, but he has no cult, and tribes trace their linkage to him via the number of remembered pig-killing festivities they have organized and not by listing Ancestral names. Between Mondo and the remembered deceased lie the *kipem bang* (the 'red spirits', meaning 'distant Ancestors'), who, though an amorphous collectivity, are very powerful in ensuring a given tribe's welfare, while the more recent dead are thought to be still active in immediate human affairs and are known by name. The favour of both these groups of departed ones is cultivated, especially during group ceremonies, because they are expected to be supportive when they witness displays of their clan's wealth. As in various (more typically eastern) highland societies, Ancestral power is specially embodied in sacred flutes at initiations. Fearful ghosts, however, as distinct from the helpful dead, are assumed to cause only harm. Thus for the Wahgi the Ancestors are a very important object of ritual concern in their own right, while focus on the war gods (as among the south-eastern Wahgi) is limited to preparations for conflict, and placation of bush spirits dependent on the magician's identification of types of sickness. Despite variations, with the coastal regions certainly showing up more parity of ritual response shared between deities and Ancestors than in the highlands, this pattern is characteristically Melanesian.

Throughout most of Oceania, interestingly, the helpful deceased are those who have received the proper funerary rites, while troublesome ghosts arise from those not properly disposed of or from those expected to carry their grievances beyond death. What distinguishes various highly ranked Polynesian cultures, though, is the listing of primogenitively legitimated chiefs back to the gods or to the traditional arrival on an island. For what they are worth historically, the longest Maori name lists, which take each tribe back to its original canoe at the landing of the 'Great Fleet', are truly remarkable in this regard, and no known oral history collected from Melanesian societies takes such a form. And in both Micronesia and Polynesia Ancestors other than chiefly ones tend only to be objects of very minor ritual activity. At meals on Tikopia, indeed, do not expect invocations of Ancestors 'in a household of no particular status', but rather their naming and welcoming by those of higher rank. The latter articulates the 'key Ancestral structure' which links all clans back to the generations of the gods, whose ancient and continuing 'Work' is celebrated in a festival involving the whole island, and who once supposedly descended on Reani peak (a space on tiny Tikopia significantly left uncultivated). On Rapanui/Easter Island, the well-known megaliths were erected for the 'great Ancestors', whose lined effigies sat facing the tribal land that they had secured and defended for the great majority of ordinary mortals coming after them.[7]

To complete our introductory survey, habitants of the cosmos are often said to include all sorts of lesser spirit agencies, though some ethnographers are more thorough in listing them than others. Ralph Bulmer has identified ten classes of Kyaka Enga spirits, ranging from the recently imported fertility goddess, through 'nature demons', Sky Beings and ghosts down to 'cannibal ogres ... and minor nature spirits ... , including tree spirits, echoes and snails'. For the Hawaiians, Valerio Valeri has been still more exhaustive, and to the great gods, kinship gods and Ancestors he adds manifesting deities, spirit predators and imaginary animals, including '*alde* the "ominous bird" '. For the Maori, James Irwin would even append the 'aborted foetus' (who joins humans as a malicious trickster), 'monsters', 'goblins', 'fairy folk' and any 'visible form' (*aria*) – by way of birds, fish, reptiles, and animals – taken by spirit-beings.[8] Voyagers have to deal with the spirits of winds and waves; hunters and hungry travellers have to avoid taking prey tabued to them – for the 'totems' sometimes lying at the origins of their own ancestry, or sacred to their society or cult, provide a protection very dangerous to flout.

Such a sensitivity for varied environal forces will remind readers that so-called 'primitive' peoples have been called 'animists' (following a usage by E. B. Tylor). Yet if animism means the belief that the whole cosmos is alive with unseen spirit-forces, as if 'all that exists, lives', as the American Chukchee shaman poetically affirmed it,[9] then Oceanian *Weltanschauungen* do not fit the conditions. The Tolai will sense Ancestral presence in birds appearing in an appropriate context; Fuyughe will avoid killing snakes in case they signal the presence of *sila*; and the Micronesian prohibition against eating porpoise is widespread; but only recognizable parts and not the whole of the visible cosmos awaken a sense of awe, ritual obligation or anxious avoidance among Oceanian peoples. In all other respects their pragmatism towards their environment is potent, and an evident 'materialism' – especially in Melanesia – governs their approaches to war and production.

PAYBACK

Oceanian cultures, as we have stated, were warrior cultures. Rare indeed were groups who escaped armed conflict with enemies, and most males had to be trained to propel spears, arrows or clubs for the recurrent round of surprise attacks and field battles. It is no longer plausible to consider traditional warriorhood in the region without contemplating its religious 'face' or its many relationships with more distinctly religious activities. There were shared, commonly enunciated reasons for fighting enemies or for taking up weapons, and such consensus justifications had everything to do with traditional belief-sytems. Most warfare in Oceania centres around revenge; if a community loses one of its number, the death must be 'paid back'. By a cumulative effect, retribution against those threatening a group's survival also built up its own sense of identity, with past victories being celebrated in song and legend, with myths explaining, if not legitimating, the necessity of taking 'life for life', and with daily 'male talk' consolidating the sense of being a people to be reckoned with and feared.

Among the 2,000 or so stateless societies across Oceania, the solidary community – or better still the 'security circle' or 'war group' – was typically small, being a lineage or clan concentrated in one or a few hamlets or a tribe made up of two or more clans bound to be supportive in times of conflict by blood ties. Such social atomization made for quick executive action, but it often meant that people who spoke the same language – tribes within the same culturo-linguistic complex, who might seem to have been ideally suited to make up a cohesive bloc *vis-à-vis* different groups – made war against each other. Even such confined-looking dots on the map as Chuuk or Ponape in Micronesia were islands divided into separate regions by conflict and shifting alliances. And if some people preyed on others further afield – like the Roviana looking for Bougainvillean heads – that is no confirmation that the aggressive culture was politically united. Even the greatest chiefly systems of Polynesia were no proof of such a unity either, at least at the time of European contact. Scanning the traditional scene, then, we are left with the virtual ubiquity of small and separated social units, always under pressure to uphold basic principles of tribal solidarity (while we concede that among some peoples, especially in Polynesia, confederating pressures were not without effect).

In Melanesia connections between war and religion are manifold. The obligation to requite a kinsperson's death usually mixes moral with apotropaic concerns. On the one hand, a death may be paralleled in community rhetoric to the loss of a hand from the body; on the other, there arises an increasing anxiety that, if nothing is done, the ghost of an unavenged warrior will turn on those who have not fulfilled a basic obligation. *'Pring pangwo'* runs an utterance of the highland Chimbu, when a member of one's lineage has fallen: 'I am guilty' (or 'I am not right in my relations with my fellows and the spirit world until I secure revenge'). Ongoing military exchanges can be found connected to all sorts of rituals – Wahgi magicians marking out lines before a battle and whistling to warn any of their side who cross it that their spiritual protection has been removed; coastal Papua Motuan specialists cracking their fingers as auspices before an ambush; warriors on San Cristobal (in the Solomons) only taking up spears after one of their number shows signs of spirit possession; war-cries and victory songs evoking the support of the dead among the Dugum Dani (in the highlands of Irian Jaya); and more. All such traditional Melanesian phenomena, together with the vigour and excitement of armed clashes themselves, especially when heroic acts are recalled in the male long- or cult-house after a day's exchange or a successful expedition for heads, justify the description 'warrior religion'. For some peoples, as with the Sepik Iatmül or the Arawe of New Britain, men were not fully initiated until they took life; or could not be received into Dalugeli, the celestial resting-place as the Huli envisaged it, unless they had fought or been slain in battle.

All documented Melanesian societies have their repertories of reasons for death (and also for sickness and trouble), and in all we find characteristic actions of response to such adversities. In the conceptual and explanatory connections hamleters draw between events, and in the sets of actions issuing because of their 'assumptive worlds', there lies what we have called elsewhere 'the logic of retribution'.[10] According to this mode of thought and operation, fighting does not stop short when weapons are set aside, for in a world of grating enmities there is also 'spiritual revenge' to contend with – the sorcerer. In the traditional situation, before colonial pacification made them highly ambivalent figures, sorcerers were valued human resources for almost all security circles, hurling 'the spear by night' when it was not in use by day.[11] Conversely, enemy sorcery was typically feared as the source of fatal illness, since deaths and serious sicknesses were almost never ascribed to natural sources, but rather to living agencies and their invisible influences. Thought by the Bena Bena (eastern highlands, New Guinea) to operate nocturnally, sorcerers come close to the hamlets of their hapless victims and blow their evil smoke. When someone dies from sickness, a renowned response of these people is 'payback running'; the dead person's spirit 'seizes' a relative, who speeds off under this possession to mark the location of the sorcerer culprit's tribe. When the time is opportune, anyone from the pinpointed group is liable to be killed in reprisal, for Melanesian payback applies between collectives and is thus 'indiscriminate' – unless prior marriage linkages with the culpable clan make a selective killing advisable.

Negative retribution is also applied as punition within security circles, the latter then acting as 'jural' units dependent on leaders' effective arbitrations to maintain internal cohesion. Each culture has its own body of prohibitions (pidgin *tambu*) and its demanding principles of loyalty and obligation; the analysis of laws, moral pressures, delicts and requitals remains a major area for study in its own right. Variations abound, though with severity the norm. In east Papua, for example, adulterers were commonly killed, but among the Wedau it was only the woman who was despatched, while for the nearby matrilineal Massim complex it was the male. In some settings, as among the Tolai, there were few misdemeanours which could not be covered by the payment of fines in precious shell money. Torture and incarceration were virtually unknown, but quick corporal punishments could inflict permanent injury, and dreaded 'shame' (or social ostracism) often awaited those violating key tabus or refusing participation in warfare. Readers should be made aware that unsanctioned violence within the community was a 'crime', and if death resulted it was 'murder', whereas violence against unallied outsiders was most often an accepted activity for group survival – unless leaders ruled that hotheads had wrongly taken matters into their own hands.

Anthropologist Donald Tuzin has produced scintillating work on the interrelation between war, religion and the maintenance of cohesion in the largest of the Ilahita Arapesh villages. Nggwal, the Cyclopean god of the Tambaran, or secretive male cult, was understood to demand the victims of revenge wars, but in this quite sizeable community high-grade initiates of the cult maintained 'social control' by deciding which deaths by sorcery derived from Nggwal, or were permitted by him, and which were not. Those from within Ilahita who were 'swallowed by the *tambaran*' as sorcery victims reflected Nggwal's internally punitive power, and such deaths were 'entered in the record [the god's] kills' by adding knots to cordylline ropes.[12] Here a sorcery death is viewed more as a divine sanction; while in other situations, as among the Mekeo (of hinter-land Papua), chiefs held the accepted power of deploying 'domestic sorcerers' to remove or warn miscreants. (Students of Melanesia should be made aware, however, that after unstable pre-contact conditions were affected by colonialism, sorcery became a problem within Melanesian villages, often amalgamated and enlarged by the new administrations, and the resulting cycles of *intra*-community suspicion should be read as a *neo*-tradition. Witchcraft, by compari-son, was a pre-contact phenomenon, suspicions against women mainly arising because they married in from other tribes, following exogamous principles, and were potentially 'enemies within' a secur-ity circle until proving themselves loyal.)

To labour negativities makes for a lopsided picture. There are very many remarkable acts of concession presenting opposite impressions of Melanesian religious life – such as peacemaking procedures, ceremonial exchanges and extraordinary acts of magna-nimity – as well as continuous group interest in the relative balances of socio-economic reciprocations. The other side to retributive logic – motives governing positive 'give and take' – comes into play here, surrounded by a host of assumptions and consensus notions in any given security circle about its dealings with families, lineages and more distant traders.

Inter-tribal alliances in Melanesia were mostly forged through marriages. Whether cultures were patri- or matrilineal, much hum-drum and not unexciting exchange came with 'free passage' between affinally related tribes (if and when war did not disrupt relations or travel). As for exchange between whole groups or distant trading partners, this was necessarily more formalized by ritual procedures. The south-west Pacific was renowned for its fascinating cycles of inter-island reciprocation. The Kula Ring – whereby valuables and prized foodstuffs circulated between the Trobriand, d'Entrecastaux and northern Massim islands – was thoroughly fortified by magical rites for safe sailing and success, and the very scene of exchanges was full of protocol – with 'opening', 'solicitory' and 'clinching gifts'.[13] In the New Guinea highland cultures, among the Chimbu and Wahgi to take two examples, a host tribe will expend immense energy to prepare pigs, foodstuffs and dances of hospitality for their allies, whose travelling parties come *en masse* to receive the extraordinary acts of generosity at the great pig-killing festivals. Hundreds of beasts are killed by bashing their heads and then lined up on the *sing-sing* ground, yet the meat is all given away to the guests, who are 'wounded' to replicate the same occasion of magna-nimity in their own tribal territories. Such mass slaughters are also sacrifical; the Ancestors are commonly provided with a grandstand in the centre of the dance area, and they are to be pleased and cajoled into a supportive spiritual force by the powerful display of the living.

By mentioning sacrifice, various elements in our discussion of Melanesian payback can be the better drawn together. Offerings and sacrifical rites before supranormal powers are expressions of reciprocity. The basic paradigm is that of exchanging goods, but the human gives visible things, while the spirit is the one who can provide the invisible power to increase the material welfare of the offerer's group (or in the case of apotropaism, can be persuaded not to take adverse action toward human beings). Such rites of reciprocity are thus forms of bargaining, or parallel to the exercises by which humans satisfy themselves that they are fulfilling obligations to each other. If certain sacrifices belong only to occasions of remarkable gift-giving to allies however, others are also enacted to receive succour in enterprises of violence. Wahgi magicians, for example, would spill pig's blood over carved and rounded spirit-stones (the prehistoric left-overs from the world's earliest horticulturists), and invoke the 'Power behind the Stone' as the War God to bring victory; the Roviana, in the heyday of their far-flung raids, placed cannibal victims side-by-side as a sacrifical launching ramp for their canoes. The emphasis, as stated initially, was on visible and material benefits.

These Melanesian patterns of payback find parallels in the Austronesian cultures further out in the Pacific. Before European contact, tribal warfare was well-nigh endemic throughout Oceania. When the great American novelist Henry Melville wrote of the 'Typee' tribe of the Marquesas enjoying a 'prodigious notoreity over all the islands', he was singling out yet another ferocious group who happened to be doing rather well in the kind of recurrent inter-tribal skirmishing we have just noted for the Melanesians. While there were classic pretexts for war – quarrelling over land, pig-stealing, rape – just as there were in Melanesia, the basic cause lay with the 'system of blood revenge', as it has been put of the Chuukese in the Marianas, groups taking from each other a life for a life (but rarely that of a culpable killer) yet with no one 'being murdered by one of his own clan'.[14] The main differences in the patterns of payback war in these Austronesian regions, especially in Polynesia, lay in the apparently better organized mode of military operations (sometimes under the direction of a noble warrior 'caste'); the greater store set by avenging the deaths (or losses) of high-ranking personages; and the more prevalent practice of taking slaves and using them or slain enemies for cannibal sacrifice. Moreover, if the remarkable social atomization in Melanesia made for constantly shifting balances of power, and few signs of either multi-tribal confederacies or radical territorial expansionism, Polynesia at least possessed the institutions for making the attainment of 'higher unities' – whether under monarchs or through marriages between chiefly houses – more possible.

Social structures prevailing through Polynesia were ramages and chieftainships. Ramages may be described as descent groups which are ambilineally defined (i.e. sometimes using the father, sometimes the mother to record the lineage), and above all organized primogenitively. If each ramage had its chief, who was appointed (if fit for office) as the 'first born', one ramage was always ranked higher than others as based on (what was at least claimed to be) Ancestral seniority. The chief whose Ancestor was designated the first chief in the story of a district's settlement, in other words, was typically acknowledged to be the paramount chief over the whole tribe (or cluster of ramages). Now if military activity was affected by this system, since survivalist decisions centred around chiefs or high-ranking warriors acting in their stead, the patterns of both punitive sanction and positive reciprocity also lent towards authoritarianism.

We must be careful of glib generalization about the Polynesian panorama. The Hawaiian, Tongan, Samoan and Tahitian societies are famed for high chiefs who had virtually unlimited power to mete out severe punishments and dipossess those infringing their decrees, yet in other groups this individualized right was severely limited, and in Polynesian enclaves nearer Melanesia – Pukapuka, Ontong Java and Tokelau – punition was carried out with barely any attention to 'status differences', and the leaving of some delicts to 'supernatural sanctions' was more obvious. In both Polynesia and Micronesia, moreover, networks of humdrum and ceremonial reciprocation were not vitiated even by the extremes of social stratification found in Hawaii, Tonga and Tahiti, because there was no one economic apex, and allied tribes were constantly exercising exchanges with each other. In Polynesia most of the everyday exchanges were between ramages within a tribal territory, with some marriages being between ramages and thus endogamous to the tribe (though with chiefs always marrying outside the tribe). Within each ramage there was also an upward flow of goods to satisfy inter-tribal ceremonial reciprocations and feasts, but only in the most

stratified societies does one notice the highly inequitable require-
ment for lower orders to satisfy the sumptuary needs of the high
chiefs or the increased sacrificial needs of the priests.

Offerings and sacrifices in Polynesia vividly illustrate the combi-
nation of positive reciprocity and negative retribution in spite of
social stratification. High chiefs or kings are often viewed as mediating the divine to humans in their role as sacrificers (backed up by
a priesthood). Hawaii is best documented in this regard. At the New
Year festivals (Makahiki) and the Temple Renewal rite immediately
following it (Luakini), the role of a king is pivotal. In the former
the king must dash a live pig to the ground, killing it without the
victim emitting a squeal and in the midst of a solemn prayer; as
'supreme sacrificer' the king is thereby securing 'friendship with the
gods'. At the finale of the Luakini, the 'great sacrifice' of hundreds
of pigs, fish, bananas, coconuts, *oloa* cloths and 'some human victims'
is offered by the king to the gods in the (open air) temple. Following
the subsiduary rite by which the priests receive their assigned portion of the sacrifices, the king supervises the distribution of cooked
pork and vegetables to all present at this great ceremony, each
family representative being given 'a share according to his rank'
down to the 'crowd of "very little" people' or the needy. Such
generosity towards the gods is deliberately designed to create mutual
indebtedness, while the king's distributions symbolize both his
mediatorship and the people's dependence on his beneficence. As
for the human victims – offered once at the New Year rite and as
many as six times at the Temple Renewal – they 'must be guilty',
whether as enemies of the tribe or transgressors within it.[15]

Elaborate sacrifices like this before effigies of the gods are only
rarely found in traditional Melanesia. Carefully laid out altars, made
of stone bricks, with a central one for burnt holocausts, are known
from the Toambaita and other cultures on Malaita (Solomons).
Cannibal victims of coastal Fiji's Viti Levu were often ritually
despatched within rings of large stones that formed a shrine. But
the complexity of Polynesia's sacrificial rites, including the dressing
of the gods by chiefs and priests (which appeared to early outsiders
like 'children playing with dolls and baby-houses'),[16] as well as the
case of virtually divinized royal mediators between gods and
humans, lent the reciprocity factor a more 'aristocratic' ceremoni-
ousness and solemnity than found elsewhere in Oceania. But we
must continue to eschew unqualified generalizations. After all,
throughout Samoa religion apparently lacked all pomp and splendid
sacrifice; and apart from priestly consultations with the war gods,

carried out in small houses next to the *mamrae* (or public meeting places on the village green), Samoan religious observances were performed in the privacy of family dwellings. Furthermore, where hierarchism and centralizing cults did exist in Polynesia, and the special sumptuary needs of royal and priestly orders had to be met by generosity from below, we are not to conclude that reciprocity had thereby been rendered less crucial or less expressive of island worldviews and religiosity. With or without a pyramidal-looking social structure, redistribution was the hallmark of Oceanic economics in general; even in Melanesia, where many societies were without chiefs, somebody had to get to the 'top' to act as the 'master redistributor'. As we shall see, once old processes of reciprocation became undermined through the impact of the West, the responses to the resulting crises were typically *religious*, because reciprocity – or the common energies put behind the constant 'give and take' of primal societies – epitomized life's wholeness. And this was reinforced by successes against enemies and the preservation of order against malefactors.

POWER

So much of our previous discussion impinges on questions of power. In modern social organization we have become used to the formalized differentiation between sacred and temporal power, and the extremes between unarmed prophets appealing to conscience and naked political force. For all the effects of secularization, however, moderns remain surprisingly aware of the curious extensibility and 'invisible hand' of power. Now primal worldviews almost always foster an image of some general occult power, usually operating for the benefit of the group and its individual members; and Oceania has provided us with the most famous word in this regard – *mana* (generally: 'spirit-power for success'). *Mana* is evoked across the borders of the regions we are discussing, from the western Solomons (among the Roviana) across to the Marquesas. Quite apart from the continuing debate about its meaning (it is not in every context a substantive noun meaning 'spirit-power') or about its pervasive importance (Tahitians and Marquesans evoked it sparingly), the *mana* concept still remains *indicative* of socio-religious preoccupations across the board.

The subject of power naturally conducts us to the issue of social leadership, authority and mobilization. In Polynesia, it goes without saying, positions of monarchs or chiefs were legitimated by appeals to their *mana*, or 'spirit-authority'. Power-holding had to be confirmed by deeds, mind you, and it did not automatically follow that a first-born son, if he did not show himself worthy, would inherit office, or that an incumbent in a chiefly office who failed to fulfil his role with valour or strength of character would face no challenge. One of the important processes entailed by increasing stratification and centralized power, it has been shown, is the transition in Polynesia from a 'traditional' to a more 'open' society, whereby chiefs emerged because they proved themselves to be supreme in battle, with new 'usurper' lineages replacing or seriously modifying the traditional priority of the senior ramage and new rulers setting up the sorts of 'dynasties' that explorers found on contact in the 'stratified' societies of Hawaii and Tahiti.[17] *Mana* went with the totality of power; victory and continued security were pulled off because a mandate of rule was confirmed by the spirit-world. Mythologies endorsed this understanding; in the reckless career of Maui, indeed, allowance is made for success in the 'struggle for power' despite his questionable parentage.[18] In the actual histories of institutions, though, compromises were often made whereby warrior chiefdoms carried out their contests for hegemony while older embodiments of tradition, such as the Tonga's sacred king or Tu'i Tonga (who held office by much stricter primogenitive principles), remained aloof and isolated from struggles in his own enclave.

The concentration of power at the social apex found in Polynesia and Micronesia, along with high ceremonial and notions of chiefly mediatorship, has reinforced an older view that these regions clearly housed 'religions', while Melanesia only managed the inferior creations of 'magic'. Certainly, the existence of virtually divinized rulers and of priesthoods upholding 'royal cults' were unknown in Melanesia – at least outside Fiji on a regional 'boundary-line' – but one must be cautious about exaggerating socio-religious differences. Melanesia, to begin with, possessed many more chiefly societies than is commonly supposed – across Vanuatu and New Caledonia, through the Solomons to Bougainville and the Trobriands, and along the Papuan coast. Chiefs unexpectedly show up in highland contexts; each Fuyughe tribe, for instance, possessed one special chief known as *utam(e)*, who in effect was the tribe's life-essence, and who was debarred from leaving his tribal territory in case the cosmos would collapse – an idea unparalleled in all Oceania. And if Polynesia is noted for 'aristocracies', they are not unknown in Melanesia either. The Roviana created a superior ruling group, for example, by colonizing the Buin in Bougainville; and on Manam Island (New Guinea islands) the *taneopoa* were a privileged 'caste' dominating the ancestral cult, war and distribution processes. Occasionally Melanesian priesthoods are manifest. John Layard has left the extraordinary account of the 'Making of Men' in northern Malekula, where, set among the megaliths left by the 'moon spirits' (or culture heroes), and symbolizing the combined male–female elements in the cult of Creator God Kabat, ten priest-like clan magicians completed the major initiation ceremony. The ten, allegedly descending from Kabat's children, had to perform an orgiastic rite to safeguard the passage of their own souls to Kabat's realm after death. In a shrine representing Kabat's female side they lay down in ritual intercourse with female representatives of the district's villages – 'to make men as Kabat had done' – despite sometimes committing incest in so doing.[19] Even in this unusual case, however, it is not a recognizable social 'caste' or priestly 'order' which is involved so much as a specialist group with ritual privileges – and this limitation applies to most cultic functionaries in the more 'traditional', less hierarchic Polynesian societies as well.

One feature of the Melanesian scene that makes the region look 'less religious', of course, is the wide prevalence of more egalitarian-looking societies led by 'big-men' or 'managers', who achieve status through hard competition rather than by inheritance. The struggles between competing *grands hommes* in the central New Guinea highlands, in fact, led to the premature conclusion that the populous, volatile and more recently contacted mix of tribal complexes in the great high valleys of the world's second largest island were decidedly more 'secular' in ethos than most seaboard cultures. With the dead being less predictable than on the coasts – often being feared as vengeful ghosts – so much appeared left to human effort, as symbolized in the fierce competitiveness and skilful organization of the big-men themselves. The spirit-powers as a whole, however, turned out to be much less capricious than at first believed, and upon closer analysis the impressive exchange systems, which received their astounding summations in ceremonial pig-kills or in the lining up of grown pigs to contest for 'big-manship' (as with the Melpa *Moka* or Enga *Te*), could not be readily disassociated from religious activity. For Melanesia the definition of religon simply has to be broadened to include the practical pursuit of material and 'biocosmic' blessings.[20] In any case, highland big-men co-operate closely with more distinctly religious functionaries, such as the 'tabued man' (or *mapilie*) among the Wahgi, who communicates with the spirits of the warrior dead and watches over the ceremonial ground from one great *Kongar*, or pig-killing, festival to another. Further, recent studies of highland leadership have revealed that, in militarily unstable pre-contact times, a big-man was much more likely to inherit his father's role than post-contact patterns of open competition suggest.

Thus far we have concentrated on the power of leadership, but that often reflects on general and collective attitudes towards power in tribal 'security circles'. To illustrate this, in the ranked Polynesian societies we find commoners or undistinguished families looking to ranked personages and priests to perform the most crucial rituals on their behalf. A common motif or ritual is for the chiefs or priests to seek divine protection for the whole community. 'O gods', runs a prayer set for an Hawaiian king:

> come save the nobles and all the men;
> O all my gods, pay heed . . .
> Preserve the just man and do him good;
> Have compassion for my land,
> And take care of the commoners.

This theme of protection is admittedly found in prayers right down the social scale – for planting, fishing and the like – and chants for protection are well known in Micronesia as well. But they conform psycho-religiously to a vertico-hierarchical opening of both the social and spiritual orders, reflecting more an attitude of dependence and negotiated *rapprochement* than 'technologic' manipulation. In Melanesia one finds more emphasis on direct transactions with the spirits by groups as virtually unranked wholes, or by small groups helped by the incantations or 'manipulative prayers' of specialists or heads of households – to make the garden grow, as a Trobriand spell exemplifies, so that it 'rises like the iron-wood palm/[and] . . . swells as with a child'.[21]

As far as the reflection of power structures in society is concerned, such ranked societies as those found in Polynesia could reflect immense authority descending from above. Not only were there slaves, or captives waiting to be sacrificial victims, but commoners were very much at the mercy of chiefly decrees. In Melanesia this was less the case. True, among the unusually powerful Roviana and Simbo a pool of slaves was kept for menial tasks and sacrifices, and captive women were set aside for 'prostitution', but the chiefs or their lineages did not have autocratic control over these persons. Certainly the chiefs had exclusive access to their own skull-houses, where *mana* was concentrated in the preserved crania of their forebears, but of greater importance were the village skull-houses, with the piles of heads brought back from raids meant to ensure blessings from the dead for the whole tribe. The blessings were visible material results of ritual and valorous action, and in fact very typical of Melanesian rites was the direct concern with increase, aversion of possible malevolence and 'concrete results' (pidgin *kaikai*), rather than a praying above for protective aid.

Much more typical for Melanesia than the Roviana case suggests, indeed, is the mixing of rites with exchange mechanisms so as to achieve summations of material surfeit and climactic displays of wealth and physical power, thereby showing that the spirits' supportive power is already in evidence. While not disputing Oceania-wide concerns with fertility and festal distributions, Melanesian ritual appropriations of Power (pidgin *paua*) appear comparatively more 'materialistic', and the social configurations matching the religious outlooks relate more to prestige gained by generosity and to degrees of indebtedness. The big-man is usually the one who temporarily borrows most so that he can then put as many people as possible into debt through his prestige-building generosity at a feast. The 'rubbish-man' is at the bottom of this – albeit relatively more egalitarian – scale; he is unimportant because he has ventured virtually nothing in the processes of production and reciprocity which 'make a man'. In Polynesia and Micronesia, by comparison, there is more a sense that ostensibly stable arrangements of power reflect and are legitimated by a tiered cosmic order.

Other dimensions to the subject of power beckon attention, but unfortunately space only allows a cursory glance over questions of custodial power, male–female relationships, specialist appropriation of power (including sorcery) and the dispossession of power. Custodianship takes a variety of forms. It can be expressed in long-term familial and kin relationships, with husbands typically holding authority over their wives (polygamy by big-men being widespread, and polyandry, as among the Melanesian Arapesh and the Polynesian Marquesans, being rare), with parents sometimes having their children adopted into the care of other (often childless) couples, and maternal uncles commonly expected to pay special and generous attention to the development of their nephews. It can also be manifested in specific ritual contexts or repeated rites meant to be dissociated from everyday relations. In highland Melanesia, for example, patriclan leaders with a cluster of pubescent boys ready for initiation will play on their affinally linked alliances to invite in the maternal uncles as stern initiators – to supervise the appropriate ordeals (such as walking on fire and then being beaten by rods while the key tribal prohibitions are uttered, as in the *Tege* intiations of the Huli). In a sprinkling of both highland and coastal cultures boys are virtually sodomized by adults in the 'men's houses' to make them grow into strong warriors (as has been long documented of the Marind Anim headhunters, southern Irian Jaya). In other cultures again, initiation at puberty is but the first in a series of graded initiations within male 'secret societies'.

Male–female relations form a complex subject involving kinship customs as much as notions of power. To generalize about religious aspects, however, we may say that women rarely achieved leadership status unless chiefly regimes or matrilineally organized societies allowed for it. We learn of only one 'queen-like' figure from Melanesia – Koloka from the Nara of coastal Papua, who was borne about by obsequious attendants on a pallet – even if we find that female chiefs were not unusual among the nearby Roro. Of the kind of influential queens one discovers in Hawaii or Tonga, however, fighting to the death with their husbands in battle, like Manona beside Kekuaokalani on Hawaii Island, we learn nothing from the 'black islands'. Bride-price ceremonies are typical appendages to marriages throughout Oceania, yet whereas some store is set on the idea of 'love gifts' to the in-laws in Austronesian cultures, in the Melanesian highlands women tended to be rated more like 'property' (together with pigs!), and in unstable military situations were often suspected of disloyalty or witchcraft (for having married in from other tribes).

Across the Pacific the great majority of women were subjected to, yet paradoxically feared by, their husbands. Men almost always had the sanction to beat their wives whenever it was deemed necessary, for instance, yet women had their own potentiality for redress. Playing on male anxiety over pollution was one typical recourse; Melpa women angry at their husbands could walk across the food they had cooked, thus exposing a meal to their polluting genitals. That already implies, though, that women's bodies could 'dispossess' power from males, which is why the forced retirement to a secluded hut during menstruation and childbirth was a typical Oceanian phenomenon. Sometimes we find a potential balance of power expressed through countervailing male and female myths, as with New Guinea highland Gimi, but in their case the main rituals consistently resolved matters in men's favour, as also did exchanges, which Gimi women could never formally initiate. Genuine enough personal clout could still be cultivated by wives as the makers of families, though, as has recently been shown of the Irian Jayese highlander Nalum; while in certain costal contexts – especially with the east Papuan Massim – 'gender power' was remarkably even.

Specialists in the appropriation of spirit-power abound through Oceania, although not all concerned themselves with positivities. Elders and priests, the latter in Polynesia especially, were the demarcators of tabu, marking the occasions, places and actions which were spiritually dangerous if not approached properly or by appropriate persons. 'Tabu/tapu' is a famous trans-Polynesian notion (often wrongly mistranslated as 'holiness' or 'sacredness'), but it has eminent applicability across the whole region. Removing restrictions of tabu, or the effects of breaking it, by supervising a return to 'the ordinary' (commonly *noa* in Polynesia), involved legal arbitration and knowledge of placatory and purificatory procedures. Politics could be involved; in any power struggle between a set of village chiefs (as among the Papuan Roro), it might suit power-brokers to delay lifting a ritual ban if an overly influential chief or elder happened to fall under tabu regulations – by accidentally touching a corpse at a funeral, for example. A sense of cosmic order also sometimes affected tabu practices; caution between male and female among the Maori, for instance, often being paralleled to the necessary separation of heaven and earth, although if ritual decisions were male-dominated in Aotearoa, on the Marquesas there were as many powerful priestesses as there were priests.

We are not to forget here the masters of navigation, or owners of canoes, or spiritual sponsors of deep-sea expeditions. Perhaps we can recapture something of the spiritual energy invested in ancient oceanic voyaging by looking at latter-day specialists of the sea. Supervised discipline of recurrent ritual is necessary on Puluwat Atoll (Carolines, Micronesia), for instance, if trading crews are to survive on sea-water. During the Hiri journeys of Papuan Motu, when pot-laden *lakatoi* were sailed to the Gulf to exchange for sago, the most crucial man on board these sturdy vessels was a 'holy man' or *helaga tauna*. He and his wife would be the original sponsors of a given canoe's voyage: they had to prepare for it with as much fasting and ritual observance as organizational skill, and the holy man had to sit centre-deck on the *lakatoi*, shut into a windowless shrine for the entire voyage – meditating for success, praying to quieten spirits of wind and waves, and becoming the last person to die should the vessel fall prey to Nara or other 'pirates'.

Spirit-mediums, diviners and healers (often females) are common enough specialists in spirit-power, and traditional shamanism and prophetism (mainly with male adepts) are also known. In Polynesia,

Samoa is famous for its augurers, who inspect animal entrails to assess the advisability of war; the Maori for omen-takers floating 'bird-man' kites; and Tahiti for its women healers alleged to be able to tell what is wrong with their clients at a glance. Because of the older contrast between religion to the east and magic to the south-west, ethnographies leave Melanesia inundated with 'magicians', yet these often turn out to merit alternative epithets. Wahgi specialists who concentrate on spiritual support in warfare, for instance, are perhaps justifiably dubbed 'war magicians' (*obokunjeyi*), yet an ordinary *kunjeyi* is someone to consult if you are sick and is thus more a healer (though finding lost items is also in his repertory).

'Magic' is a word often used to cover the securing of some special 'individuating power' or influence to wield some benefit or harm.[22] A typical benefit in Oceania is to secure a woman's love or perhaps the return of a philandering husband; typical harm-dealing is sorcery (that is, when it is being directed against one's person and group, rather than on behalf of them). Melanesia still has the reputation for being a great regional centre of magic – of specialists who heat up substances in bamboo tubes to master and 'direct the internal power of things'.[23] Regional comparisons do lend some justification for this renown. In Polynesia and Micronesia, the idea of *spiritual beings* acting on behalf of those trying to manipulate events in their favour is virtually endemic. There we are more likely to hear of some husband being 'returned . . . by the spirits' after (white) love magic, or about 'the despatching of demons' in sorcery, to take Maori cases. Much more common there, too, will be rituals of 'prophylaxis' or prayers for protection by spirits against sorcery – 'Sun-e-e . . . Ancestors-e-e . . . you know my ill fortune, . . . turn back the spirits of the death-magic', as a Gilbertise invocation has it.[24] Melanesia reveals a greater diversity of conceptions about the *modi operandi* of 'magicians', yet so much more is now known from the region that there are new demands for case-by-case analyses, for new generalizations and perhaps for a shift in terminology so as to limit the use of magic, which too often denotes something inferior to religion.

'Sorcerer' and 'sorcery' stand as justifiable categories for the whole region (while 'witches' and 'witchcraft' are best reserved for a special class of female harm-dealers rather than these terms substituting for 'sorcery', as in the older usage of such authors as Craighill Handy. Sorcerers, whether conceived as enemies outside the security circle (the typical) or else within it (the unusual), were the classic dispossessors of power. Along the Papuan and Sepik coast barely a death stood unconnected with sorcery – even those in war were explained by its effects on weapons or bodily vulnerability; while in Polynesia, loss of a chief's *mana* and thus his downfall was often put down to the spells organized by enemies or closer contenders. In some Melanesian situations, such as with the Tangu of hinterland New Guinea, the sorcerer was the despised 'non-reciprocal man', who if found performing his occult deeds would be killed. In stratified Polynesian societies where their role was highly ambivalent – as either useful in war or a potential danger to the group(s) owing allegiance to a ruler – they were the lowest ranking of 'non-commoners'. Sorcerers 'with their fetchers in all their odd costumes', for instance, processed last at the installation of a Tahitian king.[25] Sorcery is the 'dark side' to cultures fostering biocosmic vitalities or cosmically legitimated social order.

CREATIVE PARTICIPATION

As we have already intimated, artistic creations and the maternal actualization of pre-visualized 'realities' and 'order' can be crucial reflections of religious life. The physical imaging of gods and spirits in effigies, masks and emblems, the building of shrines, cult grounds and platforms, or for that matter the very layout of a village according to Ancestrally legitimated orientations, as well as the preparing of canoes, weapons, instruments, smoking pipes, lime pots, money rings, body ornaments and a host of other minor examples of craftsmanship, have all become objects of aesthetic attention in our time, but their traditional *raisons d'être* lie in the internally religious sensitivities and worldviews of their creators. The current tourist trade in Oceanic artefacts tends to produce the deception that the central preoccupations of traditional artists were decorativeness, beauty and even entertainment, whereas the prevailing traditional incentive was to evoke the relationship between the spiritual and human domains. Museum displays of 'primitive art' also create false impressions because individual items are inevitably isolated from their original context – from within the dark eerie recesses of a cult-house, let us say. With the passing of old cultural forms, careful oral history and a 'trained imagination' are necessary to reconstruct the place of the visual and the sensual in sacred and ordinary affairs. The sensual obviously includes music, and the creation of the weird sounds through such devices as bull-roarers (which outside Aboriginal Australia are prominent in Huon Peninsula cultures, New Guinea); and we are not to forget bodily movement, especially dance, and the acting out of roles which accompany the visual tokens of the preternatural side to the cosmos.

Even just accounting for the myriad relevant objects beckons a vast encyclopaedia of 'material culture'. It is best to deploy a few useful case studies to outline the iconic, sensual and imaginal dimensions of Pacific religious life. The Elema provide some useful indicators. Although none still stand, the enormous cathedral-like *eravos*, towering cult-houses with façades up to 50 metres high which dominated villages of the Papuan Gulf, were among the Elema's greatest achievements. Arranged *in seriatim* on either side of their high apses, which were accessible only to males, lay shield-like representations of environal spirits and the elongated masks which were prepared in the shrine's darkness for ceremonies in the open. Elliptical discs with designs for each lineage marked the Ancestors' presence, and were placed below the racks of heads hunted in their honour. The whole effect was to gather together the collective spiritual forces vital for group survival. As the very spatial heart of each community, the Motuan Hiri traders who came from the east in their *lakotoi*s come first to the *eravo*, paying their respects to the Elema spirits, especially to the High Goddess Kaeva Kuku, whom the Motu and the Elema both venerated.

Leading up to and then away from the *eravo*, the Elema enacted their rare and extraordinary ceremonies to receive and at the end send back the Ma-hevehe, or the mythical sea-monsters, to their rightful watery abodes. These enactments combined sight and sound so arrestingly that F. E. William's careful and vivid description bears quoting:

A moonless night has been purposely chosen, so that no parties of children will be playing on the sands; the village as usual retires early; and the only lights are those of flickering fires inside the houses. Here and there through an open door, an oblong of smoky red against the tropical blackness, you may see the inmates sitting placidly at their betel [nut]; sometimes with desultory conversation, but mostly in sociable silence. Suddenly far down the beach there is heard a noise – a faint one because of the distance, but so meaningful as to electrify every feminine soul in the village. It is weirdly distinctive, a conglomeration of voices, which defies all description. At first the round notes of shell-trumpets seem to predominate, in strangely exciting discord; but we hear also the distant thunder of many drums; and what seems like the shriek of some tremendous, superhuman voice. The shriek gives place to, and alternates with, a deep-toned roar; and the whole volume of mixed sounds swell terrifyingly, drawing momently nearer. We may now distinguish a harsh background of noise, a kind of rhythmical yet continuous rattle; and the whole is punctuated by detonations rapid and irregular like rifle-fire.

When the Ma-hevehe and those wearing its high masks approached the *eravo*, the women and uninitiated fled to their houses and it was only for novices to be initiated in the mystery. By way of controlling the potential malevolence of the sea-spirits, the masks were burnt and their ashes cast in the sea at the ceremony's end, and the owners who inherited their designs had to remember them for the next time around.[26] So much artistry is locked into this sequence of events – architecture, sculpture, design work in wood-carving and ochres, masks and body decoration, music and sound-making, dance and performance.

Oceanian artistry almost invariably arose out of religious preoccupations. The most impressive buildings were temples or shrines or male club houses in which key rituals were performed. Famous in Melanesia are the *haus tambaran* ('spirit-houses') of various Sepik cultures, rising some 40–50 metres with richly and colourfully painted spirit-figures on their façades. In the darkness of such shrines among the (middle) Angoram people lay the 'stylized effigies of each deceased male of the clan(s), cautiously carved to represent their continuing presence among the living'.[27] In Polynesia, the most renowned architectural achievements are great stone platforms (*marae*) or enclosures marking ceremonial sites. At Mahaiatea, to the south of Tahiti Island, a great stepped pyramidal *marae*, apparently still in use, was sketched at the end of the eighteenth century, and even today the Marquesas carry some comparable examples. Most of the 10-metre-high stone walls ringing the so-called 'City of Refuge' at Howauna, Hawaii Island, also still stand today. Of roofed buildings, those most remarkable were the dwellings of the Maori chiefs and *tohunga* (priests and custodians of sacred lore), and especially the great carved house (*whare whakairo*) which dominated the *marae* or meeting grounds. The complex wooden carvings on their façades, ridges and major posts, sometimes inlaid with shell and greenstone, are high points of Oceanian art in Western aesthetic evaluation. Furthermore, they richly reflect religious insights. The *whare whakairo* was a living embodiment of the tribe, and in front of it the *tohunga* supervised genealogical recitations and other chants. The parts of this house were interpreted as the body of the ancestor. At the apex of the façade was a mask-head of the ancestor or chief (usually surmounted by a full-body figure, the *teko-teko*); the sloping bargeboards were his arms with carved 'fingers' at the ends; the ridgepole of the roof was his spine and the rafters his ribs (which could be used to depict genealogies in the interior). At the porch the door was the mouth of the ancestor, a window his eye and the whole interior his bosom. The traditional mode of address used on the *marae* still expresses this reverence for the meeting-house as an ancestral person whom one approaches with such words as: 'O house! O *marae* of the father! O people gathered!'

Under the central house pillar a block of greenstone was planted as a 'luck offering', and occasionally a sacrificed slave.[28]

An obvious competitor for attention would be the monumental and mysterious Easter Island statues. They do not obviously sit in clearly cultic settings, as did many other megalithic figures and arrangements found across the Pacific, and the remarkable number and size of them on an island so far to the east of the region has given rise to many a theory. Various scholars posit South American as against central Polynesian connections; and some have been asking questions as to whether older and more recent statues serve different purposes. Not only the statues, but also the great walls, bas-reliefs and unusual stone villages could well have been built at the behest of South American Indian leadership – the Incan Empire, after all, relied on a 'maritime foundation'[29] – but the labour and thus the artistry were carried out by Polynesians, at least according to local traditions. The older statues probably represented deceased (Incan or Quechua?) overlords, while more recent erections could have resulted from a feverish response to the first, transitory visit(s) of the (Hispanic) Europeans, taken as returning Ancestors (see chapter 5).

Ranging over non-architectural and monumental artefacts, one notes how cultures have their own special achievements, 'capitalizing' on them as tokens of their identity or perhaps as prized items for trade. Fine work in wooden figurines, and in masks which combine basketry, wood, clays and ochres, have given the Sepik River cultures an international reputation; central New Ireland specialized in smaller wooden masks (*malagan*), Papuan coastal cultures in high ones made with wicker-work. The Papuan highland Fuyughe seemed to the coastalers a wild people lacking technical skills, but they had their perforated bamboo pipes, nonetheless, while their war clubs with pineapple-shafted stone heads were keenly sought for during trade with groups below the mountains. Of more distinctly religious significance were Trobriand canoe prows (those called *lagimu* and *tabiyu*) or indeed Gogodala canoes (from the Western Province of Papua New Guinea) decorated as wholes; finely painted, bone-pointed arrows presented to Samo initiates (Western Province hinterland); Maisin *tapa* cloth used in ceremonies (northern Papua); Mekeo lime pots (such as the *apu* used to signal the inviolable chiefly authority), and so forth.

Dances were almost always 'religious statements'. At ceremonial high points, dance and accompanying song evoked myth, closeness to the animals and birds of the cosmos, love magic and generative power, and mutuality or the handling of tensions between groups. This last facet is well illustrated by the remarkable compensatory *gisaro* dancers among the Kaluli (under Mount Bosavi, southern central highlands of Papua); spectators often reacted by burning the grass skirt of a good performer who had shamed them into contemplating their own past hostilities. Dancers, of course, carried their own created or well-tended paraphernalia – headdresses, painted bodies, sometimes the most startling costuming – and hardly ever performed without some kind of musical instrument present. Such instruments were typically conceived to evoke the spirits' presence, and sometimes their sounds *were* the spirits (as when the sacred flutes were sounded in Wahgi and Chimbu initiations). The least durable but nonetheless carefully constructed musical object could also be the most sacred. A certain type of bull-roarer from many Huon Gulf cultures provides a fascinating case in point, for

> the 'genuine' and indeed most fragile bull-roarer can only be whirled a few times at the height of important ceremonies in some of these cultures. As the voice of the ancestors, its temporary and successful application by a bigman will bring peace and security to his tribe, but its breakage spells utter disaster. An impressive comment on the delicate matter of presenting right relationships in small-scale, survivalist societies![30]

The configurations and principles found applying in Melanesia fit island Oceania more generally. Survivalism in conflict engendered special features in Polynesia, including variation in the styles of weaponry (such as war clubs) and other artifices of war (including brilliantly decorated war canoes). Among the Maori, successfully shrunken (commonly tattooed) heads of the warrior dead (which were later to enter the European market as prized curios) were the results of a difficult craft and the heads were designed for occasional display in a sacred grove, so that if a visiting relation or friend arrived, he could weep over the saddening object and 'cherish the spirit of revenge against those by whom [the warrior] fell'.[31] Maori kites, too, were rather special, usually in the form of bird-men and with wingspans of up to 15 metres; they were either for omen-telling, or for hovering over enemy territory so as to demoralize and beam forth malignant power. Special garments and headgear throughout Polynesia were made with status and durability in war and ceremony in view. In the Marquesas, tattooing of the whole body was more for rendering the warrior's body formidable than beautiful.

In general, we can see, the traditional artist had 'no idea of art for art's sake', but expressed aesthetic sensibilities in accordance with inherited traditions. To outsiders the exaggerated breasts and genitals of many effigies may seem to reflect the 'instinctive impulses' and 'crude unconsciousness' of 'savages', but in fact they are the typical results of applying stringent rules of the game.[32] Despite the great length of time between each Hevehe – up to twenty-five years – Elema clan designs must be visualized accurately in specialists' memories and passed on before death. The language and techniques for transferring specialization, moreover, sometimes suggest the transformation of one person into another, as with the Trobriand prow-carvers of *lagimu* and *tabuya* (see above). Again, many outsiders may respond to much Oceanian art as ugly or mon-strous. The grotesque has its purpose – to warn. Among the Maori, long-tongued carvings of the gods and ancestors remind viewers of aggression and *tapu* (and oversized heads of *mana*), while the iconic identification of each spirit – the beaked bird-spirit *manaia*, the curling merman *marakihau* and so on – is not to be overlooked. Smaller carvings, such as greenstone pendants of Tiki, the first man, were prepared as love-gifts within security-circles or between in-laws and thus not intended for trade (let alone the tourist market to come); the small elliptical wooden plaques on which Easter Island's as yet undeciphered Rongoronga script was cleverly inscribed were for specialists' use only, aiding their set prayers. Crucial for an understanding of Oceanian artistry, on reflection, is the study of the role of the imagination, which is only now beginning to receive the scholarly attention it deserves. In the world of the imagined, art, power, projections of divinity and the retributive impulse all converge.

BECOMING SPIRIT

Maurice Leenhardt, the well-known missionary anthropologist and predecessor to Lévi-Strauss at the Sorbonne, arrived at a profound insight about Houailou people (from north-east New Caledonia). They saw life as a process of 'becoming spirit', and the older one was the more one took on *bao* (the character of spirits) and shed humanness. This is an approach to life which seems to have more parallels in Oceania than less sensitive research has allowed us to see. Elsewhere in Melanesia, for instance, we learn of the Orokaiva notion that men ought to prepare themselves in life to become helpful spirits after death; and on Malekula one of the purposes of the extraordinary orgiastic rite previously described (see p. 142 above) was to safeguard 'the passage of the souls of the ten clan magicians to the land of the dead, where [the god] Kabat lives under the reef', from whence their spiritual support could be continued.[33] In Polynesia, becoming a disembodied soul could mean taking on the nature of the gods and thus returning, freely incarnating in animals or insects, to support the living. Some chiefs among the northern Maori saw themselves as having taken on the qualities of *atua* (here 'godlike power') even before death, and thus before their left eyes soared up to become as stars the watchers of their people.

Death, certainly, was an ever-present reality in traditional Pacific cultures. Loss in childbirth was hardly uncommon, women and children were very vulnerable to raids, the loss of life in fighting was high, while unhygienic habits and traditional diseases lent themselves to an already low life-expectancy (of about forty to forty-five years). The possibility of death conditioned one's attitude and behaviour. Like present-day footballers in the West, men kept to their cult or 'club' houses and abstained from sex on the night before battle (although in odd cultures, such as on Malekula, the opposite apparently applied and families discussed what had to be done if things went wrong). In Wahgi long-houses, the sharing of waking dreams was important for deciding on the wisdom of opening or continuing hostilities; and a Maori warrior would lose that extra bit of confidence if he did not awaken with an erection. Someone dangerously ill might be subjected to more questions than seemed desirable, but for the Motu it was part of the caring process as kin and elders sat around sick persons and found out where they had been recently, to whom they had spoken and from whom they had received food – to identify likely sources of sorcery or other causes. (Gaining confidence that sickness could be overcome was crucial, since so many people succumbed to a 'psychology of inevitable death' because someone 'had their hair', or nail clippings, or some part of their clothing, to work harm.) Upon the prospect of a specialist's death, naturally, there was a concern that his precious knowledge should be passed down to an elect descendant; while among Polynesians a dying chief could be propped up for the household or even the gathered tribe to hear some 'last instructions' – the *Oohaaki*, as the Maori called it – before the accession of a new ruler.

When death came, especially that of an adult male, it was an event which almost always yielded remarkable activity. Quick burials were only for unworthy or unproductive persons (including those mentally handicapped or crippled for life), and funerals were both occasions for exchange (within the security circle and along marriage links) and typical pretexts for organizing revenge activity. Simple mortuary procedures among the Dugum Dani (of highland Irian Jaya) illustrate how the two concerns are wrapped together in ritual. What those connected to the deceased person bring to a funeral depends on their moiety membership, one lot bringing pigs and those in the opposite moiety to the dead person bringing shell bands or other less commonly presented items. Small kin groups have to work out what they are to give, but before the rather 'matter of fact normal tones and postures' of exchange get underway, and the presentations are laid out on the ground, close kin enter the hamlet with a dirge and a stylized walk of mourning, by rubbing a deliberately bent leg. In the distribution which follows we see the importance of reciprocal relations among the living cemented by the dead, but 'the most important witnesses to the funeral ... are the ghosts', and especially the warrior or big-man who has just died, who is often propped up in a chair to survey the scene before he is properly cremated and his spirit given safe passage along a pre-set trail to the bush. Even in his formalized apartness, however, he will be a worrying factor for the group until his death is requited.[34]

The basic motifs of this scenario show up across the Pacific. A letter by Cantova provides the earliest documentation of a death rite – the burial of a man of high rank in the Carolines. 'The painting of the corpse with tumeric, the women's keening, the funeral eulogy ..., the kinsmen's watch over the corpse, the food, offerings left for the spirit of the dead person, and the eventual internment in a marked grave-site were all noted.[35] Chiefs' deaths were often occasions of festal distribution and conspicuous consumption, yet not before performing rites with the utmost caution and decorum. On the Lau Islands, just east of Fiji, mourners even have to restrain themselves from weeping until the chief is buried, and up to that point conch shells are blown continuously both day and night. And the urges of avengement were hardly left unevoked at the deaths of the great ones. The lost clan at a Baled chief's funeral (on north-eastern New Caledonia), for example, allowed in a band of the deceased's maternal relations to ravage trees and gardens so that the hosts felt more sharply the loss and the shame of letting the death happen (especially if it occurred in the middle of hostilities). Such an onslaught on things underscores the most important obligation of all: it gives more incentive to make the enemy suffer for its baleful success. In Maori wars, as colonial commentators reported, chiefs often requested *utu* or 'satisfaction' for their deaths, but danger lay in being made vulnerable to attack after losing a leader (and his *mana!*), so that revenge often came through putting up a fierce defence against an enemy raid.

Matters of obvious religious interest to do with death are the various procedures for the disposal of the dead, as well as beliefs about the whereabouts of the departed, and whether they can be summoned or in any sense 'judged' in another world. Disposal fashions in Melanesia are highly varied. It was an older European view that 'burying the dead' was a universal custom, but if such a theoretician as Giambattista Vico – who espoused this view and founded the first 'social science' upon its ubiquity – had looked upon the dripping pits and bone pendants of many New Guinea peoples, he would have been utterly dismayed. The Papuan Motu followed a conspicuously unpleasant-looking practice, for example, which they were quick to abandon once receiving unfavourable reactions from early Polynesian missionaries. After a few days propped up in a house, with the kinsfolk whispering requests for gifts and assistance into its ear, the corpse of a warrior was laid in a shallow, unfilled grave under the family house. The smell was the ready reminder of a needful revenge, and the widow was expected to lie down beside the decaying body in bursts of mourning, smearing decaying flesh upon her breasts as a sign of fidelity. Other people preferred the body out of the way: the Dani, as we have seen, cremated, whereas most New Guinea highlanders buried, and in the Torres Strait we learn of mummification. Common in the Papuan highlands, as with the Fuyughe and neighbouring Koiari, were high platforms on which corpses were left to waste away, the bones being later collected, washed and placed in the rock crevices of mountainsides. In other cultures – the Wam of the Sepik, for example – descendants and the bereaved wear single bones of their close kin as memorials. With the renowned case of the southern Fore in the New Guinea eastern highlands we find endocannibalism, the wife consuming the brains of her dead husband (sometimes contracting the debilitating disease Kuru), the daughter-in-law eating the penis, etc., and in this and other nearby settings feeding on the body of one's father meant acquiring spirit-power for group survival.

In Polynesia and Micronesia, even on coral atolls, burial was common, but with exhumation of the bones and the redepositing of them in crevices or groves. On the other hand, variations require some reckoning. About the Maori we learn of an ordinary man or woman or child being 'thrown into the sea', while warriors were buried in hillocks with spears stuck in the ground as 'trophies'. But there are also accounts of canoe-shaped coffins containing trussed cadavers in trees, and of open-railed enclosures on stone platforms for persons of distinction. Burial was actually not so much in evidence on contact, even if archaeology attests it, along with grave goods, for the earlier inhabitants of New Zealand. Usually bones were secretly buried in high places, but, as already shown, heads were often shrunk, or else skulls kept in carved rounded 'boxes', as reminders of revenge; although chiefs, for their part, had their bones exhumed and placed in palisaded 'tombs'.[36]

In certain contexts death accompanied death. The equivalents of 'suttee' are rare but of interest. The widows of cremated Lemakot men (New Ireland), to take one unusual case, had to be strangled and thrown on their husbands' pyres (unless suckling a child), while the elderly widows of Maori chiefs (but, interestingly, not of commoners) were often expected to hang themselves. Sacrifices accompanied all Hawaiian funerals, which were aimed first to commemorate the dead and then to transform them into Ancestral 'deities', but humans were only sacrificed at the 'state' mortuary rites of kings or very high-ranking personages, and thus only in state temples (rather than in the domestic temples or village compounds where lesser mortals received their proper respects). In these rituals the bodies of the human victims had to be correctly prepared as offerings in all the great sacrifices; killed beforehand, no blood was to be showing when they were brought to the temple, and paradoxically the victim's death was symbolically denied so that he mediated between heaven and earth and was 'transformed into the slayer's god'. The body was left with the god(s) and decayed, but the bones were then distributed, becoming insignia of power for aristocrats and priests, with the teeth attached to the living king's loin cloth, feather cloaks or personal bowls.[37] Under these circumstances, victims played more of a sacrally significant role than expected, although one finds no hint of post-mortem tasks for them as retainers of rulers, for instance, in the other world (cf. p. 7). As for the earthly memorials of Hawaiian kings, they were given tombs, and stone arrangements also marked the place where they died with their fellows (during battle).

Where the dead are conceived to be after they are fully released from the living usually provides a useful index to a community's cosmic picturing and religious orientation in general. Varied envisionings about the after-life in Oceania also reflect natural tendencies to validate the known order of the living rather than individual exercises in speculation or metaphysics. Melanesia, as usual, holds most variation, yet in fact a few commonalities can be extrapolated for all island Oceania from the plethora of notions. The dead are almost without exception understood to continue their involvement with the living. Rare indeed is the pre-contact Fuyughe view that the Ancestors departed to the highest mountain (Mount Albert Edward) to cease their concern for human problems. That would help explain the Fuyughes' singular lack of interest in genealogies – some of them cannot even remember the names of their grandfathers – as well as their anxiety about the continuing living presence of the *utame(e)* (see p. 141), even though the Fuyughe do share the well-nigh ubiquitous fear of ghosts, the haunting of those departed ones whose bodies were not properly deposited and thus could not gain final repose. The distinction between 'Ancestor' (or 'spirit') and 'ghost' is always useful to bear in mind, and if certain ethnographies labour the point about fear of 'unavenged ghosts' – as they do of the Dugum Dani and Mae Enga, for example – remember that avengement is commonly thought to 'exorcize' a spirit of its inimical aspects, turning it into a 'supportive' agent.[38] (Of course much depends on common assumptions about which ghosts to fear, your own circle's or others'; Hube magicians in the Morobe actually used to thrash the corpses of their own dead, for instance, to make the ghostly anger of the dead flare up all the more against enemies.) If one is expecting from the 'vertically oriented' religious of Polynesia and Micronesia, moreover, that the dead proceed heavenward or to the underworld, prepare for the surprise that they are also commonly felt to be rather close – in birds, fish or Triton shells, as Mangaians aver, or as insects with a nocturnal shrill, in Marquesan views.

To be sure, the capacity of the dead to visit and show interest often needs distinguishing from the 'place of the dead'. In more 'horizontal' Melanesian views, such places tend to be at known geographical locations, such as a cape (thus the Roro), or in an unvisitable lake at the end of a major river (thus the New Guinea highland Daribi), or to the west at the setting sun (the Toaripi of the Papuan Gulf), or on an 'Isle of the Blest' (the Tuma of the Trobriands). It may have been very common to distinguish (malevolent) ghosts from the (helpful) dead, as we have argued, but otherwise the abodes of the dead were usually peopled by the 'good and the bad' alike, as spiritual extensions of the living community. The picture of the 'Happy Hunting Ground', without consideration for individual ethics, generally prevailed. Very few are traditional notions of a heaven or hell. The Erave or South Kewa (of the hinterland Gulf) held that all warriors who died in battle, and the womenfolk who supported them, could ascend to 'the red place' in the sky, while the rest were doomed to permanent estrangement in an earthbound 'place of brown'. The highland Chimbu buried malefactors and unwantables in a separate burial ground, not expecting them to share the post-mortem benefits of the lucky majority. Elsewhere we hear of transmigration – among the highland Siane, Papuan islander Dobu and on South Penecost in Vanuatu, to take three instances – so that some individuals are recognized to have returned to the bosom of their families. Yet all these are exceptions, albeit very interesting and indicative of Melanesian diversity.

From Micronesia and Polynesia we expect more consistency, though we have it more from the latter region than the former. For Polynesians the dead usually descended into an underworld; thus despite above-mentioned notions of their capacity to incarnate in facets of the environment, the common imaging of a 'vertically ordered' cosmos did still pertain. The very gates to the underworld could be indicated on island shores by long-rooted trees or unusual rock formations. In the Hawaiian and Cook Islands and New Zealand there were extreme westward prominences for the leaping of souls at their departure for the Ancestral region. Souls undertook journeys which corresponded archetypally to ancient voyages to their islands from an idealized origin-point, usually eastern and named Hawaiiki, so that spirit journeying was often in a westward direction, continuing an earlier process of the living. It is remarkable, though, how these journeys were often pictured as worrying ordeals, the outcome of which sometimes depended more on luck or a kind of fate than on moral or even social virtues. Grave goods were intended to help, and the Marquesan evidence suggests that gifts were thought useful for getting past four pairs of demons barring the World of the Dead; but sometimes one's post-mortem lot, either in 'Light' (*Ao*) or 'Darkness' (*Po*), as the Raiateans of Tahiti put it, simply depended on whether the soul got itself perched on the right rock or not. On Tahiti proper the preferred place of the dead, called Miru, was apparently 'a kind of heaven', while the more typical Polynesian visioning had the places of both the successful and the hapless below sea, land or horizon.[39] In Polynesia's hierarchical societies, of course, one could expect to hear talk of chiefly ascendence to the skies – of the left eyes of Maori chiefs becoming stars, as discussed above. An extreme case of post-mortem stratification comes from Tonga, where royalty and nobles could expect bliss at the idyllic Pulotu (west of Tongatapu), while mere commoners were told they would stay back, turn into vermin and eat the soil.

We have been dealing here not just with the geography of the soul's task in negotiating an entrance to the Other World (or death, but also what we may call the 'sacred bridge' motif in comparative religion, following Jouco Bleeker). Parallel materials present themselves in traditional Micronesia, where the belief in the soul's journey to the west was very widespread. Even on scattered Melanesian islands the notion of the soul's journey and final ordeal is not absent, old expectations on Muju (or Woodlark Island) having it that one travels precariously on the back of a Great Serpent called Motetutau to paradisal Tum, and is disallowed its endless supplies of foods and intoxicants if 'an inexorable old woman' does not find the requisite 'two lines of tattooing' on one's arm. In the Wuvulu group, moreover, a Micronesian enclave close to New Guinea, what is tantamount to a vertically oriented heaven and hell makes an appearance. Each Wuvulu hamlet was taken to be both protected and ordered by guardian *puala*-spirits, whose actions were interpreted by priests. Over and above 'accidents' and sickness, 'the ultimate sanction of the *puala*-spirit was to deny a person into the wonderful villages of the dead'. Directly below these villages lay Mani Pino Pino, where waste dripped down and the evil dead ate snakes and lizards 'in a constant state of agony' until the *puala* had 'mercy ... sooner or later'.[40]

Allusions to this future reprieve raises questions about eschatologies in Oceania – as to whether there are ideas of some collective future judgement, or 'end of all things', or final convening of the living and the dead. Of last judgements one will hear nothing in traditional belief; of ends a few unusual bit and pieces, the Ipili Enga view, for example, being that everybody and every living thing will eventually disappear down a hole in the ground! As for beliefs about 'the return of the dead', a by now famous projection associated with new religious movements in Melanesia, there is no evidence of an eschatological aspect in traditional religions. Certainly there were isolated ideas that, at some unexpected point(s) the Ancestors would return 'sending abundance', as in the case of hopes documented early among the coastal Roro, who understood it to be brought from inland, presumably from their ancestral home and origin-point Isoiso Vapu.[41] A common assumption prevailed in Melanesia that the benevolent dead would return collectively to witness the great feasts, just as the individual deceased would come to eat that small portion of the meal so commonly set aside for them. As for some dramatic return of the dead, conceived to be final-looking or less a part of expected recurrences, this idea comes only under the impact of colonial intrusion. Across Oceania, in fact, notions of a completed future were next to non-existent, though of course the belief that the Ancestral state was without end – or *mo ake tonu atu* (henceforth forever) as the Maori put it – was naturally concomitant to views about the abundant life of the spirit realm. Confronting the obviously more cyclical outlooks of the islanders there came in time the extraordinary and not-to-be-expected: the denizens of the outside world.

NOTES AND REFERENCES

1 On Yabwahine, e.g. I. Lasaro, 'History of Bonarua Island', *Oral History* 3/7 (1975): 172, cf. G. Róheim, 'Yaboaine: a War God of Normanby Island', *Oceania*, 16/3 (1946): 233, cf. 319 (quotations); on Kapauka, L. Pospisil, *Kapauka Papuans and their Law* (Yale University Publications in Anthropology 54), New Haven, 1964, p. 17 (quotations), cf. pp. 16–18.

2 On Madang, esp. P. Lawrence, *Road Belong Cargo*, Manchester, 1964, p. 16 (quotation) and n. 1, cf. pp. 21–4; on Lakalai, A. Chowning, 'Lakalai Religion and World View and the Concept of "Seaboard Religion" ', in G. Trompf (ed.), *Melanesian and Judaeo-Christian Religious Traditions*, Port Moresby, 1975, Book 1, p. 89 (quotation), cf. pp. 87–8.

3 On the Maori (without Io), G. Grey, *Polynesian Mythology and Ancient Traditional History of the New Zealanders*, London, 1929 edn. p. 3, cf. pp. 1ff. Concepts of Io are taken seriously by Jack Irwin, yet currently disputed in research by Lyndsay Head, Jean Rosenfeld and Jane Simpson; we await James Veitch's monograph to arbitrate. Io is now being claimed for other islands, e.g. K. Kauraka, 'Thinking about Cook Island's

Native Religion', in *Search* (Rarotonga) 3/1 (1991): 12. On the Gilberts, we follow the famous version in A. Grimble, *A Pattern of Islands*, London, 1952, pp. 168–71.

4 J. Cantova, in *Lettres édifiantes, etc*, Paris, 1728, vol. 18, pp. 215ff; S. Wallesier, 'Religiöse Anschauungen und Grebräuche der Bewohner von Jap', *Anthropos* 8 (1913): 607ff.

5 Following Joel Taime's amplifications of W. Gill, *Cook Island Custom*. London, 1892, pp. 22–3, with personal communication 1991.

6 Grey, *Polynesian Mythology*, p. 3 (first quotation); J. Siikala, *Cult and Conflict in Tropical Polynesia*, (Academia Scientarum Fennica FF Communications 99/2), Helsinki, 1982, p. 116 (second).

7 R. Firth, *We, The Tikopia*, London, 1957 edn., p. 113, cf. pp. 28, 259, 364–5; *Rank and Religion in Tikopia* (London School of Economic Monographs on Social Anthropology 1–2), London, 1967, esp. ch. 3 (Tikopia); P. S. Englert, *La Tierre de Hotu Matu'a*, Santiago de Chile, 1990 edn., pp. 41ff. (our translation) (Rapanui).

8 R. Bulmer, 'The Kyaka of the Western Highlands', in P. Lawrence and M. J. Meggitt (eds), *Gods, Ghosts and Men in Melanesia*, Melbourne, 1965, p. 136 (Kyaka Enga); V. Valeri, *Kingship and Sacrifice: Ritual and Society in Ancient Hawaii* (trans. P. Wissing), Chicago and London, 1985, pp. 12–23 (Hawaii); J. Irwin, *An Introduction to Maori Religion* (Special Studies in Religion 4), Adelaide, 1984, pp. 39–41 (Maori).

9 Quoted in W. Bogoras, 'The Folklore of Northeastern Asia, as Compared with That of Northwestern America', *American Anthropologist*, 414 (1902): 582.

10 G. Trompf, *Payback: the Logic of Retribution in Melanesian Religions*, Cambridge, 1994, esp. chs 1, 3.

11 A. Forge, 'Prestige, Influence and Sorcery: a New Guinea example', in M. Douglas (ed.), *Withcraft Confessions and Accusations*, London, 1970, p. 259 quoting Abelam phraseology (Sepik hinterland).

12 D. Tuzin, 'Social Control and the Tambaran in the Sepik', in A. L. Epstein (ed.), *Contention and Dispute*, Canberra, 1974, p. 324, cf. pp. 321, 335; *The Voice of the Tambaran*, Berkeley, 1980, esp. pp. 140–6.

13 B. Malinowski, *Argonauts of the Western Pacific*, New York, 1922, pp. 98–9.

14 On the Marquesas, Melville (1834) is quoted in C. R. Anderson, *Melville in the South Seas*, New York, 1939, p. 91; and on the Chuukese, Mrs Treiber (1888) and others, see I. I. Oneisum, 'Chuuk Violence: Then and Now', *Micronesian Counselor* 1 (1991): 3.

15 Valeri, *Kingship and Sacrifice*, pp. 141, 229, 309–10, 311, 69 (quotations in that order), cf. Part 1, ch. 2; Part 2, ch. 5; Part 3, chs 7–8.

16 As Melville wrote of a large Marquesan ritual in the 1840s, in *Typee*, London, 1846, pp. 235–8.

17 I. Goldman, *Ancient Polynesian Society*, London, 1970, pp. 20–1, cf. also M. Sahlins, 'Poor Man, Rich Man, Big-Man, Chief', *Comparative Studies in Society and History* 5 (1963): 285ff.; B. Douglas, 'Rank, Power, Authority', *Journal of Pacific History* 14 (1979): 2ff.

18 Cf., e.g., *The Kumulipo; a Hawaiian Creation Chant* (trans., ed. and comm., M. W. Beckwith), Honolulu, 1972, p. 130.

19 J. Layard, 'The Making of Men in Malekula', *Eranos-Jahrbuch* 16 (1948):

274–5, cf. 210ff.; B. Deacon, *Malekula* (ed. C. Wedgwood), London, 1934, p. 652.

20 See esp. E. Mantovani, '*Milpela Simbu*! The Pig Festival and Simbu Identity', in V. Hayes (ed.), *Identity Issues and World Religions (Selected Proceedings of the Fifteenth Congress of the International Association for the History of Religions)*, Adelaide, 1986, cf. pp. 194ff., cf. A. Strathern, 'The Female and Male Spirit Cults in Mount Hagen', *Man*, N.S. 5 (1970): 573; Trompf, *Payback*, ch. 2.

21 K. Kamakau, quoted in Valeri, *Kingship and Sacrifice* p. 258 (Hawaiian prayer); B. Malinowski, *Coral Gardens and their Magic*, London, 1935, vol. 1, p. 169, cf. also pp. 223–4, 233–4 (Trobriand spell).

22 See R. Wagner, *The Curse of Souw*, Chicago, 1967, pp. 47–57, cf. G. Trompf, *Melanesian Religion*, Cambridge, 1991, p. 84.

23 P. A. Curti, 'L'isola di Muju o Woodlark', *Politechnico* 14 (1862): 38–9 (kind permission of translator D. Affleck).

24 E. Best *et al.*, 'White Magic of the Maori', *Journal of the Polynesian Society* 140 (1926): 323 (Maori love charm); Best, 'Ngatori-i-Rangi and Manua', *ibid.*, 139 (1926): 214 (Maori sorcery); P. H. Buck, *Regional Diversity in the Elaboration of Sorcery in Polynesia* (Yale University Publications in Anthropology 2), New Haven, Conn., 1936, p. 13 (Polynesia); Grimble, *A Pattern of Islands*, pp. 121–2 (Gilberts).

25 K. O. L. Burridge, 'Tangu, Northern Madang District', in Lawrence and Meggitt (eds), *Gods, Ghosts and Men*, p. 230 (Tangu); T. Henry, *Ancient Tahiti* (Bernice P. Bishop Museum Bulletin 48), Honolulu, 1928, p. 166, cf. pp. 157ff (Tahiti).

26 F. E. Williams, *The Drama of Orokolo*, Oxford, 1940, pp. 210–1. The roar is of a bull-roarer. Please note that at the time Williams wrote his ethnography even the western Elema had given up their raids (against the Arihava and Heuru), cf. *ibid.*, p. 71, although extreme western villages, Aimei and Iria, still retained magnificent *eravo* complexes.

27 Trompf, *Melanesian Religion*, p. 27, cf. plates 4, 6 (on Angoram and western Elema).

28 A. C. Moore, *Iconography of Religions*, London, 1977, pp. 61–2 (long quotation); J. Cowan, *Book of Maori Lore* (rev. J. B. Palmer), Wellington, 1959, p. 51 (short). For a broader study of Maori symbology, E. A. Rout, *Maori Symbolism*, London, 1928.

29 M. E. Moseley, *The Maritime Foundation of Andean Civilization*, Menlo Park, 1975.

30 Trompf, *Melanesian Religion* p. 28, cf. T. Bodrogi, *Art in North-east New Guinea*, Budapest, 1961, p. 73.

31 R. Robley, *Moko; or Maori Tattooing*, London, 1896, p. 159.

32 R. Piddington, *An Introduction to Social Anthropology*, London, 1957, vol. 2, p. 517; R. Firth, *Art and Life in New Guinea*, London and New York, 1979, pp. 30–1.

33 Layard, 'Making of Men', p. 275, cf. M. Leenhardt, *Do Kamo; la personne et le mythe dans le monde mélanesien*, Paris, 1971, pp. 81–3.

34 K. Heider, *Grand Valley Dani (Case Studies in Cultural Anthropology)*, New York, 1979, p. 123, cf. pp. 120–8.

35 Paraphrased in F. X. Hezel, *The First Taint of Civilization* (Pacific Islands Monographs Series 1), Honolulu, 1983, p. 54.

36 J. Crozet quoted in H. L. Roth, *Crozet's Voyage to Tasmania, New Zealand, The Landrone Islands, and the Philippines in the Years 1771–1772*, London, 1891, p. 65 (earlier quotations); R. S. Oppenheim, *Maori Death Customs*, Wellington, 1973, esp. p. 65, cf. pp. 60–5.

37 Valeri, *Kingship and Sacrifice*, p. 338, cf. pp. 38, 337–9.

38 A further culture-specific distinction of importance is between 'spirits of the recent dead' and the 'longer departed' (t Ancestors more properly), as previously discussed (see p. 131).

39 P. Huguenin, *Raiatea la sacrée*, Neuchâtel, 1902, pp. 179–80 (on *Ao* and *Po*); W. Ellis, *Polynesian Researches*, London, 1831, vol. 1, p. 397 (on Miru). For discussion over the years about the apparent disjunction between 'morality' and one's state in the after-life in some Austronesian societies, see also A. Bastian, *Einiges aus Samoa und andern Inseln der Südsee*, Berlin, 1889, pp. 38–9; R. W. Williamson, *Religions and Cosmic Beliefs of Central Polynesia*, Cambridge, 1933, vol. 1, pp. 288ff., vol. 2, pp. 1ff.; E. G. Burrows and M. E. Spiro, *An Atoll Culture*, New Haven, Conn., 1957, pp. 207–11.

40 Curti 'L'isola di Muju', pp. 38–9 (Muju); A-C. Lagercerantz, 'The Process of Change in Wuvulu Island' (unpublished typescript, New Guinea Collection, University of Papua New Guinea), 1980, pp. 2–3. In some Melanesian cultures there are ideas about 'spirit villages' – variously placed under lakes (Haliai, New Britain), on treetops in the forest (Samo), or sometimes in the sky (Erave).

41 L. A. Navarre, 'Notes et journal, June 1888–July 1889' (handwritten MS, Catholic Offices, formerly Yule Island, subsequently Bereira), Yule Island Mission, 1889, p. 90 (Tchiria village beliefs, Roro).

5 Cults of intrusion

By the year 1601, and through the publication of a crude map (showing the Carolines, Marianas, north New Guinea and most of the Solomons), the Pacific islands had become part of the 'general history' of humankind.[1] Through their voyages of exploration, even if they seem rather tame beside the extraordinary adventures of the Pacific islanders long before them, the Europeans of the so-called 'modern period' created the possibility of a global history and a complete registering of the world's peoples. By 1610 the Pacific had truly become a 'Spanish lake'. Guam, Magellan's 'discovery', had been a Spanish colony for forty-five years; de Mendaña had explored the Solomons twice, hitting las Marquesas on his second tour; and de Torres had passed through that crucial strait between Australia and New Guinea which bears his name in 1606. Of our three regions Micronesia was known best first, because the Spaniards tended to converge on it while establishing an alternative route to the Indies. The passing of the seventeenth century saw more of Polynesia known, this time through the Dutch (Tasman to New Zealand and Tonga, Roggeveen to Easter Island and Samoa), while by the end of the next century, especially after de Bougainville's Melanesian excursions and Cook's three matchless voyages across the whole face of Oceania, few landfalls of significance remained off mariners' maps. Australia, of course, was not circumnavigated until 1803, twenty-three years after Cook had claimed it for the British, and its great heart was barely known even by the mid-nineteenth century.

Despite the exploits of a few doughty explorers and miners, the deep interior of the great island of New Guinea remained the world's 'last unknown' at the beginning of the twentieth century. By that time, most of the rest of the Pacific islands had experienced the 'fatal impact' of so-called civilization for a good fifty years or more.[2] Religious war had racked Tahiti and Tonga in the 1830s as the results of muskets and missionaries. Epidemics borne by contact brought unpredictable waves of depopulation, most noticeably during the mid-century. New Caledonia had become France's penal colony in 1864 and the Maori Wars had raged in New Zealand from 1860 to 1872. Sandalwood forests had been virtually decimated to serve Chinese markets after more and more American merchantmen plied the Pacific and islanders scrambled, often all too violently, to secure the trade, while Peruvian slavers had been abroad to drag off human fodder in such isolated places as Easter Island and Niue (especially in the 1860s). Copra and sugar plantations had already been worked on many an island (with Indians being sent as labourers to British Fiji as early as 1879), and not only had the recruiting of Melanesian (*Kanaka*) labour to the Queensland cane fields already ceased, with Australian public opinion being outraged over the notorious capturing or 'blackbirding' of islanders in the 1870s, but colonial Australia had turned against immigrant labour altogether by the next decade. It was in the 1880s that German presence was felt in the Pacific, although Germany received a serious setback with Australia's takeover of New Guinea and New Zealand's seizure of German Samoa in the opening year of World War I (and Germany's attempts to keep some western Solomon and south Micronesian islands beyond that time were doomed to failure). Up until World War II, the interests of the French, the British and the Dutch went on unchecked in Oceania. After the Japanese incursions in the western Pacific were forestalled, pressures for decolonization were set in train in the post-war era.

The pattern of contact and interaction was, however, very uneven in each of the large regions we are considering. In each great island complex, interchange with outsiders was typically concentrated on recognized ports-of-call, and various outliers tended to go unnoticed, until missionaries were ready to show an interest in reaching new enclaves of lost souls. By the time Rennell Islanders in Polynesia were ready to receive Christian missions in 1936, for example, shortly after patrol officer James Taylor and his company first entered the great Wahgi Valley in the New Guinea central highlands of Melanesia in 1933, the American city of Honolulu numbered over 110,000 inhabitants and New Zealand's Wellington about 146,000. Any overview of islander responses to outside intrusions cannot really do justice to this unevenness and to unique local conditions. Furthermore, although our ordering of materials for convenience presents movements of adjustment in a chapter separate from our examination of indigenous Christianity, it must be stressed that the two are interlocked. This being acknowledged, we will proceed to plot major phases in organized islander reactions against external impact and colonialism, discussing the various types of movements that emerged and asking whether there have been different emphases of protest and expectation at different times and places.

CULTS OF VICTORY AND PROSPERITY

Because the powerfully armed outsiders first used the islands only as temporary stop-overs, and because such individual beachcombers and missionaries who did stay longer were first accepted by one indigenous grouping or alliance rather than others, the chiefs of Micronesia, Polynesia and eastern Melanesia naturally sought ways by which newcomers and their goods could be turned to their advantage in ongoing inter-tribal conflicts. The items most effective in upsetting a local balance of power were muskets. With the arrival of the *Antelope* at the Palau group in 1783, for example, the *ibedul* (great chief) of Konor was only too willing to enlist the help of the English seamen in massacring his arch-rival's people on Melekeok. By 1808 the notorious (and aptly named) Charles Savage was in the thick of Fijian battles fighting for Naulivou, chief of Mbau, shooting enemies out of range of their traditional weaponry and adding to the feasts of a society already well sated by carnage and cannibalism. Even missionaries got caught up in the process of 'upgraded' warfare. As founder of the New Zealand Mission from the infant colony of New South Wales, Samuel Marsden expressed his utter dismay in the 1810s that his personnel were trafficking in muskets; yet to have any impact among people so preoccupied with exchanges and their signification, what else could his men do? – or so argued Thomas Kendall, in the hope that the guns served only for hunting. White trading, however, was not necessary to fuel some of the local fires. Tongans despatched virtually the whole crew of the *Port-au-Prince* in 1806 with the aim of securing the new goods, especially axes and firearms, in a new game of prestige and victory that nine years earlier nearly produced a disastrous unmooring and wreckage of the first (London Missionary Society) vessel to the so-called 'Friendly Islands'.

These activities – the channelling of alien influence by certain 'pocket Napoleons'[3] to suit their circles of power – were but extensions of tradition through the incorporation of new factors. Matters were different if the encounter(s) with outsiders were tantalizingly temporary and mysterious or if, *per contra*, these newcomers began undermining religio-political structures. Instances of the first kind arise when, as with Captain Cook at Kerakekua Bay, Hawaii Island, in 1779, the visitors were taken to be supranormal. Revered as the returning Lono, God of Agriculture, Cook might have provided grounds for some significant cultic readjustment, had not some of the islanders stolen his rowing boat for its precious nails. Panicking over their captain's isolation, Cook's crewmen opened the hostilities which resulted in the great navigator's end.

It is quite possible that a good number of the megalithic statues on Easter Island reflect a much earlier extraordinary burst of 'cultic energy' and innovation – arising from just that kind of encounter in which numinousness far outshone the bare facts of material exchange. Perhaps the Spanish landed on Easter Island before the Dutchman Roggeveen did in 1722; indeed perhaps it was an all too brief landfall for the ill-fated lost caravel of 1526. If so, the Romanian scholar Dragos Gheorghiu, though poorly arguing his thesis, could well be right in his surprising inference that some of the megaliths were created (or reoriented?) in a manic attempt to attract back the bearded Spaniards (as returning Ancestors with astounding cargo) after the 'trauma' and 'enigma' of encounter 'inflamed' the islanders' imagination, and produced an obsessional-looking response among an utterly isolated people.[4] Unlike the older rows of figures, many of the statues near the quarry of Rano Raraku face out to sea – one with a sailing ship carved on its chest – while the beginning of an avenue is laid in the westward direction of departing vessels. Internal war, oral traditions suggest, racked the island after the effort, and the Polynesians who had laboured for their long-eared (South American?) overlords rebelled, pushing over most of the older creations.

As for reactions of the second kind, to the efforts of outsiders to dismantle the old institutions – and we think mainly of missionaries – the early contact experience produced a few (pro-)traditionalist responses running counter to movements of Christian conversion. By 1808, for example, the London Missionary Society (LMS) had been established on Tahiti for eleven years, but it then ran into trouble. Its early work coincided with the growth of the new cult of Oro, God of War, a deity beginning to be worshipped over a greater number of tribal areas than any other god, and one whose popularity was directly connected both to the pursuit of victory with introduced fire-power and the struggle between chiefs for paramountry and control over the highest symbols of power – the main Oro idol. The young Tu (son of King Pomare I and later Pomare II) was hoping the missionaries would be as useful as the mutineers from the *Bounty* had been for gaining military supremacy, but it was not LMS policy to trade in muskets, and in any case Tu's arrogance produced a general reaction against the Pomare family, with the rise of opposing, power-seeking chiefs and a widespread will 'to restore the ancient form of government to the island'.[5] Pomare I was virtually exiled, and was joined on the Leeward Islands by the missionaries, who persuaded him to adopt Christianity and provided him with incentive to secure dominion over the whole Tahitian group. If Pomare's successful holy war against the protagonists of the Oro cult and its old aura of power brought mass conversions in its train, however, the new monopoly of power he created threatened older reciprocities. The missionaries were also implicated, since they received assistance from villagers' labour and offerings for their auxiliary work, including the publication of books in Tahitian, yet did so without providing material *re*distribution; thus rebellion and anti-missionary activity soon appeared in the guise of a 'syncretism'. The institution of traditional prophetism became the vehicle for appropriating spirit-power for resistance and for securing direct access to the new God, whom rebel prophets now proclaimed as opposed to mission law and as opening a new order of freedom. This Mamaia movement, as it was called, grew in such strength that in 1833 a battle ensued between chiefs in the opposing camps. The 'heretical' rebels were crushed by Pomare IV.

Certain features comparable to those of Mamaia reappear in subsequent protest activity and new religious movements in the Pacific, and are worth highlighting. A crucial source on Mamaia's origins has it that one 'Teau, deacon of the church at Panaria' manifested strange behaviour (through some kind of altered state) and then announced himself to be 'Jesus Christ'. In 1828, moreover, came reports that Mamaia followers anticipated God would send 'a ship load of cloth from the skies... wine from heaven in bottles, and cows out of the clouds'.[6] Both these motifs, of course, had everything to do with victory and prosperity. Mamaia was about acquiring more powerful *mana* than was ostensibly available to the dominant faction; it was revivalist and therefore what Ralph Linton would term 'nativistic' in trying to regenerate something of the influence of the old prophet-diviner and of the travelling priest-like purveyors of a unified cultism (formerly focused on Oro). But Mamaia was also innovative in adopting a partly Christian face and in its advocacy of licence (e.g. sexual freedom for supporters).

Anthony Wallace might just as easily place it among his 'revitaliz- ation movements', as a collective effort to create a more satisfying culture.[7] In the history of Pacific islanders' varied group responses to contact and colonialism, some blend of retrogression and exper- imentation usually pertained – in different measures. The identifi- cation of a leader with a divine figure, however, and the hopes for the coming of cargo call for special comment.

For introductory purposes, it is worth exploring how some of our earlier distinctions between vertical and horizontal cosmic orien- tations have implications for the comparative study of responses to colonialism across the Pacific islands. Melanesia, of course, is much more famous than the other regions for so-called 'cargo cultism', or group agitation in expectation that European-style goods would issue out of the spirit-world. That is not completely absent from movements outside the south-western zone – we see something of it in Mamaia and perhaps on Easter Island much earlier – but it is not characteristic. And certainly the way Mamaia advocates con- ceived the new goods to be coming from the heavens reflects a distinctly Polynesian vertical cosmology, while by comparison Mel- anesians typically looked to the horizon. The claim of divinization, however, or of being a 'finisher' (*faaoti*) with the final message of God, as one Mamaia prophetess designated herself, is a common feature of protesting and adjusting movements in Austronesian chieftain societies. With the chiefs' mediation of the divine made questionable by the Gospel, the new power has to be grasped at its source and the divine mediator of the Bible must needs be brought to earth. And not just for spiritual purposes in such movements, but also for political and material results.

Insofar as the cargo cults and 'mediator cults' of both Micronesia and Polynesia project the coming of a final-looking scenario, in which cult followers are the beneficiaries of a cosmic Result and the unwanted colonials and detractors removed, one can talk loosely about millennarian movements. Some care should be taken, though, lest sociological categorization betray historical realities, because islander hopes for a future 'show-down' can be much more limited and far less eschatologically panoramic than some theoretical gen- eralizations about cross-cultural millenarianism suggest. Just the arrival of tinned bulk-beef in plenty will do for some cargo cultists; just the reversal of social control will be enough for most protestors.

Certainly in the history of Melanesian adjustments, at early stages in the contact history of given cultural complexes, leaders' hopes focused on transformations which would ensure military and economic dominance for their people – by harnessing the spirit-power necessary to overturn the newly intrusive order. Elements reflecting tendencies in both Melanesia and Polynesia are manifest in Fiji's Tuka movement (1883–5), in which Ndugumoi, a traditional priest from the hill country of Viti Levu, renamed himself Navosakakandua ('He Who Speaks Once', or 'Chief Justice') and declared that the world was fast approaching *tavuki* (or a Great Reversal), through which Whites would serve Blacks, and chiefs, (who by this time often abetted White causes) would change places with those commoners who now followed them. Navosakakandua, significantly, had the alleged power of bringing God down to earth in his temple séances.

Such a response to incipient colonialism has its parallels throughout New Guinea history. A prophet arising from the eastern Fuyughe, for instance, brought at least six tribes of the Sauwo Valley into opposition against mission and police influence. This was Ona Asi, who snatched a sacred pig tusk from a glade of the neighbouring Seragi and was thereby seized by a more-powerful-than-ordinary *sila* called Bilalaf (in 1910). With the spirit of this Cosmic Serpent, Ona could harness environmental forces to bring down thunder and lightning on the outsiders, and at one point he even predicted a great catastrophic earthquake if Blacks so much as looked upon Whites. His movement had its heyday between 1933 and 1942, during which time he borrowed both from the Ten Commandments to frame new laws and from neighbouring groups to introduce new rituals. If Fuyughe traditions gave the Ancestors little part in the affairs of the living (see p. 158 above), Bilalaf announced that they would bring *susum* (goods) in abundance, for his was a desperate hope that there were occult powers and sources of abundance in the universe which would eliminate the threat to his people's security.

Among the Wahgi, only a decade and a half after Taylor's party trekked to their valley from the Goroka outstation in 1933, there occurred an extraordinary ritual of despair – a kind of deformed, exaggerated *Kongar* or great pig-kill – to bring about a miracle of wealth and power for the participants. The instigator of this so-called 'Madness' was Goitaye Dolpa of Mur hamlet, who instructed his followers to wash wrappings of fungi, long leaves and lengths of wood in a mountain lake where he had seen the dead making wealth (*mongi*). After these items had been borne in a line down to the specially built cult-house beside the traditional ceremonial grounds, days of vigorous dancing and outbursts of mock violence followed in the desperate effort to transform these objects into steel axes (or shell money), valuable bird of paradise feathers and (most significantly) guns. The fever for a grand reversal of fortune attracted representatives from many previously hostile tribes – both to regain lost prestige caused by the Whites' superior fire-power and to secure apparently unlimited access to key valuables both old and new. In these Melanesian movements, leaders made no claims to divinity and the materialistic interest was paramount, but, wherever they were in the island Pacific, strong collective reactions close to contact always reveal a great concern with renewed group strength or security.

OF KINGS AND CARGO

It was above all during the hundred years between 1830 and 1930 that the Pacific islands experienced the far-reaching effects of both missionization and the imperial pretensions of European powers. That is a century of events famous for the various postures of Polynesian kings and chiefs bent on enhancing their power or containing a White takeover, and for the emergence of Melanesian cargo cultism (earlier called the 'Vailala Madness'). We have already seen how the alliance between missionaries and a powerful chieftain family plummeted Tahiti into the throes of a new kind of ideological conflict. In other Polynesian islands both the circumstances of religious change and the responses to it by ruling and powerful families were different; and in Melanesia what we would describe as prosperity cults of early or limited contact situations can be compared to cults, less traditional and more affected by Christian prosleytism, which arose in societies experiencing longer interaction with outsiders.

On the Hawaiian Islands, moves towards political unification under the great Kamehameha I were immediately followed by a severe undermining of old cults just before the coming of the American Presbyterian missionaries. After her husband's death in 1819 the renowned Queen Kaahumanu became 'premier' to his weak successor King Liholiho. An impressive 300kg beauty and famous surfer, she initiated sweeping reforms to end many of the traditional tabus (*kapu*), including those which had traditionally subjected women. After organizing a feast on Maui in which Liholiho broke *kapu* by eating with women, both nobles and commoners joined in a rampage to destroy effigies and temples. Missionary presence from 1820 onwards suited Kaahumanu's projects, and her encouragement of the king and other chiefs to adopt the new faith and its (Calvinist) rules brought an unprecedented religio-political unification by the time of her own baptism in 1825. A quarter-century later, however, with a population torn between the pull of two worlds and depleted by epidemic disease, an agreement called the Great Mahele resulted in massive land sales in favour of White settlers, who had taken advantage of a pacified Hawaii. By 1894 the White cartel – which had formed an Annexation Club and forestalled the move by Queen Liliukalani to legalize a new constitution giving voting rites only to true Polynesian Hawaiians – took over the islands through a local American coup. The royalists (who had by this time turned to the Church of England) tried their hand at America's one and only revolution, but they were flushed out of the bush and their bomb-stores uncovered. In the wake of the Spanish-American War, the United States reneged on the policy of non-interference and annexed Hawaii in mid-1898. Kaahumanu's clever reformism under-cut the old feudalism only to make possible a new one – and one dominated by unscrupulous sugar barons rather than missionaries.

In Tonga, by contrast, where mission influence remained stronger and imperial interference slight, traditional royalty prevailed, but only after the victorious 'secular' chief Taufa'ahau absorbed the role of sacred ruler as well, after the last Ti'u Tonga had died. Under the 1852 constitution the powerful Taufa'ahau, renamed King George, was the divine king, and was in a good position both to dictate Tonga's religious policy despite missionary competition and to ward off threats of colonial annexation (cf. p. 183 below). To the deep south, the Maori were not so fortunate. Pressures to open up land for new settlers inevitably led to war in the North Island. Anti-White tribes rallied, significantly enough, around a 'king' (in 1857): Potatau I was an elected king presiding over a Maori council of state, judiciary and police system, with the hard task of stopping inter-tribal war and retaining land. Out of this King movement came the psychological strength to confront the Whites militarily during the 1860s, except that by 1872 the Maori had been beaten back into their enclave in the North Island's west central region.

In New Zealand indications of religious innovations came first with the wider adoption of what was originally a district War God, Maru; but this neo-traditional development was overshadowed by the emergence of the renowned Hauhau extremists in 1864. During the Second Taranaki or Maori War of 1864–5, Hauhau fol-lowers displayed extra daring because of the belief that the shouted spell 'Pai Marire, Hau! Hau!' would make them impervious to Euro-pean bullets. This was in spite of the fact, however, that Te Ua, the prophet of this movement (which is better named Pai Marire, 'good and peaceful'), did not advocate a military response at all. Instead he encouraged his supporters to move away from war theatres to let God do the destroying for his chosen people – 'the house of Shem' or 'Tiu, or Jews' – even while bearing the comforting message of the revealer Gabriel that those who did get killed would be 'glorified,' . . . [and] stand here on the roof of clouds'.[8] With the defeat of the Maori, the King movement developed into a new religion, a mix of traditional and Christian elements under Tawhiao, King Potatau II, which lasted to the 1890s, while Hauhau was transformed by Te Kooti, one of its later guerrilla activists, into a separatist church which lasts to this day (see p. 184 below).

With reformist Kaahumanu, King George's role as Ti'u Tonga and the Maori kings, we sense the pull of traditional views about sacral rulers mediating between heaven and earth; with Te Ua and Te Kooti, appeals were made to a direct access to the divine which by-passed the time-inured nexus of political and religious authority. What happened in Samoa during the middle decades of the nineteenth century also illustrates the diverging of chiefly and distinctly religious mediatorship. Samoa possessed its paramount chiefs, who were recognized as such – and ceremonially installed by kingmaking orators – because they were suitable by birth, holders of the highest titles and thus personages of *mana* 'to whom gods and men crowded'.[9] If one such 'royal son' held sway in the west and the other in the east, however, there was a constant jostling for supremacy among the various chieftains, and once Christianity was introduced there tended to be competition between them for the support of the new divine power(s). By 1845 the LMS, Wesleyans from Tonga, Catholics and numerous tiny movements called 'sailor sects' all had their footholds, and this diversity suited a decentralized social system and a culture which possessed few obvious focal points for its old religion; not even temples, altars, idols or cultic offerings. In the 'sailor sects', then, as with early indigenous experiments with Christianity, it was perhaps to be expected that leaders would be presented, or present themselves, as divine mediators, epitomizing a given region's claimed access to the newly discovered, supreme source of *mana*, and so making the 'foreign religion' very decisively 'one's own'.[10]

For some of those following the Samoan freelance missionary Siovili of Eva (sometimes called Joe Gimlet), for instance, 'the Son of God' had come to dwell 'among them' in the body of an elderly woman, and she among other Siovili prophets could communicate

directly with 'the Great Spirit'. Others regarded Siovili himself to
be Jesus. Churches were built, acquired books were muttered over
in rituals, and hymns were sung in the hope that worshippers would
receive a cargo ship sent by 'the King of the Skies'.[11] Perhaps it is
the way such developments reflected the importance of each locality
and chieftainship that is of most consequence here, for it was the
confusingly decentralized nature of Samoan religio-political affairs
that actually rescued island society from potential disintegration in
the long run. A diffused, almost irrepressible opposition was kept
up during periods of land alienation to foreign settlers or companies
(1860–70s), and of direct colonial rule under Germany (1889–1914)
and New Zealand (1914–62). How Samoa avoided the fates of the
Hawaiians and Maori is thus of great fascination in itself. Yet in
the history of more distinctly religious reactions to Western
intrusions, the appearance of divine mediators in the Siovili cult also
provides a clue to a characteristically Polynesian tendency: the turning to a 'divine human' figure to secure cosmic order (or reordering
in a time of crisis).

Indeed, even in those Polynesian and Micronesian settings where
chieftainship systems are more 'traditional' and less 'stratified' (see
p. 138 above), outbursts in which Christianity is radically recast in
indigenous terms reflect this tendency very dramatically. The
Rennell Island reception of three different missions in 1936, for
example, resulted in the various tribes' claim that traditional priests
and mediums had now been appropriated by God, and this led the
tribes to divide themselves into three sectors, one for each incoming
mission. Central to the change was Tegheta, the adopted son of
Taupongi, the priest of Nuipana on the shores of Lake Tegano.
After turning against his father while under traditional-looking possession, he sent off three messengers 'to heaven' to bring back calico.
When they did return bearing new goods (from a neighbouring
settlement), Tegheta had the courage to announce his own divinity
and then broke strict tabus by having sexual intercourse with his
classificatory mother and sister (Taupongi's wife and daughter). With
a more general, chaotic breakdown of socio-sexual tabus ensuing,
as well as other seizures and messages by adepts, what missionaries
could only describe as 'Nuipana Madness' finished with the high
chief's division of the people – to accept the defeat of the old gods
and embrace Christianity in the three regions of south, east and
west.[12]

A little earlier than this, on Onotoa in the southern Gilberts, a
shortlived 'new sect' sprang out of the LMS mission (1930–2) that

viciously recoiled against the presence of Catholics on the atoll. A certain Ten Naewa declared himself God's prophet with a new revelation, that God was going to descend on the island in person. With a rather surprising theological quirk he was soon declaring himself 'Father of God' – thereby becoming superior to the awaited God the Father – and surrounded himself with women, his 'Sheep', who fell into trances at his command and two of whom were aspects of Christ. His 'Swords of Gabriel' were men who brought the threat of death against those heedless toward his prophecies. When the promised hour – their 'millennium' – came and went without event, Naewa and his Swords turned on the enemy, and after processing in a contorted dance managed to kill two Catholics.[13]

Aside from such extraordinary claims by the guiding stars of these last two movements, and of course preoccupations with the disclosures from heaven, reported intimations of madness and frenzied collective expectation will immediately remind many here of earlier and pre-war manifestations of cargo cults in Melanesia. After all, before Lucy Mair gave scholarship the attractive and alliterative phrase 'cargo cult' in 1948, various religio-political disturbances in colonial Papua and New Guinea were called the 'Vailala Madness'. This curious denotation hails from some extraordinary phenomena along the Vailala River, among the Elema of the Papuan Gulf, from 1919 to 1922. Taken at its onset to be a visitation of the Holy Ghost, the local LMS Pryce Jones wrote favourably in his diary of collective praises in the Spirit and an enhanced generosity toward the church, whereas the later (more oral historical) report by the government anthropologist F. E. Williams made unfavourable judgements – about 'gibberish' rather than glossolalia, 'hysteria' instead of spiritual transformation and 'automania' as against possession. This movement was noted for its rejection of tradition and 'the destruction of native ceremonies' (such as the Hevehe masks), and for episodic anticipations of returning Ancestors who would come from across the seas in a ship laden with European goods.[14]

The prime motivation for the Vailala agitation was the desperate concern to re-engage with the Ancestors and thus shore up the defences of both the dead and the living against the destroyers of local autonomy. By 1918 the Territory authorities required the Elema to pay an annual head-tax, and to grow rice – a non-traditional, unwelcome crop – to make their district pay. The local LMS missionary abetted the colonial cause but promulgated a message of radical spiritual change, which villagers in the Vailala movement embraced on their own terms, possibly through the influence of freelance itinerant preachers from Port Moresby, and certainly because 'new men' claimed access to the spiritual power necessary for group regeneration. Crucial early on was the prophet Harea, who foretold a new order without sorrow, sadness or hunger. By 1921 it was Evara, a man more military in style, with his uniform and medals and his 'make-believe' radio station, who was to the fore. Both figures encouraged collective trance states as the means of receiving new power and as a preparation – a kind of *rite de passage* – for a promised world of abundance. The cargo, however, is best interpreted as a by-product of the Ancestors' return than the object of materialistic desire. The coming of European-style goods, indeed, symbolized a 'total salvation' which combined spiritual renewal with concrete results.

What may be termed the 'classic cargo cultism' of the inter-war period typically tended to combine agitation to bring on the saving intervention of the dead or Jesus with the arrival of items, often including guns, which would rescue the Blacks from inferiorization and military subjection. The role of agitation is nicely illustrated by unpredictable outbreaks of *Adventnachten*, as the Dutch missionaries called them, in the Biak-Numfor region of Irian Jaya, feverish dances into the night meant to bear in their train a cosmic transformation. Far to the east, dreams of political reversal show up clearly in the proclamations of Stephen Pako on Buka Island in 1932 that a 'cargo ship' would arrive 'with iron, axes, food, tobacco, motorcars, and, significantly, firearms', and that work in the gardens should therefore cease forthwith.[15]

Lest the point be missed that the political annexation of all the Oceanian peoples we are discussing was by nations that possessed monarchies – and that appeals to kingship were therefore bound to show up in indigenous responses to imperialism anyway – we should note that Melanesia had its small share of 'King movements'. In 1931, a priest interviewed one of the four 'Black kings' of the Negrie-Yangoru complex from the hinterland Sepik and was told that the dead 'were making all sorts of things for the people', and that 'iron pots, tinned food and kerosene' would surely come, even though 'the whites were holding these things back and [wrongfully] selling them' to the local Blacks. Six years later a self-declared 'Black king' emerged further east among the Tangu (of hinterland Madang), collecting his own taxes, debarring the followers from attending mission schools, performing his own baptisms (of genitals, not heads) and promising that the Ancestors' cargo-laden ship was soon to arrive. Such were the innovative teachings of Mambu, who taught that the Whites diverted to themselves cargo which was rightfully the *kanakas'* by 'removing the labels and substituting their own'. His subversive thoughts soon got him into a coastal gaol.[16]

The resentments underlying cargo cult outbursts, we already sense, has everything to do with the breakdown of reciprocity between intruders, with a plentiful enough supply of new and wonderful goods, and the indigenes with an exasperatingly limited access to them. The altercations created by the cultists are on the one hand negative – they are disturbances to get back at threatening forces and in that sense are in the tradition of revenge activity – but on the other they involve projections of an ideal time of positive reprocity to come. Political realism and the effects of the missionary pacifism typically deter agitators from military action (though that was indeed tried in odd quarters) while profound eschatology as promised in the Bible engenders collective images of a presaged miracle – a totally new order of perfected rather than disfigured reciprocations.

While the quest for cargo makes its appearance in the contact history of wider Oceania – with Tongans after booty, Siovili songs beckoning ships to Samoa and Rennellese messengers seeking calico in heaven – Melanesian yearning for the new goods is much more pronounced. This does not reflect any imagined difference between Polynesian religiosity and Melanesian magic; it rather bespeaks the 'materialistic' concerns of traditional Melanesian religions – especially in the sense that the visible fruits expected to arise from ritual activity (which could include 'sacrificially' destroying one's property as an act of commitment to the spirits) were to express the plenitude and excitement of life. Little did earlier generations of colonized 'natives' realize it, but the cargo was destined to arrive among the islands in what were previously unimaginable quantities – at the time when all Oceania was drawn into world war.

INSPIRATIONS OF WORLD WAR

Changes wrought during World War I – with the dismantling of the German possessions in New Guinea, the Solomons, Micronesia and Samoa (in 1914) – were minimal when set beside the extraordinary developments of World War II. By December 1942 virtually all Micronesia was Japan's and the Japanese front line extended to the Northern District of Papua and Guadalcanal in the Solomons. In their massive counter-offensive, the Allies massed personnel and military equipment at strategically crucial points, producing uncanny spectacles of wealth and power as a result. During 1944–5 over one million servicemen passed through the Momote Airbase alone (on Los Negros Island, Manus), with ducks and armoured vehicles spewing out of cargo vessels and a four-lane bitumen highway built from one side of the island to the other. Impressive bases were set up around Polynesia, especially on Tonga and tiny Tutuila (in American Samoa) and across eastern Melanesia outside the war zone (Fiji, Efate and Espiritu Santo – now in Vanuatu – and New Caledonia). Within the war zone itself the 'liberating' troops massed at camps on the northern coasts of New Guinea – at Lae, Saidor, Wewak and as far west as Meokwundi in the Biak-Numfor region; and they kept flushing the Japanese out of the atolls until the final assault on Okinawa (March 1945).

The careers of some new religious movements were inextricably bound up with the events of the war. Tagarab of Milguk (Trans-Gogol, Madang) was credited with predicting the bombing of Madang township by returning Ancestors in the guise of Japanese servicemen. His followers believed the real name of God was (the local deity) Kilibob (see p. 124 above), and for failing to reveal this, even missionaries were now being made to suffer with the other Europeans. Kilibob intended cargo for the Madangs, a changing of their skin to white and a cosmic upheaval, but Tagarab's dreams came up against the harsh realities of Japanese rule and he was eventually shot for protesting. To the north some Batari cultists on west New Britain tried to make use of the Japanese occupation to expand their activities, although their 'missionary', isolated on Bali Vitu Island, was arrested by a daring Catholic catechist who acted under the impression that Australian rule still applied. To the west, the greatest of all Biakese prophet-figures (*konoors*), Angginita Menufeur of Imsumbabi Island, was arrested first by Dutch and then by Japanese local authorities (mid-1942). Committed to her vision of a new order of abundance (*Koreri*), many of her faithful formed the 'America Blanda' Army to free her from gaol. Proclaiming her queen of an independent New Guinea and convinced that a magic oil would render their bodies invulnerable, up to 2,000 Koreri 'warriors' were shot dead by Japanese rifle-power (in a collective 'martyrdom' which has given subsequent inspiration to today's anti-Indonesian Liberation Movement, the OPM).

Far to the east, the remarkable movement known as Maasina (so-called 'Marching Rule', 1944–54) took its cue from the wartime presence of both Black and White American servicemen working as equals in the Solomons. The British authorities found themselves embarrassed by anti-colonial enclaves, especially on Malaita and San Cristobal, where disciplined organizations were bent on the autonomous collection of taxes, court hearings, the imposition of fines, drills, and the framing of regulations for the total ordering of society (including conformity to the Ten Commandments, Sunday worship, etc). One implication of this kind of activity was a very distinctly religious one: the setting up of a separatist or independent church. The first of these in Melanesia was founded in the Admiralty Islands by the great Paliau Maloat, who, after his many experiences abroad – patrolling with James Taylor in the highlands, and officiating as sergeant-major of the Rabaul police under the Australians and the Japanese – returned to his home island of Baluan (south of Manus) in 1946. An ecclesial independency resulted, and we shall investigate the Paliau church and others comparable to it in the next section. Maasina joins other movements we have mentioned, however, by pointing rather obviously in a political direction. As protests against European hegemony, as attempts at self-determination and as expressions of spiritual independence, various 'native disturbances' have in one way or the other laid the foundations for the new nations of the Pacific. Odd rebellions – Ponapeans against the Spanish in 1898, the 1927 Malatian Massacre of District Officer Bell and his assistants, etc., – need recognition here so that the variety of Pacific responses is better conveyed; as do anti-tax agitations, strikes, boycotts, co-operatives and eventually political parties.

In post-war cargo movements both great and small, moreover, the links between the pursuit of political and economic power and religious interests became all the more apparent in the greater concern with money. The war itself brought an influx of dollars to certain Pacific sectors, while slow but steady monetarization of the islands marks the post-war era. Co-operatives established around the Pacific were the typical organs by which villages could build up financial reserves and a renewed sense of local autonomy as collectives, although in Melanesia their collapse was often followed by the exasperations of cargo cultism. One hallmark of post-war cargoism is the fund; money was collected by leaders and stowed for group contingencies (and all too often individual leaders' sumptuary needs). The number of exercises in the 'magical multiplication' of money also noticeably increased after 1945. A prime object of the well-known Tuesday table rituals among the many coastal Madang villages loyal to the Yali Singina of Sor (1948–75) was to make more money; that is, to please Ancestors and so gain access to cash. Cult leaders' access to money also confirmed their political clout.

Money, after all, was one crucial key to the cargo, and as the effects of colonialism deepened during the 1960s and 1970s, the differences between experiments at *bisnis* (private enterprise) and rituals of cargo cultists were often blurred. Many Mengen took up the instructions to 'keep passbooks', put their 'money in the bank' and 'keep the Ten Commandments' as advocated by the heroic Koriam Urekit (from Ablingi Island), who campaigned along north-east New Britain coast to secure a seat in the first elected Parliament of Papua and New Guinea in 1964; but these same supporters typically held that Koriam's 'work' was a sign of the Ancestors' collective return, and that the dead by a mere wish could bring into being houses of permanent building materials, streets, cars, indeed all that constituted a city like New York! A comparable excitement over money and its possibilities came with the emergence of the Mount Hurun movement (centring on the Malambanja village in the Negrie-Yangoru complex of the Sepik in 1971), with ten-dollar subscriptions being collected for a 30,000-strong membership of the new Peli Association and a slick, fancily dressed (but non-literate) 'clerk' Jimmy Simbago found shuffling papers around in a square fibro building called 'the office'. The grand vision of this movement, however, was the miraculous event set for 7 July 1971, when the removal of unwanted geodesic markers from the sacred mountain would release from it cargo and great plenty, or so the apocalypticist Matias Yaliwan prophesied. Overlooking Malambanja red boxes were buried in an artificial cemetery; the money placed in them at night might be procured if one could get home without one's eyes being diverted to the left or right. In the village cult-house itself one found 'flower girls' swilling money in dishes of water, their male guardians clasping their breasts from behind (and sometimes having intercourse with them) in a nocturnal ritual of multiplication. The mastermind of the new rituals was Peli's manager and Yaliwan's right-hand man, Daniel Hawina.

The flashpoints or the moments of most intensity in many such movements occasionally brought a breakdown of traditional sexual tabus and a propensity to acts of violence, the latter sometimes aimed against Whites or expatriates, but most often against local detractors. Under its president John Teosin, the Buka Island Hahalis Welfare Society developed the so-called 'Baby Garden', initially designed for young men and women to have free access to each other as the expression of Teosin's 'naturalistic' philosophy and his movement's rejection of mission constraints. When the Society was ceremonially opened in 1962, in fact, a public ritual mime of sexual intercourse between young men and women was enacted at Hahalis village. To secure his social experiment, Teosin's offsiders also had very effective methods of dispensing with opponents by ritual beheading; to maintain independence Hahalis also held well-known anti-tax demonstrations against the Australian colonial government and (as we shall show in the next section) established an alternative church. On Bougainville proper around this time, Torau cultists of Rorovane village stripped themselves naked of their *laplaps* in the committed hope that a cargo ship was arriving, and when nothing happened the men ran up and down a mountain to make it appear. Anger was turned on the local Catholic catechist and parish priest because they stuck to their clothes, and these two narrowly escaped death. This was the same year – 1960 – when an ambush of local mission personnel was planned among the Kiriaka (on Bougainville's west coast), but it came to nought with a quick radio warning to a local government post about the cult plot. Toward the island centre in Nasioi country, Damien Damen began organizing his own subscription system for the Ancestors in 1962, and then created what became known as the 'Fifty Toea (or cent) cult', which in turn provided spiritual backing to opposition against Bougainville Copper Limited mining at Panguna, and thus to the Bougainville Rebellion (1989–91).[17]

By comparison with Micronesian and Polynesia, Melanesia has been a sea of troubles for post-war colonialism. Various outbursts of dissatisfaction, cargo cultist or not, were precursory to eruptions arriving at the end of the twentieth century. There have been disturbances at the point of independence: the OPM gained impetus once it was clear (by 1965) that Indonesians and not Melanesians would run western New Guinea; the Bougainvillean bid to remain out of Papua New Guinea's independence in 1975 was a foretaste of the later rebellion; both Jimmy Steven's rebels (on Espiritu Santo and its outliers) and adherents of the Jonfrum cargo movement were at their most agitated on the point of Vanuatu's 1980 independence, partly through French instigation. Leftist Kanaks at the barricades on New Caledonia (1984–8) and Colonel Rabuka's two Fijian coups (1987) further bear out the impression of Melanesia's greater turbulence, both countries possessing mines and poor labour conditions. Micronesian and Polynesian peoples, in contrast, apart from such exceptions as Tonga, West Samoa and Palau, were either too 'outpopulated' (as in Hawaii and New Zealand) or generally too dispersed to agitate effectively for freedom (that is, until recent times). Even during the international movement for decolonization (in the 1970s), some groups opted to remain under the protection of bigger powers, reaping economic and social security benefits into the bargain (e.g. the Cooks, Niue). In terms of more distinctly religious developments, however, and more particularly the emergence of independent churches, wider Oceania joins Melanesia in offering its fascinations. Let us turn now to these phenomena.

YOUR OWN CHURCH

When 'King George' managed to couple the roles of 'secular' and 'sacred' chieftainships on Tonga in 1852, he created a cultural problem. In traditional terms, combining these offices might have granted him both political and religious paramountcy, yet Wesleyan–Catholic missionary competition appeared to prevent the desired religious unity, and the persisting presence of the foreign missions implied that he was not fully in control of all Tongan affairs. Near the end of his reign (in 1875), however, the problem was solved by allowing the king to be 'divine' and a constitutional monarch at the same time, with control over a church of his own – the Free Church of Tonga. Due to the offices of the controversial Wesleyan missionary Shirley Baker, who interfered in politics rather more than his colleagues approved of, this 'independent church', the first of its kind in the Pacific, broke ties with the mother church in Australia, and King George thereupon ordered all Wesleyans to join his own church. It did not work so well, and left two minority groups – one old Wesleyan and the other Catholic – disengaged from royal control. Even his persuasive successor Queen Salote could not ever succeed in bringing the two separated Wesleyan (or Methodist) components together. The anomaly remains, and so this is how Oceania's first ecclesiastical 'independency', quite unlike any of the others to follow, became an 'established church', not by any means a piece of 'maverick sectarianism'.

What, though, is meant by 'independent church'? Here we take our frame of reference from Bengt Sundkler and other Africanists who have been documenting the multiplicity of African independencies for a good generation or more.[18] An independent church is one which is founded by an indigenous (religious) leader in opposition to or as a secession from an older, introduced mission or sect, with the adherents of the separating movement wishing to remain or to present themselves afresh as 'a church'. Perhaps the Tongan case does not fit perfectly. It depends where one places the emphasis: on Tongan royal prerogative or on the fact that, in the beginning at least, a European presided over the day-to-day running of the church (Baker's friend Watkin). In other Polynesian settings, however, the indigenous factor has been blatant. In the wake of the Taranaki Wars, for instance, the young Te Kooti Te Turuki, who had been wrongly condemned to penal servitude in the Chatham Islands for allegedly spying for the Maori 'rebels', escaped back to New Zealand with his followers in a 'latter-day flight out of Egypt'. On the Chathams he had laid the foundations of Ringatu, a faith in which the Maori were firmly identified with ancient Israel. Turning the Whites into the Amalekites, whom God wanted swept from the land (cf. 1 Sam. 15:3), Ringatu was earlier a 'prophet cult' to followers who engaged in guerrilla attacks on White settlements and took God's support of Israel's victories as a legitimating precedent (1869–71). By the 1880s, though, it had begun developing into a 'church', so that today it presents itself as 'established' and as 'a Maori Christian Church'.[19] Its ministers are called by the traditional Maori term *tohunga* (experts), and their special tasks include caring for the sick, maintaining a rigidly correct form of service and teaching strict, traditional-looking rules about the body, water usage and planting.

At the beginning of the twentieth century the fruitlessness of Maori attempts at physical protest was all too evident, and church separation became the order of the day. At the present time there are about ten independent Maori churches. The best known founder among these was Tahupotiki Ratana, who started the Ratana church in 1928 (now 20,000 strong). A series of dreams and visions confirmed his belief that God had empowered him as a healer and as the vehicle by which the Maori would turn away from old tabus and ancestral relics to become faithful to God. Support for him from the mainstream churches was strong until Anglicans reported that he added to the Trinitarian formula 'and the true angels'. Soon isolated as a schismatic, he formed his own church, ordaining its 'bishops', 'apostles' and 'leaders of worship'. His widely proclaimed gift as a healer attracted many needy visitors, both indigenous and White, to the village of Ratana (North Island of New Zealand), and in his role we find, once again, the characteristically Polynesian concern with 'mediatorship'. If King George as 'divine king' sat between God and the Tongans, Ratana was 'the mouthpiece of God', as many hymns allude to him, and following his death in 1939 he has 'tended to replace Christ in many of the congregations'.[20] In the church's iconography the beginnings of his separate church are symbolized by a ladder linking an aeroplane (heaven) to a car below (earth), this partly denoting that for Ratana political and religious goals became intertwined. He insisted on the Whites properly ratifying the 1840 Treaty of Waitangi, and persuaded Prime Minister M. J. Savage to let the Maori field four candidates for Parliament.

The Polynesian saga continues. Of most recent interest is the movement surrounding Apii Piho on the Cook Islands (mainly Rakahanga). In 1987 she announced that she was Jesus Christ, a rather fascinating self-identification in our world of Indian Divine Mothers and Western feminist evocations of God as the Great Mother – but once again, for Polynesia, the appeal to sacral mediatorship is indicative. Mrs Piho even challenged a television interviewer in New Zealand, where she has many Cook Island followers, that she would take off her clothes and reveal she was indeed a man and thus Jesus if the television company donated NZ$10,000 to the work of her new church!

Melanesia, for its part, has thus far yielded up as many as eighteen independent churches; a third have arisen from pre-existing cargo movements. Historically the first was Paliau Maloat's church, which he founded in 1946 as the Baluan Native Christian United church on Baluan Island, south of Manus (see above). Paliau's catch-cry was *gutpela tingting* (right thinking), and he meant by that a rejection of all that was bad in the 'old fashion' (or tradition) and an embracing of the 'new fashion' (his version of Christianity). In his theological myth-history, called the 'Long Story of God', he placed Baluan and the Manus group firmly in the theatre of cosmic history, so that the islanders were meant to receive his radical reduction or telescoping of the 'Bible story' as their new myth. By implication Jesus was judged at his trial by an Australian official, and the nations to be judged by God are those who have given the New Guineans a bad time. Australia will go the way of Germany and Japan unless it changes its attitude, and God will use America as his liberators. Large Paliau churches were built of traditional material on the islet of Mouk (off Baluan), and at Mbunai, south Manus, where a huge, somewhat suburban-looking village was built by his followers (who included Usiai groups from the centre of Manus as well as the Manus themselves). From these churches Paliau and his 'lieutenants' preached Sunday sermons and led the liturgy, which consisted of the Catholic Mass in pidgin with the central pages – covering the offering of the bread and wine – ripped out. Paliau supporters were to avoid attendance at both the Catholic and Liebenzell (Lutheran) Missions.

With his rapidly spreading fame, Paliau walked a tightrope with cargo cultism. He openly dissociated his movement from excesses of cargo expectation – from the 1947–8 Johnston Island cult called 'The Noise,' for instance, when isolated villagers longed for the spectacular arrival of a cargo ship – yet on monitoring the fund collected for his organization he played on villagers' unrealistic expectations that money was multiplying rapidly, and by the 1970s was constantly dipping into reserves to satisfy both his own sumptuary requirements – as feast organizer, political campaigner, etc. – and his penchant for new projects, such as land purchases at the Manus provincial capital of Lorengau. Averting temporary yet massive defection in his church, by 1984 Paliau was very much back on top of things. His protégé Paliau Lukas had purchased Lorengau's biggest store, the first floor being used as the church's offices; an impressive site overlooking the same township was acquired for a church building; a new manifesto ('the little white book') was published; and claims were made that the new provincial government should recognize Paliau's special political authority over Manus as comparable to its own. What is more, by 1991 Paliau was knighted – not long before his death.

Nowhere in all these proceedings, however, was Paliau rated as divine. A *profet*, to be sure, who received a vision of Jesus while he was still in Rabaul (see p. 180 above) and who bore a message because of his encounter; but not a divinized mediator. By and large Melanesian movements stop short of turning sacred leaders into incarnations of deity. Some New Guinea cases leave one with a sense of old cargo cult energies being continued with good management, as if the leaders answer the continuing need to 'get back' at the missions by taking a leaf out of their book and thus setting up a competitive *sios* (church) or *lotu* (form of worship). After the Hahalis Welfare Society lost its attractions on Buka, for example, John Teosin was runinng his new church, called Hehala, along with a popular nightclub. His people the Halia, he has maintained, had their own Jesus in Buka tradition, the heroic Mattanachil. After stopping warfare, ordaining good custom and performing healing miracles, Mattanachil went up to the heights of Tehesi (a volcano on north Bougainville) from whence he shall return in power at some unknown hour. The Whites can worry about their Jesus, but the Buka have their own local welfare to address, and their open-air 'sacrificial feasts' (*hets*) to the deity Sunahan are above all meant to increase the island's fertility.

Previously, various nocturnal rituals of Hahalis were performed to cajole the Ancestors into returning with European cargo; now, because of its bad press, cargo cultism is eschewed in a matter-of-fact manner. Something comparable happened with the Peli Association after the arrival and passing of the great event on 7 July 1971. Daniel Hawina had to face the inevitable criticism that nothing had really come from removing the markers from Mount Hurun (see p. 181), and in a vehement argument one of his relatives, Markus Kenna, who also happened to be President of the Negrie (Catholic) Church Council, sardonically challenged him with the words: 'You can start your own church, if you are man enough'.[21] With the more obvious presence of the Canadian New Apostolic Church missionaries at this time (1980), Hawina sought to do just that. Coming and going on tourist visas (until the East Sepik provincial government legislated against their coming altogether in 1981), the New Apostolic missionaries became more and more dependent on Hawina as a permanent fixture and skilful manager. Peli's old 30,000 strong membership was transferred to Niu Apostolic; Hawina soon inherited the church leadership and the box of ecclesiastical paraphernalia – sacramental vessels, service books, even a black suit and false tie – to go with it. Cargo cultism was abandoned, Hawina and his delegates performed baptisms freely, and in 1981 he was working on a local theology.

Such blatant pragmatism, however, is matched elsewhere by independencies with more manifestly spiritual *personae*, because they have incorporated (even while adapting) Western styles of worship and theology with greater seriousness. Up until 1975, for example, the Nagriamal Federation Independent United Royal Church, which was founded by Jimmy Stevens in 1965 and became strong on Espiritu Santo and such outliers as Aobe, received a good deal of support from Church of Christ missionaries. The two foremost ministers of this church defected from that denomination, yet carried much of the liturgical and theological style from it into Nagriamal. As the heroic leader of this church, Stevens, who was placed in a government prison as a rebel from 1980 to 1991, was certainly extolled as a new Moses, but never divinized. Even to the very east of Melanesia, on Fiji, the reverential epithet for the founder of the remarkable Congregation of the Poor, Sekei Loaniceva, is 'Vunawai', which means the 'Physician Anointed by Jehovah'.

Admittedly, there are odd Melanesian claims to self-deification –

often by psychologically disturbed individuals wanting to start new cults, as Burton-Bradley has shown.[22] Occasionally women become the locus of a virtually divinized mediatorship; in 1984 Bikana Veve of the Rigo area, Papua, founded an independency partly on the basis of her claim to be pregnant by the Holy Spirit, like Mary; and in the mountains of west New Britain among the Kaliai, a holy woman was acclaimed as Jesus. Of the better known Melanesian churches, however, only with the renowned Christian Fellowship Church (New Georgia, Solomons), and Yali movement ('Wok belong Yali', Madang, New Guinea), does one find an extremely strong emphasis on messiahship and occasional (though hardly uniform) claims of virtual apotheosis.

Silas Eto, othewise remembered as the Holy Mama, led a breakaway church from the Methodist Mission in 1960. The phenomenon of *tatura* – 'a form of mass enthusiasm which involved drumming, crying out, fainting and collective involuntary movements in church services' – convinced the Roviana, his people, that the Holy Spirit had visited them from 1956. Trained as a Methodist pastor-teacher under the great New Zealand missionary J. F. Goldie, Eto went on to organize church building, primary schooling, development projects, a ministry serviced by the Theological Education Fund of the World Council of Churches, anti-logging activity and a political campaign to lay the foundations of the Western Province of the Solomon Islands – among other things! Of all the leaders of the Pacific independent churches, he is the one most reminiscent of the white-robed, Black messiahs and Zulu Zionists of Africa. It is small wonder that some of his followers believe that '*he winim Got* (He supersedes God)', and even Eto sometimes spoke of himself as the fourth 'Man' of the Trinity through which the *mana/minna* of the Godhead was mediated to humans.[23]

As for Yali Singina, the great (Allied) war hero and the organizer of the most widespread of all cargo cult organizations, he was bound to be divinized by some of his followers at his death in 1975. The fact that Yali named his adopted son 'Jesus' already foreshadowed such a move, and in the cunning systematizations of Beig Wen, his itinerant secretary and the great old man's would-be successor, Yali has been turned into the Madangs' messiah, who came and showed 'the good road', like the Whites' Christ, and who will return at some unknown point in the future with the collective body of the Ancestors. Under Beig a stop has been put to cargo cult talk and the movement is presented to outsiders as an alternative church, the house of a *minista* sitting on Madang's main road, and Professor

Peter Lawrence's famous book about Madang cargo cults is presented as a kind of Old Testament.[24] The New Testament is Yali's sayings written down in an old exercise book, and last seen in his old village of Sor (Ngaing area, Rai Coast).

Thus we see how, in the fascinating processes of adjustment, Oceanian peoples have not been the passive victims of change or unquestioning recipients of external influences, but have been 'wrestling with the angel' of Encounter to test the strength of their own long-inured cultures. What we have viewed in this chapter, we concede, are altercations very often borne of misunderstanding, or 'erring acculturation', as van Baal has aptly described it.[25] Pacific peoples have harboured a range of possibilities for the cosmos – the divinization of humans, the coming of the cargo, the return of the dead – which modern Westerners consider to be unrealistic, magical or even plainly nonsensical. These hopes for astounding transformations have been rather naturally articulated, moreover, at the very time when the time-honoured, lithic order of existence seemed to reach an end – with the coming of the mysterious intruders. The newcomers, with their extraordinary technology and their preached message of changed lives, bespoke great transformations themselves and thus carried to the Pacific 'eschatological implications'. It is small wonder that some responses to their impact were millenarian or cargoistic or open to quite miraculous events – even if always with the indigenes' own interests being confirmed. We will remind you, however, that other responses were reactive and retaliatory, and in any case some of the traditional sting of 'payback' still lies in the tails of cargo cults and independent churches just described. And again, as the next chapter indicates, most other responses involved entry by groups into the mainstream of the process usually called Christianization, although in this process, too, the people of Oceania have generally not been noted for passivity and the mere replication of European ways. A new survey called *Winds of Change* on the rapidly growing revival of spiritist religious groups will vouch for that.[26]

NOTES AND REFERENCES

1 In A. Herrera, *Historia general*, Madrid, 1601, the map being by Juan López de Velasco. In contrast, the cartographic frontispiece to Walter Raleigh's *Historie of the World*, London, 1614, does not cover the Pacific.

2 G. Souter, *New Guinea: the Last Unknown*, Sydney, 1963 (New Guinea); A. Morehead, *The Fatal Impact*, Harmondsworth, 1968 (Pacific more generally).

3 For the phrase, cf. J. C. Beaglehole, introd. to *The Journals of Captain James Cook on His Voyage of Discovery, The Voyage of the Endeavour, 1768–1771* (Hakluyt Society Extra Series 34), Cambridge, 1955, p. clxxii.

4 D. Gheorghiu, *Un 'Cult al Cargoului' din Renaşere (Uniunea Artiştilor plastici din România; revista arta*), Bucharest, 1988, p. 8 *et passim*. Cf. also Langdon, *The Lost Caravel*, Sydney, 1975 (both interpretations require caution).

5 J. Jefferson, *LMS South Sea Journals*, 1801, quoted in Jukka Siikala, *Cult and Conflict in Tropical Polynesia* (Academia Scientarum Ferricae, FF Communications 99/2), Helsinki, 1982, pp. 225–6.

6 J. A. Moerenhout, *Voyage aux Isles du Grand Océan, etc.*, Paris, 1837, vol. 2, pp. 501–2 (on Teau); W. P. Crook, *LMS South Sea Letters*, 1828, quoted in Siikala, *Cult and Conflict*, p. 241 (cargo).

7 R. Linton, 'Nativistic Movements', *American Anthropologist* 45 (1943): 230ff; A. C. Wallace, 'Revitalization Movements', *ibid.*, 58 (1956): 264–6.

8 P. Clark, *Hauhau: The Pai Marire Search for Maori Identity*, Auckland, 1975, p. 10; cf. B. Elsemore, *Like Them That Dream: the Maori and the Old Testament*, Tauranga, 1985, pp. 110–13.

9 G. Pratt, 'The Genealogy of the Kings and Princes of Samoa', in *Report of the Second meeting of the Australasian Association for the Advancement of Science* (Sydney), 1890, pp. 662–3; cf. D. Freeman, 'Some Observations on Kinship and Authority in Samoa', *American Anthropologist* 66 (1964): 557.

10 Siikala, *Cult and Conflict*, pp. 194–5.

11 G. Turner, *Nineteen Years in Polynesia*, London, 1861, p. 107, cf. pp. 106–9; D. Freeman, 'The Joe Gimlet or Siovili Cult', in D. Freeman and W. R. Geddes (eds), *Anthropology in the South Seas*, New Plymouth, 1959, p. 195, pp. 185ff.; and for a broader discussion, L. D. Holmes, 'Cults, Cargo and Christianity: Samoan Responses to Western Religion', *Missiology* 8/4 (1981): 471.

12 S. H. Elbert and T. Monberg (eds), *From the Two Canoes: Oral Traditions of Rennell and Bellona Islands (Language and Culture of Rennell and Bellone Islands, vol. 1*), Copenhagen, 1965, pp. 401, 409, cf. pp. 401–14.

13 H. Nevermann, E. A. Worms and H. Petri, *Die Religionen der Südsee und Australians* (Die Religionen der Menschheit 5/2), Stuttgart and Berlin, 1968, p. 77; A. Grimble, 'Religious Disturbances', in Great Britain, Colonial Office, *Gilbert and Ellice Islands Colony Report for 1929–30*, London, 1932, pp. 31–4, cf. Grimble's, *A Pattern of Islands*, London, 1952, pp. 93–100.

14 F. E. Williams, *The 'Vailala Madness' and the Destruction of Native Ceremonies in the Gulf District* (Territory of Papuan Anthropology Reports 4), Port Moresby, 1923, pp. 4ff., 31ff., *et passim*. G. W. Trompf foreshadows a reassessment of this movement in the light of neglected unpublished materials.

15 P. Worsley, *The Trumpet Shall Sound*, London, 1970 edn., p. 125, cf. F. C. Kamma, *Koreri*, The Hague, 1972, pp. 106–7, 111–12, 125–7, 134–44, etc. on Biak-Numfor movements.

16 B. Kubitza, 'Cargo Cult Activities at Kaiep in the 1930's', *Oral History*

8/2 (1980): 88 (four kings); K. Burridge, *Mambu*, London, 1960, p. 185 (Black king).

17 M. Fathers, 'Revolution in Paradise', *The Independent* (UK), 27 July 1991, confirming G. W. Trompf, *Melanesian Religion*, Cambridge, 1991, p. 233.

18 See esp. B. Sundkler, *Bantu Prophets of South Africa* (1948), London, 1961 edn; D. B. Barrett, *Schism and Renewal in Africa*, Nairobi, 1968.

19 Elsmore, *Like Them*, pp. 142, 145; G. X. Misur, 'From Prophet Cult to Established Church: the Case of the Ringatu Movement', in L. H. Kawharu (ed.), *Conflict and Compromise*, Wellington, 1973, p. 97 *et passim*.

20 J. Irwin, 'Tahupotiki Wiremu Ratana', in J. Hinnells (ed.), *Who's Who of World Religions*, London, 1991, p. 322; cf. J. M. Henderson, *Ratana* (Polynesian Society Memoir 36), Wellington, 1972 edn.

21 P. Gesch, *Initiative and Initiation* (Studia Instituti Anthropos 33), St Augustin, 1985, p. 112, cf. also p. 326.

22 B. G. Burton-Bradley 'The Psychiatry of Cargo Cult', *Medical Journal of Australia* 2 (1973): 338ff.

23 Trompf, 'Independent Churches of Melanesia', *Oceania* 54/1 (1983): 51–2 (both quotations).

24 P. Lawrence's *Road Belong Cargo*, Manchester, 1964.

25 J. van Baal, 'Erring Acculturation', *American Anthropologist* 62 (1960): 108ff.

26 M. Ernst, *Winds of Change: Rapidly Growing Religious Groups in the Pacific Islands*, Suva, 1994.

6 Missions, Christianity and modernity[1]

In the year 1992 an astounding fact presented itself to the outside world: an estimated 95 per cent of people on 25,000 islands in Oceania acknowledged their involvement with some Christian tradition or another. A century and a half previously, over 95 per cent of the habitable portions of this vast island realm had heard nothing of the Bible or a proclamation of the Gospel. The difference, of course, has everthing to do with the processes we call missionization, evangelization and conversion. These processes were set in train by European churches who sent personnel to 'save souls' lost in 'heathen darkness'. As we shall confirm, though, those who adopted the new faith were not like empty vessels waiting to be filled. It does no justice to island peoples to imagine that they were duped by foreigners, unable to make choices in their best interests and thus suffered under new religious regimes they did not deserve to have foisted upon them. Much modern criticism against missionaries, certainly, can be helpful; the very notion of active missionization has and should come under scrutiny and energetic debate. On the other hand, the historical records no longer justify the conclusion that a scattered, physically vulnerable bunch of isolated 'do-gooders' were responsible for the Christianization of the Pacific and the demise of the old cultures. In what follows we find that the Christianization involved 'people movements' – transformations of religious allegiance and commitment by word of mouth at the village level, and by families, clans and tribes and sometimes whole culturolinguistic groups – and most of the action was in the hands of the indigenous peoples.[2] They had traditional repertories and criteria for deciding upon religious change; they also had the common sense to discriminate between the types of newcomers they experienced and between what lay behind the new messages and their bearers' behavioural enactment of it. It is sheer romanticism to expect that they would not attempt some religious adjustment, let alone radical conversion, moreover, because it was not just the missionary message which called for a response; in fact it is remarkable how Christian preaching was so widely and seriously received when so much else by way of technical wonders and widening geographical horizons affected this previously 'untouched' (some might say 'untainted') part of the globe. Of course at this point in time there is anxiety for the Pacific churches that many more 'messages' from the global village – via radio, television, new supermarkets, etc. – are circulating to capture the islanders' attention.

MISSIONS TO SAVAGES

A brief catalogue of foundation missionary work has its own merits. By being selective, the pattern of both the denominational and the imperial influences of Europe can be conveyed in a nutshell. In 1668 the Jesuit Diego de Sanvitores began work on Guam, and by 1722 Cantova, from the same order, began in the Carolines. The Catholic foundation period in the Pacific was very early and very Spanish. Protestantism's impact waited until the nineteenth century. The famous LMS vessel the *Duff* lay off Palau in 1797 but went on to sow the seeds of the Gospel in Polynesia in the same year, bringing ministers James Cover, John Eyre, John Jefferson and Thomas Lewis to Tahiti and some of their lay supporters to Tonga and the Marquesas. The LMS, being interdenominational, included personnel from Anglican, Congregationalist, Methodist, Presbyterian (and later Quaker) persuasions, and its effects on the spread of Christianity much further afield were momentous. While avoiding duplication of work by Presbyterians in Hawaii (Hiram Bingham Sr. being sent by the American Board of Commissioners for Foreign Missions [ABCFM] in 1819) and by Wesleyans in Tonga (Walter Lawry, from 1822), the LMS worked westward to the Cooks (through Robert Bourne and John Williams) in 1821, Samoa by 1830, and beyond to Vanuatu (the New Hebrides) in eastern Melanesia, where Williams was clubbed to death on Erromanga in 1839. Samuel McFarlane came to Lifu in the Loyalty Islands (New Caledonia) in 1859 to provide stability to work already begun by Samoans and Rarotongans; and still later, in 1874, William Lawes and a cluster of Polynesian pastors were landing on the shores of Papua, Port Moresby becoming their main base.

At that late stage much had happened with Catholic affairs and the other Protestant missions. Fathers of the Congregation of the

Sacred Hearts of Jesus and Mary began in Honolulu in 1827, Manga-reva in 1834 and the Marquesas four years after (where Gracia and his confraternals began important linguistic work). French gunboats provided this same Order with a toehold on Tahiti in the same year (1838), setting the tone for Catholic–Protestant competition elsewhere. France often sought to protect its interests wherever Catholics, especially French nationals, opened new mission fields – on Futuna in 1841 (after Peter Chanel died as a martyr), on Tonga in 1842 (Joseph Chevron) and on New Caledonia in 1848. The last three initiatives were by Marists, who were at work on the Solomons and Bougainville by the very end of the century. The Marist Order was established as recently as 1836 and 'Oceania was its first mission-ary effort', so that it is the less surprising that three Marists arrived in the North Island of New Zealand in 1838, being somewhat of a foil to Samuel Marsden's Anglican emissaries.[3]

Marsden's special passion, the New Zealand Mission, had com-menced with his own journeys across the Tasman from Sydney harbour in 1814 to missionize for the Anglican Church Missionary Society. The work of the Church of England naturally expanded with the White settlement of New Zealand, and it was through a curious anomaly of ecclesiastical jurisdiction that George Selwyn, the first Anglican Bishop of New Zealand by 1841, noticed that his diocese included the Solomon Islands, far to the north. Through his consecration of Coleridge Patterson as Bishop of Melanesia in 1861, the Melanesian Mission was truly born; and high Anglicans of their ilk had begun work at Wedau, Papua, before the nineteenth century's end. Wesleyan Methodism was naturally spread to Fiji by neighbouring Tongans, with White Australian missionaries becoming involved by 1835. A generation later Methodists, under George Brown, were at work in and around Rabaul, New Britain, ten years before Germany began developing its New Guinea colonies in 1885. They also pioneered in the Louisiade and d'Entrecasaux Archipel-ago, east Papua, under William Bromilow (in 1891). Presbyterians were operating in Vanuatu by 1848, and the ABCFM opened its Micronesian Mission in 1856. The Lutherans, for their part, were comparative latecomers, though two German Lutherans, Geissler and Ottow, were sent to Doreh Bay (Geelfink Bay, west New Guinea) in 1855, heralding a long line of Dutch Reformed missionar-ies to the area. From 1885 Lutherans formally began their labours in lands zoned German, the Australian-based Johann Flierl begin-ning at Finschhafen (Morobe, New Guinea). Lutheran presence deflected some of the activity of the French Sacred Heart (MSC)

mission away from New Britain to the Papuan coast, with the well-
known Yule Island station (west of Port Moresby) being founded in
1885.

All the above developments created missionary spheres of influence, often prompting imperial annexations and certainly condition-
ing the denominational styles still found today in the various regions
of the Pacific. The history of a later phase of missionization by
minor and 'sectarian' groups is patchy and much more difficult to
cover with a thumb-nail sketch. An early organization of interest
was the Queensland Kanaka Mission to Malaita in the 1880s (this
becoming the South Sea Evangelical Mission to the central Melanesia region as a whole), and there are Baptist groups, the Church of
Christ (see p. 187 above), Swiss Brothers, Brethren, and the Salvation Army to consider among 'conservative evangelicals'. Seventh
Day Adventist (SDA) presence was surprisingly early – work beginning at Sogeri outside Port Moresby as early as 1908 – the SDA
following eventually becoming proportionately bigger among Melanesians than anywhere else. Newly emergent Mormonism (as the
American Mormon Missionaries) was early on Hawaii (1844), which
is significant considering they eventually built the only denominational university in Oceania there. Parallel to this was the 1844
arrival of Mormonism on the Tuamotus, east of Tahiti, where lay
their stepping-stones to other South Sea locations – surprisingly to
conservative Tonga by 1891 – and on to a growing popularity in the
twentieth century, especially after America's victory in World War
II. Along with SDAs and Jehovah's Witnesses, the Mormons have
been frequently criticized for 'sheep stealing' by missions and
churches pre-established in given areas. Of course once the central
highlands of Papua New Guinea became more accessible after the
war, opportunities were snatched by a plethora of minor (often
American fundamentalist or Pentecostalist) 'Gospel hawkers'. With
up to eighty different groups present in and around Goroka and
Kainantu during the 1970s, the Eastern Highlands Province
appeared to be the most missionized place on earth. Indonesian
policy, less trusting towards foreign missionaries, made for differences in the west New Guinea highlands, though less mainstream
forms of Protestantism – especially the Pacific Christian Church
(which started as the independent Unevangelized Fields Mission in
swampy west Papua in 1932), Baptists and SDAs – gained a wider
influence there than heavier competition might otherwise have
allowed.

To analyse the complexities of Pacific mission history, one has to develop a working sense of stages. In any sector of Oceania chosen for study, it will be helpful for working purposes to periodize years of foundation, establishment (with colonial connections of major missions being noticeable) and the shift from mission to island church. Macroscopically, too, one has to be prepared for differences in church approaches to missions from one era of European civilization to another. The Hispanic impact in Micronesia, for example, reflects European values less sympathetic towards 'savage' peoples than those emerging among expatriates in a more liberalizing post-Enlightenment ethos. On the other hand, even in the nineteenth century, there were some island peoples and systems of government that commanded greater respect from Whites, the latter being unable to avoid their own preconceptual contrasts between 'more civilized' light-skinned Polynesians and dark-skinned 'primitive' Melanesians. Through training our discriminatory sense, of course, one can come to appreciate how missionary attitudes were generally more sensitive to the needs of islanders than were the approaches of other newcomers, such as beachcombers, miners, settlers or officials – and the local peoples very soon detected such differences themselves (as well as the importance of isolated Christian souls, such as Robert Louis Stevenson on Samoa, who were 'chummy with the natives').[4] There were attitudinal divergences within groups of arriving church personnel, nonetheless, so that one needs to assess which individuals or denominations were more or less tolerant toward island traditions, or more or less likely to pass off pre-existing beliefs more as Satan's darkness than as vestiges of some original (and general) revelation.

In the early Hispanic period there was an obvious difference between clergy who fulfilled their duty on behalf of crews plying the high seas, and individuals who took pity on the island peoples exploited at the voyagers' hands. The great Bartolomé de Las Casas was renowned for accentuating that very difference in opposing Spanish treatment of Meso-American peoples (1540s), as also was Peter Claver, who openly and pointedly licked the sores of the African slaves landed in Columbia by trans-Atlantic trafficking (1630s). Thus it was that Sanvitores returned to Guam because he so despaired over the treatment of the indigenes by Spanish transients. Once Sanvitores and his companions opposed the Ancestral cult, however, and traditional sexual freedoms in the 'bachelor houses', the mission ran into serious trouble. Personnel, including the Jesuit Father himself, were killed, giving rise to long tribal (or the Chamorro) wars.

Lines of the spiritual battleground always had to be drawn some-where by the missionaries, unless one is persuaded, like a Thomas Kendall, that the way of life one encounters is better than the one offered by the mission message. Catholic missionaries, one will find, were generally less deprecating of primal culture than were Prot-estants. About matters of sexuality, admittedly, they could be highly sensitive, and often were the sexual favours of Tahitian and Marque-san beauties spurned by celibates who looked as though they needed good spouses. On the other hand, a recurrent theme of Catholic missionary visions has been the recovery of insights about the divine which had been suppressed by savage cultures. Such an understand-ing goes back especially to that great (and probably dark-skinned) bishop from North Africa, St Augustine, who, while notorious for stressing humanity's original sin as a contaminant inherited from Adam, also argued that something in us survived the Fall: the image of God. All members of every culture have their *imago Dei*; but their deeper memories (*memoria*) have to be awakened, so that they come to know where their true origins lie and thus rediscover who they really are (or were meant to be). We are just now begin-ning to realize the importance of these insights for Catholic mission work (starting with the Jesuits) and for countering that folly of trying to eliminate all pre-existing beliefs, even if they did not seem to be 'religious'.

Protestant missionaries, by contrast, were very much affected by Reformed doctrines of 'the depravity of Man', and looked to a complete replacement of total darkness by the Gospel's Light. Souls needed saving from the snares of Satan, or else they needed to hear the World, for the Gospel was to be preached to all nations before Christ's return (cf. Mark 13: 10). And for Protestants, those of the nineteenth century particularly, the civilizing process – of pants instead of penis gourds; soap-washed rather that fat-smeared bodies; schools, not male cult-houses – was inseparable from the Gospel. In their quest for an individual change of heart Protestants were thus rather more prone to criticize the native for being 'earthly, sensual, [and] devilish', even though hardly alone in deprecating indigenous ethics.[5] In the long run these differences clearly betoken how the Catholics were milder in the undermining of traditions, although some Protestant expectations for change were more extreme than others. Charles Abel's trade-oriented mission in Papua, for example, involved separating children from their families to train them for a whole new way of life on Kwato Island (in the 1910s especially);

the SDAs, for their part, instructed Melanesians to give up those Pacific favourites pork and crab for Levitically clean meats.

Protestant and Catholics, at least up until the post-war era, vehemently disputed between themselves, and Protestants commonly trundled out the argument that the local heathenism and Romanism were hard to distinguish. Sectarian wars were very rare, but inter-village brawls erupted and damage was caused to church property where denominations were in close contact. It was obvious from the very beginning, though, that missionaries of all persuasions shared basic commitments to bring peace between warring tribes, to turn every arena or 'resting place' of human sacrifice into 'a cow-pen', as Wyatt Gill put it of old Rarotonga, to create new communities, and to serve the local peoples – some, like 'the hero' Father Damien who lived with exiled lepers on Kalanpape peninsula of Hawaii's Molokai (1873–89), doing so in the most inspiring ways.[6] By 1900, in any case, Oceania was noted for its mission spheres, with whole tracts or islands being the domain of one mission or another, and conflicts being limited to borders or disputed zones. The era of pioneer martyrs was closed – perhaps its end was marked by the death of the great James Chalmers, the LMS 'king' of the Papuan coast who lost his life trespassing in a great cult-house on Goaribari Island (western Gulf) in 1901 – and after that the consolidating of mission stations became the order of the day. The story of missionary foundations in the Pacific, though, would hardly be complete without also considering the critical role played by islanders themselves.

ISLANDERS AS MISSIONARIES

It is obvious that Christian teachings could hardly be conveyed without missionaries learning and attempting translations in local languages, which they did. Hours upon hours had to be spent with patient islanders, many unnamed and unknown, who alone could make the mastery of a new tongue possible. Those who so 'turned talk', indeed, were the first local persons to participate actively in the missionary process. More important were those who accompanied the Europeans in their preaching, or who, after appropriate preparations, took on a mission field by themselves. Being an islander missionary among one's own people, of course, was always trickiest because of the inevitable pressures to be reabsorbed into the culture, and by far the most effective emissaries of the Gospel were those left to manage with strangers, and who became new-comers themselves in far distant lands.

The saga of islander missionaries has just begun to be written. The practice of using helpers from among new converts in a neighbouring context is both old and continuous. Just outside Oceania were the earlier contacted Philippines, and Sanvitores took a group of Filip-pino catechists with him to Guam. The odd Filippino was to play a significant role in later Pacific mission history; Emmanuel Natera, for example, a stowaway who got to Thursday Island and was then recruited to help MSC, had an extraordinary impact on the Catholics in Papua, especially after marrying a Roro. When the great Jesuit Francis Xavier journeyed as far as the Moluccas far back in 1546, he sprinkled his holy water on peoples also destined to render service in Melanesia. Dutch Reformed missionaries made use of Ambonese *gurus* (teachers) along the northern reaches of west New Guinea, and archives about their activities still await analysis.[7] During the so-called interregnum period, when Holland fell to revol-utionary France (1795–1830), the LMS intervened in the Indies to send Ambonese to work on the south side, toward Berau Bay, and this slice of history needs better documentation. Of greater moment for Oceania as a whole, however, was the training of Polynesian mission personnel, many of whom played a crucial pioneering and pastoral role in Melanesia and Micronesia.

The ABCFM experiment in Hawaii was partly inspired by the presence of one Opukahaia at Yale, New Haven, Connecticut in 1809. As an orphan, maltreated by his foster parents, he persuaded the captain of a fur-trading vessel to take him from Hawaii to the land of the Whites, and, being affected by what he learned of Christianity on board, impressed Yale reverends so much that they sent him to the Cornwall Mission School, Connecticut. He died, however, before Hiram Bingham and Asa Thurston set sail, yet not without a vivid description of the mores these two would face. He was, in any case, the first in a series of native Hawaiian mission helpers. At the end of the century an American survey could rejoice that 'the Hawaiian churches became self-supporting' (from 1860), and thus, confusing as it may seem, were independent in the sense that they were no longer organized from Boston. 'Native Christians', the report added, were 'actively engaged in the work of sending the gospel to distant lands', that is, to the Carolines, Marshalls, Gilberts and even the Marquesas.[8]

Most impressive among the islander missionaries, though, were those from central Polynesia. We can already sense how important they will become when LMS missionary William Ellis seized the opportunity to visit the Binghams and their colleagues on Hawaii in 1822. Kaahumanu the reformer accompanied the Ellis' Tahitian companion Auna on a tour for 'some weeks ... to different parts of Hawaii', and, with the Tahitian tongue being intelligible enough, the effects were crucial – the local governor wanting to read and write, a young chief desirous to hear the Gospel, and villages at one place destroying 'no fewer than one hundred and two idols' in a day.[9] Of the central Polynesian groups, it was of course the Cook Islands group and Samoa which spawned the greatest number of teachers and pastors. Some sixteen years after the LMS began work on the Cooks, the famous Takomoa Theological College was erected, dominated by a handsome two-storeyed building on Rarotonga (from 1839). Not long after, near Apia in Western Samoa, a training centre of comparable importance for evangelizing the Pacific was set up. This was Malua Theological College. Its inception in 1844 came only nine years after the LMS commenced work on Savai'i Island. By 1895 as many as 142 ordained native agents and 184 native preachers were abroad in Samoa itself, with 7,713 scholars in 209 schools (mostly native run). Malua College itself was a stately, well-arranged campus with twenty buildings. In contrast to this latter development, the Catholic experiment to take Samoans to Sydney for training was disastrous both psychologically and financially.

Even before Takomoa and Malua passed its first graduates, certain Polynesian helpers had their hands full in the opening up of eastern Melanesia. Take Vanuatu, for example. Lalolangi, Salomea and Mose were left on Tanna in 1839, and reinforced by Pomare and Vaiofanga the following year – which was a fatal one, for they all fell ill and both Salomea and Pomare died. Two Samoans tried Erromanga and were starved out (1840), so that the LMS took out four Erromangans to Malua (1849), these apparently being the first Melanesians to be trained theologically, and then sent them back home to work with two Rarotongan couples (1852). Simeona the Samoan had been laying the groundwork on Aneityum six years before Whites (mainly Presbyterians) arrived. New Caledonia has a comparable history. Samoan and Rarotongan teachers preceded Marists to this group – on the Isle of Pines by 1840, on the south coast of the main island and in the Loyalties the following year – and their courage in the face of the unknown and threats of death was astounding. The story of Ta'unga o te Tini, who had previously helped with Bible translations on the Cooks, is particularly arresting.

After his dramatic experiences at Tuauru and Yate in southern New Caledonia, he wrote up an account of his adventures in Rarotonga.

An old chief of Tuauru gave Ta'unga and his companion Noa his friendship, but the Melanesian tongue was so difficult and sounded to the newcomers 'like the noise made by turkeys'. Having a good ear, Ta'unga mastered the language in six months and those interested in his teachings were numerous enough to warrant the building of a church. An epidemic in the region made his position dangerous, however, and signs that outsiders were being blamed for the deaths came with the massacre of the crew and missionaries on the *Starr* off the Isle of Pines (late in 1842). Two men later tried to kill Ta'unga near Yate, but their spears just missed him in his flight over a river, and when he found that the Yate villagers had killed and cooked one of his attackers as a punishment for their designs, he managed to redeem the other before a similar fate befell him, arguing that the remaining man was his 'share' and that he wanted a 'servant'. This survivor became a faithful member of Ta'unga's household; but the Rarotongan's troubles were not over. Tuauru villagers blamed him for the death by sickness of the chief's daughter, and only the chief's denial of the charges saved him; then the chief of the Isle of Pines turned up on the mainland blaming the Tuauruans for the epidemic, only to give in when Ta'unga bravely greeted him and preached to him that God was angry for people being deceived by the Devil and making 'the world . . . full of idol worship'.[10]

If Ta'unga escaped the threatening locals, for others they presented less problems than did certain outsiders. Take Iotia and his companions Ngatikano and Taditi, for example, who after their training at Takomoa were left on the almost forgotten and isolated island of Penrhyn (now part of the Cooks) in 1854. Talk about Christianity by a previously shipwrecked White – Mr Lamont – prepared islanders for the work of these three, which proceeded effectively for ten years before White missionaries showed any attentior.. As Joel Taime has recently shown, though, poor Iotia was taken off by Chilean slavers just before contact was renewed from Rarotonga. The three teachers were rewarded with $250 (Chilean) for releasing Penrhyn islanders for the promised opportunity of good labouring jobs in Latin America. Alas, Iotia and all those potential slaves carried off with him were never seen again.[11]

Looking again to Melanesia, another part of its edges to be affected by Polynesian mission work was Fiji, although in this case it was rather carried out by Tongans newly trained by the Wesleyans.

Tahitians were in the Lau group during the 1830s, yet as early as 1835 it was a Tongan, the accredited preacher Josua Mateinaniu, who was sent as a kind of scout to mingle with the many Tongans on the eastern side of Fiji proper, and his teaching produced a very favourable response. Given Tonga's long-standing political interest in this region, however, it was King George himself who played a crucial role in Fiji's Christianization, for, although Whites were labouring there for souls (from 1839), they could not secure the conversion of the most powerful chief – Cakobau. After a visit to Sydney in 1854, where he was received with state honours, King George promised to visit Cakobau's islet stronghold of Bau with the splendid gift of a schooner. 'I wish, Cakobau', the king's communication ran, 'you would *lotu* [= worship the Christian way]', and this, followed by a long interview with Joseph Waterhouse, persuaded Cakobau to change course. On the following Sunday (30 April) he was at church with his priest, more than forty wives and the rest of his family! From then on the largely Methodist history of Fiji was assured.[12]

Fijians subsequently enter the missions side-by-side with Polynesians, with evangelization occurring further west. Tupou College, established on Tonga in 1866 by the inspired organizer J. E. Moulton, elevated the standard of higher learning in the Pacific and serviced Wesleyan/Methodist ventures above all. Thus when George Brown pioneered in New Britain and Bromilow in eastern Papua, Fijians as well as Polynesians went with them. It was in reprisal for the murder of one of his Fijian colleagues (Reverend Sailasa Naucukudi), in fact, that Brown mounted a small punitive expedition, a somewhat unmissionary exercise for which he was disciplined by the Methodist Overseas Mission in Australia in 1878. Along the Southern Papuan coast, by comparison, Polynesians alone were in operation (from as early as 1872), for the LMS. Put ashore at villages along their coast, sometimes with their wives, they had to fend for themselves in very unhealthy, usually malaria-ridden country – and, being without immunity, 103 out of 203 of them died of illnesses. Others, of course, were killed. They were given guns, but only to shoot into the air as a warning, a ploy which worked for Rau at Balawaia (because the chiefs opted for peace thereafter) but not for others (such as the faithful Tauriki, who fell prey to a raiding party at Motumotu).

Once acceptance was granted, the inhabitants of central Melanesia were remarkably willing to consider the South Sea newcomers' opinions about changing customs. When the Rarotongan Piri arrived among the Motu at Boera (1874), to take one vivid example, he soon came across the stench of the dead under the houses and the custom of widows smearing themselves with putrefaction (see p. 156 above). His instantaneous disgust for the practice made the chiefs abolish it forthwith! Around the same time to the north, on the Duke of York islands, the Fijian Misiali undercut the claim that the Waira people had to steal produce from neighbouring tribes because of their own poor soil, for he successfully harvested huge yams near their settlement. These newcomers could amaze with their new ways. That the rather frail little Rarotongan Ruatoka was prepared to carry sick people to the Moresby mission station for help stunned the Motuans; they feared that the ghost would haunt the carrier if the sick person died. As late as 1947 many Nasioi on Bougainville were persuaded by Methodist Tongan pastors to eat 'a meal in public' for 'the first time', whereas previously they ate in family groups to avoid sorcerers securing food scraps.[13]

In various other respects – through introducing health measures, better housing, new dances, let alone schooling – the South Sea islanders were great innovators. One often sees them caught, however, between the distance, even arrogance, of the White missionaries, who rarely considered them properly trained, and the local Blacks. Towards the latter the South Sea teachers developed a reputation for authoritarianism and the corporal punishment of schoolchildren, so that they made up a middle stratum in 'the colonial pattern' comparable to Asian groups in the secular sphere.

We are not to forget that many converts from central Melanesia played their role as missionaries also. Some individuals have become renowned for their courageous evangelism. In the later 1880s, the Anglican deacon Clement Marau was left by himself to work on Ulawa (in the eastern Solomons). A Banks Islander (north Vanuatu), he had to rely on Mote as a *lingua franca* and a helpful Ulawa go-between Walter Waaro. The turning-point in his work came when he persuaded a wedding procession to pass by a sacred grove where a vengeful place-spirit was thought to dwell, but when no calamity befell the people they had 'a proof for themselves' that the old religion was questionable and Marau's message true.[14] Other Melanesian workers found themselves in a world of strange customs, but kept their equanimity. To illustrate this, when Pastor Hosea Linge finished his studies at George Brown College (on Ulu Island, Duke of York group) in 1917, he was posted to Omo, on the northern end of New Ireland, and was not long after asked to conduct the funeral of an old woman. He willingly did so, but to his amazement he saw the body taken to the bush and burnt. 'A cremation of the dead' was utterly foreign to the practices he grew up with in central New Ireland, where shallow, smell-engendering graves were built close to the houses; but Hosea's training had made him more critical of his own people's methods of disposal, which were traditionally meant to induce revenge, and more tolerant of strangers' customs when they did not obviously conflict with the Bible.[15]

There are many more stories of Black missionaries from central Melanesia. One thinks of Hughie Wheatley, born of a White settler and a Roviana mother in the western Solomons. He was a young beneficiary of the mission under J. F. Goldie, the New Zealand Methodist (p. 188 above), and later entered the Fiji School of Medicine in 1933, not long after its inception. When appointed to back up newly developing Christian work on Rennell Island as Medical Officer, one could say he was the first known Melanesian doing missionary work among Polynesians (1937). He and his wife died in Rabaul during the Japanese occupation, and it is from there, too, that one learns of the great Catholic catechist Peter Torot, who was killed by the Japanese while keeping his church alive during the absence of European Fathers and Sisters. The disseminating influence of local Catholic catechists and Lutheran evangelists cannot be underestimated. Lutheran missionaries first entered the New Guinea central highlands (1920), and in their wake evangelists and their families were sent into the most populous and turbulent territories in all Melanesia. Kâte families from the Morobe who were prepared for mission work in Finschhafen recalled something of the agony of cultural isolation, trying to persuade tribespeople to dispense with the traditional items – by burning spears and shields in a pyre, and smashing sacred stones – to mark the turn to a new life.

Our survey will have left the impression that Protestants did the lion's share of pioneering work by islanders, and that assessment is fair. Catholic history has admittedly had some significant failures with some of their Polynesian emissaries. Three Tahitians were brought to Peru as early as 1772, trained in the Viceroy's palace at Lima and were then sent back in the following year to spread news about the benefits of both the Catholic faith and Spanish civilization, but they had no effect, although even the two White priests who followed them, and who preceded the LMS in the Society Islands by twenty-three years, did not last long there. Elsewhere Catholic Polynesians did not make good 'groundbreakers', and a lack of systematic training for their difficult tasks is a key explanation of this. But once European priests and Sisters established their bases, that 'small nucleus of native catechists' they drilled was always vital, and it was especially this group 'who gradually promulgated the teachings of their . . . masters.'[16] Training for the Roman priesthood, we should note, was traditionally more arduous academically than preparing for a Protestant pastorate, and thus the indigenization of the clergy has come late to Pacific island Catholicism; but now that the number of Polynesian priests is multiplying there has become a need for them to serve even in Latin America, where priests are in short supply. (This last point reminds one that islanders can take on missionary activity outside the central Oceanian region, as Methodist Fijians have done in the Northern Territory of Australia, and priests in Honduras, Belize and Costa Rica on the opposite side of the Pacific.)

Space deprives us of further details, but enough to conclude that Pacific Christianization, though initiated by Europeans, was largely disseminated by indigenous people themselves, including those who passed on the messages into lineages and along affinal links of communication. That persons with only a smattering of the new religious knowledge were involved in this process meant of course that confusions, feats of imagination and unexpected turns of logic resulted. The new religious movements we have already considered are thus more explicable against this background. When H. Schrencker, the LMS missionary at Orokolo, reflected on the so-called 'Vailala Madness' among the Elema in the Gulf in 1921, for instance, he noted his worries about strangers (presumably from the east), in an area too large for his proper supervision,[17] and the effects and unwritten history of many such independents cannot be ignored.

INDIGENOUS CHRISTIANITY

The Christian message is mediated through cultures; the Europeans and other newcomers brought their versions of it, and the islanders interpreted it with their local preconceptions. In the process of translating the Bible, pre-Christian vernacular terminologies begin to be transformed into recognizably Christian outlooks. At the grassroots, evangelization or formal education do not result in a strong acculturation into Western (or global) styles of thinking – as Pacific island senior high schools, seminaries or universities tend to produce – and we rightly expect to find village Christianity to be distinctly 'indigenized'. Observers of Western Christianity are used to differences between 'folk elements' in the rural areas and the more intellectual or speculative pursuits of Christian 'suburbanites', and so they anticipate comparable divergences in Pacific contexts. What they find is that, with the obvious exceptions of Hawaii and New Zealand and perhaps now also Tahiti and Rarotonga, the great majority of islanders dwell in the village, and what they make of Christianity is our present concern. What is made of it by educated elites, and especially by the emergent group of ecclesiastically and university-trained theologians, we shall leave to the final section.

In principle, it is fair to assert, the Christian proclamation is not directed against culture as such. Its bearers affirm and endorse culture, in fact, when institutions, laws, customs, practices, social forms and beliefs either anticipate or already conform to the Biblical vision for the world, while these bearers will challenge or oppose those cultural forms which do not. Variant applications to this principle of discrimination, however, have complicated all mission history. The perennial spectrum has run between the intolerant and the more liberally minded, and in recent centuries conservative theological minds who have imposed stringent new regulations on indigenous peoples have appeared in sharp contrast to those who left alone as much of local tradition as did not threaten the Gospel's claims on life. As the result of variant demands, the expressions of island Christianity take on distinctive forms, most obviously between denominations but sometimes within them.

Worship is one area offering some interesting comparisons. There is a typical uniformity in the phenomena of the Catholic Mass across the Pacific, but then, intriguingly, high church liturgy prevails in virtually all indigenous Anglican contexts from Papua New Guinea to Hawaii. The powerful singing of introduced hymns is noticeable in Lutheran and traditionally Methodist circles, while in what have been LMS areas the endowing of traditional chants with a hymnic quality – so-called *peroveta* or prophet songs – is a dominant motif. When the LMS Papuans combined with the Methodists of the Louisiade Archipelago, New Guinea Islands and the western Solomons to form the United Church in 1968, not a few tensions arose over musical issues in 'mixed' urban congregations! Part of the interest in these teething pains lay in the fact that, for the Methodists, the contents of the *Methodist Hymn Book* had become a kind of neo-tradition, and after almost a century of enjoying and harmonizing with them, it was hard for other sounds – including the high pitched or nasal chanting of Papuan women who loved their *peroveta* songs – to be accepted as worshipful. The Papuans for their part have made from the *peroveta* tradition so many brilliant compositions of their own. Only when pressed would they acknowledge the long-term impact of Polynesian musical creativity from the east, the intensity of which can still be felt on Communion Sundays in the great Protestant temple at Papeete, Tahiti (when each village group powerfully sings its heavenward praises in turn), or on the special occasions, Easter Day, Mother's Day or Whit Sunday (as recently well-documented of Islander churches in New Zealand).[18]

Theological strains in the rural areas of given regions often reflect the background of the Whites who first organized the mission. Melanesian pastors in Lutheran churches on the eastern side of Papua New Guinea, for instance, reflect liberal Protestant theology and concerns for social justice known among their White Australian and German mentors, while preaching in the Wabag Lutheran church among the Enga in the New Guinea highlands is very much affected by the theological conservatism of the Missouri synod in the United States. Patterns of worship affected by charismatic or pentecostal tendencies vary in their appearance again. In the urban Christian Life Centres, often led by amazingly articulate islanders, we find that the raising of the hands, the praying in tongues and the testimonies to personal faith can be easily paralleled in White Pentecostalist churches in New Zealand, Australia or Honolulu. By comparison, many services on the earthern floors of churches built under the Finnish Pentecostalists among the Wiru (southern highlands) will recall traditional religious attitudes, collective repentance being carried out with a characteristically droning wail, and excited worship sometimes involving a shaking (pidgin *guria*) quite comparable to that traditionally experienced by this people, in times of bad harvests, prevalent sickness and other adversity.

What happens to places of worship through the creativity of local persons is another matter for comparative interest. Because of Polynesian influences, traditional LMS areas are noted for their wooden, rather squat English-style churches, with Gothic windows and stained glass, and for the village competition to build bigger and more impressive ones. Catholic churches are typically more elongated in Melanesia, and often thatched, and interest will lie less in windows than in other iconic forms. Crucifixes and sculptures of Mary make for interesting study, as Father Theo Aerts has not long since shown, especially when pre-Christian stylization (often through distending faces and limbs) shows up.[19] In one of the Stations of the Cross painted on the wall of a Catholic church among the highland Melpa, intriguingly, Pilate is depicted as an Australian official with a slouch-hat, while Christ is a Blackman with a crown of thorns (see also p. 185 above).

The outward practice of the religious life can hardly be neglected in this analysis. One always senses one is arriving at an Adventist village, for instance, because there are no pigs to be seen and tethered goats are usually about. Mormon presence will be known, of course, by the number of white shirts and black pants. In most Protestant circles, villagers are less likely to worry about eating their own totems; in Catholic settlements the opposite tends to apply. Catholics, too, will generally be less anxious about attending persisting traditional ceremonies, especially if they are openly blessed by the priests or tolerated by them. At most Wahgi pig-kill or *Kongar* festivals, for example, a priest will now say Mass beneath a Cross planted in the centre of the *sing-sing* ground – before the main dances begin. An eager group of communicants can always be assured, yet meanwhile highland members of the Swiss Brotherhood church will be glowering at their fellows winding their way to the ceremony. As for Lutherans, their church allows them to attend, but they will have already killed their pigs and given them away separately, so as to dissociate their actions from the Ancestral cult, since the clan dead are supposed to glory in, and be pleased by, the mass sacrificing of beasts.

Overall, the visible effects of Christianization appear greatest in Polynesia and Micronesia, which generally leave a picture of clean little villages dominated by a church, and a plentiful array of houses made from permanent building materials. Coastal Melanesia is in many respects similar. Traditional ways seem all but expunged, though the experience of village life will soon reveal how many pre-Christian beliefs, rituals and customs still survive, usually subsisting in a symbiotic relationship to local Christian practice. Pre-contact behaviour patterns that sit awkwardly stand out starkly. On Puka-puka in the Cooks, for one case, an annual ritual of temporary promiscuity persists (*poroaki*), near Christmas, when girl or boy sponsors match partners both married and unmarried for one day of the year. Such a phenomenon recalls a smattering of orgiastic rites documented in traditional Polynesia (e.g. the Marquesas) and presents an ethical challenge to Christians. But the issues about the relationship between old and new beliefs are manifold. Go looking for a Roro if he is hunting, for instance, and even if he is a United Church deacon he will explain that he did not catch anything because someone was looking for him! Old practices die hard; with plants for a quick abortion available on various west Micronesian atolls Catholic women in trouble will find it hard to resist taking them. The local Pacific cosmos is still replete with spirits. In virtually every society the dead will be conceived as having a continuing interest in the living, usually being supportive and readily accessible. Malevolent spirits will still be abroad, sometimes in a more traditional guise, sometimes as demons accepted along New Testament lines. If fear of sorcery barely exists in some quarters – on the Cooks, for example – elsewhere, as in coastal Papua or the Sepik, it is highly pervasive. In some settings where 'custom' is highly resilient, old ways will remain in a kind of constant debate with Christian beliefs. Trobrianders, for instance, have to decide whether the dead still go to the Isle of Tuma or to the Christian heaven, and some say that they go first to one and later to the other.

A crucial element in the acceptance and indigenizing of Christian worldviews is the application of retributive logic (see pp. 133–40 above). In the early critical stages of conversion, old assumptions about the rewards and punishments of the spirits were tested against evangelical claims. Those who expected that a desecration of traditional shrines or an entrance into tabued places would bring the punitive anger of the old gods were proved wrong. The new deity being preached thus seemed more powerful. In some cases, of course, it was highly desirable to take on board such a powerful God and traditional principles of payback were immediately linked to the new deity. When the LMS *Messenger of Peace* arrived at Savai'i (Western Samoa) in 1830, it was just what the powerful chief Malietoa needed to gain supremacy after the recent death of his rival Tamafaiga (a death the family feared would be avenged and against which threatened vengeance they needed spiritual fortification). In other situations, the old logic is applied and acted upon time and again, yet to no effect. Many Erromangans (Vanuatu) became thoroughly demoralized because they expected that either Christianity or the tradition to which they temporarily reverted would save them from sickness (mainly dysentery). 'But nothing worked',[20] and a real crisis came here to a long-inured, basically endemic mould of traditional reasoning in the islands – that religion brings material protection or concrete results. By comparison, most islanders were converted to Christianity when significant experiences proved the new God appeared obviously supreme over the old spirit-ordained sanctions – when Christian Pomare IV proved victorious over 'the heathen' in battle on Tahiti (p. 169 above), when nothing happened to the wedding procession which deacon Marau sent through a sacred grove on Ulawa (p. 203 above), when missionaries' medical care worked better than traditional healing practices, when missionaries chose to build churches on old sacred sites in eastern Papua and the local spirits did nothing to stop them, and so on. But the conviction to change, we can infer, was mostly in terms of the traditional retributive logic, which in turn was to be reinforced by the Old Testament principle that God visibly rewards the righteous and requites the evil.

The practicalities of payback, of course, have been very much affected by conversion. In most cultures (but not yet in a few highland ones) tribal warfare was halted. People were encouraged to foster the virtues of positive reciprocity – of 'caring and sharing' – and village life was left only half as interesting and effervescent, in fact rather colourless if the missions also opposed traditional dances and exchange ceremonies. Some excitement was left over from tradition, however, in being able to explain events in terms of rewards and punishments, praise or blame, so that a shark death here or a motor accident there would be (and still is) put down by village consensus to a significant cause, and usually a non-natural one. Pacific village life, in and out of the church ambience, is very much about making sense of what is going on in a world in which God, the dead and malevolent agents constantly interact with the living. Old styles of reasoning persist in the plethora of talk, but new explanations intertwine with the old. Among the Hula-Aroma-Velerupa people (coastal Papua), for instance, sorcery no longer explains most deaths. Good persons dying nasty deaths can be martyrs, and bad persons killed by sharks may be deemed punished by God. It depends on the outcome of 'talk'. Sometimes new explanations crop up: a university student dying of bone cancer who died back in the village was said to have been contaminated by the Whites.

Sorcery, we must note, is both an idea and (at least a presumed) practical side to payback which has outlived the demise of tribal fighting. Examining it in relation to indigenous Christianity is an important area of research. In some cases (as among the east Papuan Massim), Christian leaders are widely believed to hold their authority because they are also powerful sorcerers; in other situations, as with the Waria (northern Papua), sorcery has surprising acceptance as part of the checks and balances of power. Along the central Papuan coast, there is a wide fear of others' sorceries – for roads and motor boats allow Gulf and Dobu practitioners too great a freedom of movement. In the face of this perceived rising threat to life, villagers sometimes express the fervent hope that a great Christian revival will sweep sorcery away (and indeed some small 'search and destroy' movements against sorcery in Melanesia have virtually succeeded in this; as among the Maringe, Ysabel, Solomons).[21] Other coastal Papuans, however, make some defence of sorcery by saying that the greedy and non-reciprocal – those who build big village houses for themselves out of public service salaries – are quite justly the butt of jealous neighbours who employ sorcerers to bring the arrogant down.

With this last thought we see how sorcery is conceived to be something like a punitive sanction. Even after colonial control was replaced, neo-colonial governments kept the power of serious punition – of heavy fining, gaoling or capital punishment – as their preserve. At the village level what we find is that moral pressure (both Christian and traditional), sometimes sorcery, and local courts handling minor offences and disputes, are the only institutions keeping some sense of legal and executive autonomy alive. Under these circumstances, villagers often perceive Christianity to be essential – 'the seat of our survival', as one indigenous Anglican priest expressed it for the Maisin (coastal Oro, northern Papua), because it does not punish and order around like the government, and it challenges the vindictiveness of sorcery. And of course for today's majorities departing from the Christian faith would spell material disaster and the withdrawal of blessing. Mormon Tongans put the general 'metatechnologic' outlook of Pacific peoples very aptly: 'God rewards hard work in fulfilment of family and church obligations, and punishes social transgressions with economic hardship, ill health, physical deformity, infertility and bad luck.'[22]

Becoming Christian, we hasten to add, has stages to it. Some people were daring in the degree of commitment they showed to take up their faith; many people lived split lives between the call of the cow horns to the mission station church and the obligation to be at a traditional sacrifice and feast (a common Fuyughe problem); while others again who were strong traditionalists into old age suddenly became the devoutest Christians. What leads a group to abandon its most splendid rites is sometimes hard to explain and a link to retributive logic is not always so clear. The Tikopia ritual cycle called 'The Work of the Gods' had no practitioners 'after the disastrous epidemic of 1955', while when the Motu of Boera finally abandoned their old fruit harvesting festival it was because the war, especially the Japanese bombing of Port Moresby, had somehow rendered it irrelevant. Sometimes the end of a lineage brings a customary form to an end, as on Fiji, when in 1966 there died 'the last of the great traditional chiefs' (this being Ratu Terita of the Lau group, Prime Minister Ratu Kasese Mara's father), and the tabu against weeping before burial and the continual blowing of conch shells apparently applied at his funeral for the last time (see p. 156 above).[23]

In a poignant oral account, Robert Pulsford tells how the last great Hevehe ceremony was put on by the Elema at Orokolo (cf. pp. 149–50 above) to see whether or not the local LMS missionary, Benjamin Butcher, considered it compatible with Christianity. Butcher, a rare missionary in the Pacific for his interest in comparative religion, was approached by the chiefs after the Hevehe for his assessment. He responded that it was highly acceptable and a great credit to Elema culture, although there was one activity which was not essential to the ceremony itself, which was better removed, and that was the practice of adult men taking a woman of their choice for three days of lovemaking during the proceedings, each partner making a tattoo on the other's back for memory's sake yet promising never to return to each other again. That comment was enough; the Hevehe was never put on again. F. E. Williams, the government anthropologist whom Butcher had courteously invited to the event, returned to Port Moresby to begin writing his *Drama of Orokolo*. At its conclusion he quite misleadingly asserted that the mission was responsible for the Hevehe's demise. Actually it had been the people's choice, yet whether it was because one ritual component could not be removed without affecting the whole, or whether the sanctioned sexual licence was a favourite part of the entire affair, can only be surmised.[24]

The promptings to take a leadership role in the church, and the daring to conduct a community in a new religious direction, even to take Holy Orders, is a fascinating and immensely important area for study. The psycho-spiritual preparations for such roles requires investigation to understand how certain individuals commit themselves more strongly than others to promulgate the new faith. A vivid dream of Christ rescuing the dreamer from the death-bearing Devil, to take one known case, can lead a person to evangelize by recounting the experience. A near-death experience of being sent back by Christ to earth led the young Koitabu woman Iora Boiori (the 'Miracle girl') to begin work as a healer near Port Moresby. The first Black Lutheran bishop among the Morobe people of New Guinea, Zuruwe Zurenuo, often preached about a miracle which was utterly determinative for his life: when his real mother discarded him at his birth and threw him on the river bank, her sister later discovered him at the water's edge, his sticky little body covered with ants, and she brought him up as her own – to be God's servant in due course. How young Kasa, daughter of the chief of Oua (Tonga), became a nun in the Society of Mary is comparably moving in islanders' terms. Given as an adopted daughter to Father Tremblay, Kasa was taken to live at Maufanga mission, where she felt the call to Sisterhood. Returning home at the time of her father's death, her aunt scorned her sense of vocation and managed to get her treated as *motu* – outside the circle of security and reciprocity. When Kasa's cousin was eaten by a shark, however, the villagers were soon asking, 'What have we done to make God angry like this?' and felt sorrow for trying to prevent her 'from giving herself to God'. Once a nun, Kasa dedicated herself to work in the village of her birth.[25]

Tried in the heat of resilient tribalism and foreign sectarianism, the island churches of the Pacific have emerged from their crucibles.

PACIFIC THEOLOGIES

Most major churches in the island Pacific are now organizationally autonomous and whenever possible economically self-supporting. In all the churches deriving from mainstream Protestant denominations, indigenous ministers or pastors now outnumber expatriate personnel, and since the late 1970s the localization of clergy has gone on apace in the Catholic arena (most noticeably in Melanesia, where Catholics had lagged behind). The new leadership – including a strong block of Black bishops in the United Church of Papua New Guinea and the Solomon Islands (formed 1968), and such impressive episcopal figures as the Anglican Ambo (north Papua), the Lutheran Zuruwe (Morobe) or the Catholics ToVarpin (in Papua) and Singkai (on Bougainville) – have naturally held their flocks within the prevenient ecclesiastical traditions of their missionary predecessors. But as the influences of institutionally entrenched expatriates have lessened, the pervasion of an ecumenical atmosphere has increased, and at no time more obviously than in the 1970s, after the Pacific Council of Churches and the Melanesian Council of Churches were formed (in 1961 and 1965 respectively). These councils had Catholic as well as mainstream Protestant representation, and indeed, especially considering such a Catholic protagonist as Father Patrick Murphy was involved in both organizations, were uniquely ecumenical for the whole Pacific region. Admittedly, sectarian Protestants (except for the Salvation

Army) did not want council membership, for an Evangelical Alliance of the South Pacific Islands was formed as early as 1964, and eventually also a Pentecostal Council (1980).

During the processes whereby missions were transformed into the 'Island Churches of the South Pacific', a confusing array of institutional modifications occurred and names changed. Some island groups established churches grounded in island locales. The old LMS congregations on Western Samoa, for instance, became the Christian Congregational Church of Samoa (in 1961) and in the Cooks became the Cook Islands Christian Church (operating alone by 1965); and when their members migrated abroad – to New Zealand, Australia or Hawaii – the emigrant communities have tended to look back home for pastors. By comparison, some churches took names distinguishing their theological stance, as did the LMS-originated *L'Église evangelique* on New Caledonia (1960), for instance, and *L'Église libre*, which tried to 'free' itself from European constraints when the rebellious French Protestant Charlemagne responded to the pressures of disaffected villagers (1960 as well). Straddling disparate western Melanesian cultures, the Asia Pacific Christian Mission (formerly the Unevangelized Fields Mission) changed its name to the Pacific Christian Church in 1966, for although remaining more obviously a 'Mission' in Irian Jaya, it responded to an impetus in western Papua New Guinea to build an 'indigenous church'.[26] These few examples must needs suffice.

Along with all such alterations came significant developments in the training for the ministry. Among the most famous of emergent institutions are the Pacific Theological College (PTC) in Suva, Fiji, providing for the Protestant churches of the central Pacific from 1966; and the Catholic Holy Spirit Seminary, outside Port Moresby at Bomana, a 'little Vatican' surrounded by colleges of the different orders working in Papua New Guinea (1962 onwards).[27] The Pacific-wide growth of sectarian Protestantism has also been served by higher institutions: by the Christian Leaders Training College at highland Banz, in Wahgi country, for evangelical groups; by the Pacific Adventist College, again outside Moresby; and by the Mormons' Brigham Young University, Hawaii. Government tertiary institutions have carried courses in Religious Studies, with degree programmes in indigenous traditions, new religious movements, mission history and missiology being developed most systematically at the University of Papua New Guinea and the University of Hawaii (during the 1970s). Three institutions – the ecumenical Melanesian Institute at Goroka in highland Papua New Guinea, the government-funded Institute of Papua New Guinea Studies in Moresby and the Institute of South Pacific Studies attached to the University of the South Pacific, Suva – have disseminated a vast amount of literature about Pacific religious life.

Tertiary education, including that made available in such First World contexts as Australia, New Zealand and the United States, has engendered regional theological activity of great interest. Two theological journals currently operate, and both symposia and mission journals have allowed a variety of 'Black' and 'tan' theologians to be read across Oceania, and to a lesser extent internationally.[28] It behoves us to conclude this book by assessing the styles and emphases of islander theologians since the 1970s. This is not easy, and the selection of figures and ideas discussed will not satisfy all theological pressure groups. Some will ask, why not say more about the theology of independent churches? Why not take more note of conservative or fundamentalist or charismatic theological positions, which are highly influential, even though they may seem to duplicate White conceptual moulds? But inevitably we shall fasten on minds of intellectual stature, who are at the cutting edge of contextual theological work and are thus exploring the relationship between tradition and Christian faith with a mature and sensitive grasp of both.

The extent of visible Christianization is already so great in Polynesia and Micronesia, needless to say, that tensions between the Christian and the traditional have virtually dissipated in most quarters. Christianity has become the new tradition, and big issues concern how to keep it alive in the face of secular competitions – mass media influences, capitalism, tourist luxury and the beckoning attractions of Honolulu, Auckland or Sydney. Occasionally one neo-tradition numerically dominates the others, so that the idea of legislating for a state church and against minorities which have a disproportionate access to resources (e.g. equal radio time) presents itself – as on Tuvalu (formerly the Ellice Islands). In general, in any case, central Polynesian and Micronesian theological exercises have tended to be rather complacent in accepting, conserving and reinforcing the neo-tradition rather than radicalizing it.

The work of the most eminent Polynesian theologian, Sione Havea, is obviously significant for its constructive questioning and invitation to bring about change or revitalization in a conservative ethos, even though it also illustrates some of the vulnerabilities of most Pacific theology to date. There has been a powerful stress by Havea, who has been Principal of PTC (and incidentally is physically large enough to match the king of Tonga!), that one does not have to be Westernized before becoming Christian. And if a proper contextualization or 'Pacificness of Theology' is to be achieved, it will be through alleviating island Christianity of its foreignness and transforming it instead 'into a first-hand, native-rooted Good News to the Pacific'. Just as Jesus took symbols and metaphor from the daily life of the Jews, Pacific theology asks why it is that island church practice and thought moulds should reflect so much importation, when local ingredients for a reframed theological outlook abound – in the coconut, fish, fruit, even Kava: 'I am quite sure that if Jesus had been born to a coconut culture, he would have used the coconut instead of bread and wine.' The coconut tree features as Havea's central theological image, and it is significantly a vertical one, with the coconut falling like water down to the lowest level; if it floats it 'finally lands on a new situation, . . . sets roots to grow and bears fruit'.[29]

The message of the moveable coconut is that of flexibility, and as such is a powerful challenge to the *status quo*, yet much more decidedly the religious *status quo*, so that Havea's theology rarely looks as if it will challenge governments. In contrast, the late Tongan Catholic Bishop Patelesion Finau more than once clashed with King Tauf a'ahau Tupou IV over the Tongan nobility's unjust wielding of power; the younger Guamese scholar V. Diaz has taken on both American imperialists and Catholic hierarchs with a blend of Marxist analysis and radical theology; while in the Marquesas, where the traditional priestesses were strong, women take initiatives in conducting worship that are highly unusual in the Catholic world.[30]

In Polynesian contexts where White domination matches that of Australia, as in Hawaii and New Zealand, we can expect theological challenges to political establishments. An extreme example is the 'revolutionism' of Hone Ka'a, the Maori priest who is the Anglican representative on the Churches Council of Asia and the Maori representative on the World Council of Churches. His has been a message of liberation for the Maori and against the land theft, paternalism and demoralizing attitudes of the Whites. Less bombastic, though no less critical of White hegemony in a nation priding itself on good race relations, is Ranganui Walker, Professor of Anthropology (Maori Studies), at the University of Auckland, defender of tradition and advocate of a 'Maori renaissance.'[31]

It is in more turbulent Melanesia, however, where the politicization of theology has been more evident. Apollinaise Ataba, Catholic priest, initiator of the Kanak cause on New Caledonia this century and mentor to Jean-Marie Tjibaou, saw in the Incarnation the raising up of 'our human nature ... to the level of a superior being', so that we could see ourselves as individuals yet equal in a 'universal brotherhood of man', not unequal under the caste-like arrangements of a French colony.[32] Radical Kanak theologians – Catholic Tjibaou and Protestant Pierre Qaeze alike – have deplored the inflexible structures of the churches, and particularly French-dominated Catholicism. Tjibaou actually abandoned his priesthood because the Catholics back-peddled over decolonization. Before being killed by protagonists for a more revolutionary position, he tried hard to apply non-violent tactics and was realistically committed to a multi-racial society. Such Fijian radicals as Suliana Suwatibau and to a lesser extent Sevati Tuwere have shown comparable commitments in another eastern Melanesian setting, although their statements extolling multi-ethnicity and social peace have been in the face of Melanesian racism. Colonial Rabuka's two coups (of 1982) unleashed anti-Indian and 'anti-heathen' sentiments among the Methodist majority. Unlike the PTC, which stood up against such prejudice, the Fiji-centred Methodist Training Centre for ministers (Davu Levu) bent with the new political forces, and fundamentalist M. Lasaro, as the incoming Methodist President, used the coups as an opportunity to demand a strict public morality, including Sabbatarianism, from the populace.

In other Melanesian trouble spots, theologies of social justice have been aired, even if with varying implications. On Vanuatu, Anglican Father Walter Lini's involvement in politics meant that Biblical values could be evoked in the movement to remove French and British presence, the demise of Condominium of the New Hebrides being marked by a national anthem which seems more like a hymnic praise to God. But the prolonged imprisonment of rebel Jimmy Stevens (see p. 187), together with the apparent tendency of the Vanuaaku Party government to impeach opponents in the courts, gave the impression that Lini wanted to hallow his own Establishment with law and divine justice on his side (until his defeat late in 1991). Far to the west, by contrast, voices as disparate among the west Papuans as exiled Max Ireeuw (with a Dutch Reformed background), Dr. Daniel Ajamiseea (working for the Catholics at Chundrawasi University, Djayapura), and Joshua Daimoi (a Baptist who became Principal of the Christian Leaders Training College, Papua New Guinea) have insisted on social justice for their people, in anxiety over Indonesian neo-colonialism (especially Javanese officialdom, military intervention, the transmigration of easterners

to Irian Jaya and the recent (1994) decision of the Jakarta government to expatriate 200 foreign missionaries to allow more room for
other faiths to operate).

In the centre of the region, practical theology has been extremely
important on Bougainville. Important among the peacemakers
during the 1990–3 war of secession, for example, have been three
eminent churchmen: one-time Catholic Father John Momis, the
architect of Papua New Guinea's provincial government system and
the visionary of a respecting, co-operating, accepting, egalitarian
and 'classless' Christian society; Bishop Leslie Boseto, former
United Church moderator and a Solomonese who has strongly advocated the 'ministry of reconciliation' and the constant critique of
negative 'payback'; and Catholic Bishop Gregory Singkai, who,
though responding sympathetically to Bougainvillean popular pressures to secede from Papua New Guinea, has always abhorred and
written against violent solutions.[33] These men have addressed Papua
New Guinea's most serious crisis, yet most theology in Papua New
Guinea has been forced to deal with its many turbulences – the
problems of revenge killing, sorcery, urban 'rascalism', political in-
fighting, industrial disputes – and, even if in a somewhat unsystem-
atic way, theologians have attempted to integrate noble traditions
and the Christian Gospel to build a post-tribal *communitas*.

Along the Tongan Havea's lines, Melanesian theological voices
have been raised in protest against the foreignness of Christian
practices, those preventing Melanesians from responding to God in
ways authentically their own. Denominational entrenchment in the
church runs against the grain of nation-building, producing a species
of neo-tribalism and blocking strong tendencies towards ecumenism
in Melanesia. The continuing Europeanization of the church makes
it all the more difficult for crucial cultural resources to be reappro-
priated as integral features of a contextual and 'Melanesianized'
Christianity. So have argued such important Papua New Guinea
thinkers as Poloukou Pokawin (as Premier, Manus Province),
Bernard Narokobi (PNG, former Minister for Justice), Utula
Samana (PNG, former Minister for Education) and John Kadiba
(when lecturing at Nungalinya College, near Darwin).

Elsewhere there have been other quests for authenticity of a
different ilk. In the Torres Strait, Anglicanism has been celebrated
by Dave Passi, hero of the historic Australian Mabo land-rights
decision, as the most appropriate replacement for tradition, because
its hierarchism parallels the old sacred isolation of the *zogoga* priesthood. In the Solomons, Esau Tuza and Michael Mailiau have both

pointed to charismatic styles of worship which are more 'natural' outcomes of the islanders' transition 'from the old to the new times', and such views, especially Mailiau's formulation of them, tend to foster 'spirit-filled', Pentecostal or manifestly joyous services of worship. Other Solomonese of his persuasion have been important evangelists in parts of the New Guinea highlands.

Old-fashioned missionary institutions, of course, will continue to have their appeal. They bear a certain stability with them – or solace, as when Cyclone Isaac hit in 1977, for example, and Tongans found themselves singing old words which nonetheless epitomized the Christian alternative to traditional retributive logic:

> Judge not the Lord by feeble sense,
> But trust him for his grace;
> Behind a frowning providence,
> He hides a smiling face.[34]

Distinctly foreign beliefs and praxis will continue to have their attractions. The strength of Seventh Day Adventism for many Melanesians is its 'regimen', despite some of its utterly 'unPacific' expectations; it demands a strict adherence to rules and sets up an ordered series of tabus commensurate with the imposition remembered from the past. The attractiveness of Mormonism for various Polynesians lies in the notion that they are remnants of 'lost tribes' from Biblical Israel – an idea reinforced by other twentieth-century pictures of Polynesia as the place of a great ancient civilization or with a providentially decreed future. Mormonism's vertical and anthropomorphic theology also needs noting: God is distinctly 'up there' on a planet (called Kolob), propagating everyone who is born on earth and being visualized as a divine Man. The Mormon church (of Jesus Christ of the Latter-Day Saints) is also a wealthy institution bringing obvious material benefits to those who work for it. Islander apologists for all these positions are emerging.

Island theologians are left with a wide range of problems to tackle across the vast ocean. Tribal war continues to rack the highlands, for example; both West Papua and Bougainville seem likely to be running sores, and threats to the region's democratic future abound. From Micronesia (the fishing rights issue on Kiribati, suicide on Truk, diminishing resources on Nauru and Ocean Island) over to the most exploited patches of Polynesia (with Hawaii, American Samoa, French Polynesia and Easter Island, all overused for defence and/or tourism), there are challenges which demand spiritual, not merely secular attention. All sorts of social psychological problems, associated with development, rapid change and the slowness of the churches to respond, demand a sound pastoral theology, as the Kiribati scholar Maroti Rimon has recently argued.[35] With these and other problems peculiar to other parts of Oceania, it is harder than we think for Pacific or even regionally oriented theologians to develop their ideas and recommendations with a sense of common ground. Yet the intertwining historical threads we have been plotting, the healthy ethos of ecumenism, and the common pursuit of a sense of identity and relative autonomy, are making Pacific theologies both possible and necessary.

NOTES AND REFERENCES

1 Portions of this chapter were used for the *South Pacific Journal of Mission Studies*, 4/1 (1994), pp. 21–4.

2 Cf. A. R. Tippett, *People Movements in Southern Polynesia*, Chicago, 1971.

3 Thus D. R. Simmons, introducing Fr. C. Servant, *Customs and Habits of the New Zealanders 1838–42* (trans. J. Glasgow), Wellington, 1973, p. 3. For Marist beginnings on Wallis and Futuna, see J. Hosie, *Challenge*, Sydney, 1987.

4 A. Safroni-Middleton, *Sailor and Beachcomber*, London, 1915, p. 197. Note, however, that missionaries often had rules to ensure that they could not get 'too close to the natives' for their own good. See D. Langmore, *Missionary Lives* (Pacific Islands Monograph Series 6), Honolulu, 1989, p. 129.

5 See S. S. Farmer, *Tonga and the Friendly Islands*, London, 1855, p. 159 for the phrase. We are not to forget the few missionaries who found it hard to keep up their own ideals in the Tropics – turning to drink, for instance.

6 W. Gill, *Cook Island Custom*, London, 1892, p. 17; Engelbert, *The Hero of Molokai* (trans. B. J. Crawford), Sydney, 1954, pp. 114–234; cf. G. Daws, *Holy Man: Father Damien of Molokai*, Honolulu, 1973.

7 Especially those at the Hendrik Kramer Institute, Oestegeest, near Leiden, Holland.

8 W. W. Scudder, *Nineteen Centuries of Missions*, New York and Chicago, 1899, p. 143, cf. pp. 142–4.

9 W. Ellis, *Hawaii*, London, 1842, p. 44.

10 Ta'unga o te Tini, 'Tuauru: a Cook Islands Mission to New Caledonia' (trans. M. Crocombe), in R. Crocombe, *Polynesian Missions in Melanesia*, Suva, 1982, pp. 79, 96, 100, cf. pp. 80ff.

11 J. Taime, 'The "Christianization" of Tongareva (Penrhyn) Island' (Bachelor of Divinity Thesis, Pacific Theological College), Suva, 1983; cf. M. Crocombe, *Cannibals and Converts*, Suva, 1983 on the training of these three Cook Islanders; H. E. Maude, *Slavers in Paradise*, Canberra, 1981 on the Peruvian slave trade.

12 J. Garrett, *To Live among the Stars*, Geneva and Fiji, 1982, p. 114, cf.

pp. 102ff., cf. D. Scarr, 'Cakobau and Ma'afu: Contenders for pre-eminence in Fiji', in J. W. Davidson and D. Scarr (eds), *Pacific Islands Portraits*, Canberra, 1976, pp. 95ff.

13 S. Latukefu, 'Oral History and Pacific Islands Missionaries: the Case of the Methodist Mission in Papua New Guinea and the Solomon Islands', in D. Denoon and R. Lacey (eds), *Oral Tradition in Melanesia*, Port Moresby, 1981, p. 184. That Tongans were on Buka and Bougainville shows that organizations other than the LMS sent South Sea islanders (the first one to Buka being the Fijian Usaia Sotutu, sent by the New Zealand Methodist Goldie, while the Lutheran Rhenish Mission in German New Guinea used the Samoan Jerome Ilaoa, among others, in its work).

14 [C. Marau], *Story of a Melanesian Deacon: Clement Marau* (trans. R. H. Codrington), London, 1874, p. 68, cf. pp. 58ff.

15 H. Linge, *An Offering Fit for a King* (trans. N. Threlfall), Rabaul, 1978, p. 19, cf. pp. 18–20, 58–61.

16 To quote R. C. Suggs, *The Hidden Worlds of Polynesia*, London, 1963, p. 55 on the Marquesas.

17 H. Schrencker, 'Orokolo Annual Report, 1921' (LMS I, 3, District Reports 1921–3; formerly LMS Archives, Metoreia, Port Moresby; subsequently Archives, New Guinea Collection, University of Papua New Guinea).

18 B. K. Duncan, 'Christianity: Pacific Island Traditions', in P. Donovan (ed.), *Religions of New Zealanders*, Palmerston North, 1990, pp. 130–1.

19 T. Aerts, 'Christian Art from Melanesia', *Bikmaus* 5/1 (1984): 47ff.

20 D. Shineberg, *They Came for Sandalwood*, Melbourne, 1967, p. 167, cf. also p. 176.

21 G. M. White, *Identity through History: Living Stories in a Solomon Islands Society* (Cambridge Studies in Social and Cultural Anthropology 83), Cambridge, 1991, pp. 111–12 (Ysabel).

22 T. Gordon, 'Inventing the Mormon Tongan Family', in J. Barker (ed.), *Christianity in Oceania, Ethnographic Perspectives* (ASAO Monograph 12), Lanham and New York, 1990, p. 207; and on the Maisin above, Barker 'Mission Station and Village: religious practice and representation' in *ibid.*, p. 190; on metatechnology, see W. C. Tremmel, *Religion. What Is It?*, New York, 1984 edn., pp. 62–6.

23 R. Firth, *The Work of the Gods in Tikopia* (LSE Monographs on Social Anthroplogy 1–2), London and Melbourne, 1967, p. v (Tikopia); J. Knox-Mawer and P. Carmichael, *A World of Islands*, London and Sydney, 1968, plates 42–52 (Lau).

24 See F. E. Williams, *The Drama of Orokolo*, Oxford, 1940, pp. 432ff; cf. B. Butcher, *Many Faiths, One Essential*, Sydney, n.d. [1950s]; and Pulsford, pers. comment, 11 September, 1991.

25 E. Tremblay, *When You Go to Tonga*, Boston, 1954, p. 266, cf. ch. 29.

26 C. Forman, *Island Churches of the South Pacific*, Maryknoll, NY, 1982 (general); [Anon. UFM] *The Indigenous Church*, Port Moresby, n.d. [1970s] (APCM/PCC).

27 T. Aerts and Trompf, 'The Catholic Missions: a Case History', in G. W. Trompf, *Melanesian Religions*, Cambridge, 1991, p. 182. This seminary was actually first founded at Kap, near Madang, in 1962.

28 *Pacific Journal of Theology* (1981–); *Melanesian Journal of Theology* (1985–); J. D'A. May (ed.), *Living Theology in Melanesia: a Reader* (Point Series 8), Goroka, 1985; G. W. Trompf (ed.), *The Gospel is Not Western*, Maryknoll, NY, 1987.

29 S. A. Havea, 'The Pacificness of Theology', in *Mission Review*, (December 1977), p. 4; 'Moving towards a Pacific Theology', in *ibid.* 19 (April/June 1982), p. 5. A recent decision taken by the Cooks Islands Christian Church, initiated by Joel Taime, replaces the Communion bread with coconut meat and milk ([Cook Islands Christ. Ch.], 'Akapapaanga i tetai au manako ki te uipaanga maata', single page mimeograph for General Assembly July 1991).

30 P. Finau, 'One Day our Children will Laugh at How Foolish We Are', in *Matangi Tonga*, January-February, 1991, pp. 3ff.; V. Diaz, 'Pious Stories: Chamorro Cultural History at the Crossroads of Church and State', in *ISLA: a Journal of Micronesian Studies* 1/1 (1991): 9ff.

31 Ranganui Walker, *Nga tau tohetohe: Years of Anger*, Harmondsworth, 1987, p. 161, cf. pp. 168ff., 210ff.

32 A. Atab, *D'Atai à l'indépendance*, Noumea, 1984, pp. 177–8. Tjibaou was more affected by the Old Testament and its complimentarity with indigenous 'socialist' solidarity of Melanesian clan life, a point reflected in the interview in *Les temps modernes* 464 (March 1985), p. 1599.

33 J. Momis, 'The Christian Vision of a New Society', in Trompf (ed.), *Gospel*, p. 163, cf. pp. 160–5; L. Boseto, *I Have a Strong Belief* (ed. G. Bays), Rabaul, 1983, pp. 34.

34 *Methodist Hymn Book*, 509 verse 4; cf. S. A. Havea, 'When Isaac Came', in *Mission Review* 19 (April/June 1982), p. 12. The point became relevant again when the Samoas were hit by a devastating cyclone in 1991.

35 M. R. Rimon, 'Kiribas: a Cultural Empirical Theology' (Masters in Theology thesis, University of Sydney), Sydney, 1992.

Select bibliography

This list of references contains works which we consider to be most useful for readers wishing to expand upon the material in our text. Of necessity, it is highly selective. Wherever possible, we give preference to works in English and to books rather than articles. The list is ordered in accordance with the sections of each chapter.

Introduction

The peopling of Oceania

Bellwood, Peter, *Man's Conquest of the Pacific: the Prehistory of Southeast Asia and Oceania*. Auckland, Sydney and London, 1978. (The most comprehensive coverage of Melanesian, Micronesian and Polynesian prehistory.)

Jennings, Jesse (ed.), *The Prehistory of Polynesia*. Cambridge, Mass., 1978. (Solid collection of articles on Pacific prehistory, including articles by such a key investigator as R. C. Green.)

Suggs, Robert, *Island Civilizations of Polynesia*. New York, 1960. (Out of date, but still the best general introduction to the prehistory of Polynesia, and interpretative issues.)

Terrell, John, *Prehistory in the Pacific Islands: a Study of Variation in Language, Customs and Human Biology*. Cambridge, 1986. (A useful introduction to the problems of interpreting prehistoric evidence in the Pacific islands, with a chapter on burial practices.)

Trompf, Garry, *In Search of Origins (Studies in World Religions 1)*. New Delhi and London, 1990. (Discusses the problems and prospects for those hoping to reconstruct something of prehistoric religions, with emphasis on Australian materials.)

White, J. Peter and O'Connell, James, *Prehistory of Australia, New Guinea and Sahul*. Harmondsworth, 1982. (The best available introduction to the prehistory of the Australian mainland, Tasmania and western Melanesia.)

The invention of the religions of Oceania

Keesing, Roger, 'Creating the Past: Custom and Identity in the Contemporary Pacific', *Contemporary Pacific* 1/1–2 (1989): 19–39. (Some challenging deconstructions of Western inventions of Pacific cultures.)

Lévi-Strauss, Claude, *Totemism*. Harmondsworth, 1969. (Gives the history and a critique of 'totemism'.)

Smith, Bernard, *European Vision and the South Pacific 1768–1850: A Study in the History of Art and Ideas*. Oxford, 1960. (A lucid study of early European images of the south-west Pacific.)

Steiner, Franz, *Taboo*. Harmondsworth, 1967. (Overviews the origin and uses of the concept of 'tabu'.)

Swain, Tony, *Interpreting Aboriginal Religion: an Historical Account*. Adelaide, 1985. (A survey of European interpetations of Aboriginal religions.)

I AUSTRALIA

1 Tradition

General

Berndt, Ronald, *Australian Aboriginal Religion*. Iconography of Religions, section V., Leiden, 1974. (A detailed work but difficult for the new student and poorly organized. The plates are superb, the data sound and thorough.)

Charlesworth, Max; Morphy, Howard; Bell, Diane; and Maddock, Kenneth (eds), *Religion in Aboriginal Australia: an Anthology*. Brisbane, 1984. (A welcome collection of readings with useful introductory sections by the editors.)

Eliade, Mircea, *Australian Religions: an Introduction*. Ithaca, NY, 1973. (A clearly argued overview of Aboriginal religions, but with a misplaced emphasis on High Gods and sacred centres.)

Maddock, Kenneth, *The Australian Aborigines: a Portrait of Their Society*. Harmondsworth, 1974. (The best general introduction to Aboriginal society, with three excellent chapters on religion.)

Swain, Tony, *Aboriginal Religions in Australia: a Bibliographical Survey*. New York, 1991. (An annotated and classified bibliography of all published works on Aboriginal religion, with extensive introductory chapters.)

Worms, Ernest A. [and Petri, Helmut] *Australian Aboriginal Religions*. Richmond, Vic. 1986. (Translation, from the French [sic], of the Aboriginal section of Nevermann, Worms and Petri's *Die Religionen der Südsee und Australiens*, mentioned in the Introduction. Dated.)

The Dreaming

Edwards, William (ed.), *Traditional Aboriginal Society: a Reader*. Melbourne, 1987. (Contains W. E. H. Stanner's famous 'The Dreaming' as well as other excellent articles on Aboriginal religion.)

Myers, Fred, *Pintupi Country, Pintupi Self: Sentiment, Place and Politics among Western Desert Aborigines*. Washington, DC, 1986. (A very rich ethnography. See especially the chapter 'The Dreaming: Time and Space'.)

Cosmology

Berndt, Ronald and Catherine, *The Speaking Land: Myth and Story in Aboriginal Australia*. Melbourne, 1988. (The best general overview of Aboriginal mythology.)

Rose, Deborah, *Dingo Makes Us Human: Life and Land in an Australian Aboriginal Culture*. Cambridge, 1992. (A vivid discussion of cosmology in the Victoria River District.)

Stanner, William, *On Aboriginal Religion*. The Oceania Monographs no. 11. Sydney, 1959–61. (A brilliant analysis of the correlative structure of Murinbata myth and rite.)

Maintaining the cosmos

Munn, Nancy, *Walbiri Iconography: Graphic Representation and Cultural Symbolism in a Central Australian Society*. Ithaca, NY, 1973. (A pioneering study of the role of iconography in the maintenance of society and cosmos, with a chapter on 'increase' ceremonies.)

Turner, David, *Return to Eden: a Journey through the Promised Landscape of Amagalyuagba*. New York, 1989. (An inspiring discussion of the logic of Bickerton Island spirit-land structure and its ecological implications.)

The emergence of life from land

Montagu, Ashley, *Coming into Being among the Australian Aborigines: a Study of the Procreation Beliefs of the Australian Aborigines*. London, 1974. (A thorough study of Aboriginal procreation beliefs, containing detailed regional investigations.)

Women and land

Bell, Diane, *Daughters of the Dreaming*. Melbourne and Sydney, 1983. (An invaluable overview of Warlpiri and Kaititja women's religious life.)

Making men

Elkin, A. P. *Aboriginal Men of High Degree*. St Lucia, Qld., 1977. (The standard survey of men's 'higher degrees' of initiation.)

Meggitt, Mervyn, *Desert People: a Study of the Walpiri Aborigines of Central Australia*. London, 1962. (Contains one of the fullest accounts of an initiation ceremony to be published.)

From life to death

Morphy, Howard, *Journey to the Crocodile's Nest*. Canberra, 1984. (A fine documentation of death beliefs and burial ceremonies based on a funeral for a Yolngu child.)

The Australian/Pacific islands divide

Thomson, Donald, 'The Hero Cult, Initiation and Totemism on Cape York'. *Journal of the Royal Anthropological Institute of Great Britain and Ireland* 63 (1933): 453–537. (The most useful general account of a Cape York religious tradition with good sections on Koko-Yao Hero cults.)

2 Cults of intrusion

General

Kolig, Erich, *Dreamtime Politics: Religion, World-view and Utopian Thought in Australian Aboriginal Society*. Frankfurt, 1989. (Contains useful information on most known post-European cults.)

Swain, Tony, *A Place for Strangers: towards a History of Australian Aboriginal Being*. Cambridge, 1993. (An extensive survey of Aboriginal religious responses to contacts with outsiders.)

The Macassans/the All-Mother cult

Berndt, Ronald, *Djanggawul: an Aboriginal Religious Cult of North-eastern Arnhem Land*. London, 1952.

Berndt, Ronald, *Kunapipi: a Study of an Australian Aboriginal Religious Cult*. Melbourne, 1951. (This and the preceding work together form the best accounts we have of All-Mother songs and rituals.)

Invasion/the All-Father cult

Howitt, Alfred, *The Native Tribes of Southeast Australia*. London, 1904. (The standard account of the All-Fathers of the south-east, although Howitt rejects the possibility that they were recent innovations.)

Mathews, R. H., 'The Bora of the Kamilaroi Tribes'. *Proceedings of the Royal Society of Victoria* 9 (1897): 137–73. (An imperfect article in many ways, but contains honest observations of European influence on Bora cults.)

Mulunga and the millennium

Siebert, Otto, 'Sagen und Sitten der Dieri und Nachbarstämme in Zentral-Australien'. *Globus* 97, 3 (1910): 44–50; 97, 4: 53–9. (The only observer to recognise Mulunga's millennial theme.)

Cults from the pastoral world

Koepping, Klaus-Peter, 'Nativistic Movements in Aboriginal Australia: Creative Adjustment, Protest or Regeneration of Tradition'. In *Aboriginal Australians and Christian Missions: Ethnographic and Historical Studies*, ed. T. Swain and D. Rose. Adelaide, 1988. (For English readers, an invaluable summary of German sources on Kimberley religious innovations.)

Kolig, Erich, *The Silent Revolution: the Effects of Modernization on Australian Aboriginal Religion*. Philadelphia, 1981. (A pioneering monograph on the effects of Western economies on Aboriginal religion in the Kimberley.)

Shaw, Bruce, *Countrymen: the Life Histories of Four Aboriginal Men as Told to Bruce Shaw*. Canberra, 1986. (Wonderful stories including fascinating reflections on Djanba and Boxer.)

The war and cargoism

Glowczewski, Barbara, 'Manifestations symboliques d'une transition économique: Le "Juluru", culte intertribal du "cargo"'. *L'Homme* 23 (1984): 7–35. (The best account of Djulurru available.)

Petri, Helmut and Petri-Odermann, Gisela, 'A Nativistic and Millenarian Movement in North West Australia'. In *Aboriginal Australians and Christian Missions: Ethnographic and Historical Studies*, ed. T. Swain and D. Rose. Adelaide, 1988. (An English translation of the key account of the Jesus/Jinimin development.)

3 Missions, Christianity and modernity

General

Swain, Tony and Rose, Deborah (eds), *Aboriginal Australians and Christian Missions: Ethnographic and Historical Studies*. Adelaide, 1988. (Thirty-three articles on topics ranging from mission histories to Aboriginal religious responses to Christian thought and practice.)

Missions and missionaries in Australia

Harris, John, *One Blood: 200 Years of Aboriginal Encounters with Christianity*. Sydney, 1990. (A detailed chronicle of an enormous mission history.)

Mission world views and Aboriginal resistance

Tonkinson, Robert, *The Jigalong Mob: Aboriginal Victors of the Desert Crusade*. Menlo Park, Calif. 1974. (A well-known account of how Jigalong Aborigines retained their tradition in the face of a strong missionary presence.)

Two laws or one?

Calley, Malcolm, 'Pentecostalism among the Bandjalang'. In *Aborigines Now: New Perspectives in the Study of Aboriginal Communities*, ed. M. Reay. Sydney, 1964. (The classic statement detailing Bandjalang syncretism.)

Adjustment and alliance

Berndt, Ronald, *An Adjustment Movement in Arnhem Land: Northern Territory of Australia*. Paris, 1962. (The first monograph on an Aboriginal religious response to Christianity. Invaluable documentation.)

Thompson, David, *'Bora is Like Church': Aboriginal Initiation and the Christian Church at Lockhart River, Queensland*. Sydney, 1985. (Tantalising rather than exhaustive data on the association of traditional Boras and the modern church.)

The medium and the message

Berndt, Ronald, 'Surviving Influence of Mission Contact on the Daly River, Northern Territory of Australia'. *Neue Zeitschrift für Missionswissenschaft* 8 (1952): 1–20. (Contains translations of the Mullukmulluk and Madngela Christian myth cycle.)

Evangelical revivals and the move towards an indigenous church

Gondarra, Djiniyini, *Series of Reflections of Aboriginal Theology*. Darwin, 1986. (Australia's most noted Aboriginal theologian reflects on the Arnhem Land revival, ecumenism, the Uniting Aboriginal and Islander Congress and other recent Christian developments.)

Pattel-Gray, Anne, *Through Aboriginal Eyes: the Cry from the Wilderness*. Geneva, 1991. (A strong statement of Black liberation theology prepared for the World Council of Churches.)

Reinventing the eternal/reclaiming a place

Davis, Jack et. al., *Paperbark: A Collection of Black Australian Writings*. St Lucia, Qld., 1990. (An excellent selection of Aboriginal literature giving a strong sense of modern aspirations and spirituality.)

Maddock, Kenneth, 'Myth, History and a Sense of Oneself'. In *Past and Present: the Construction of Aboriginality*, ed. J. R. Beckett. Canberra: Aboriginal Studies Press, 1988. (Contains a full listing of Captain Cook myths from across Australia, which are compared with Macassan myths.)

Mother Earth

Swain, Tony, 'The Mother Earth Conspiracy: an Australian Episode'. *Numen* 38 (1991): 3–26. (A more extensive account of the material presented in this text.)

II PACIFIC ISLANDS

4 Tradition

General

Goldman, Irving, *Ancient Polynesian Society*, London, 1970. (The best work relating islander religions to social fabric, although one must be wary of his evolutionist orientation.)

Parratt, John, *Papuan Belief and Ritual*. New York and Washington, DC, 1976. (The only survey of Papuan traditions; sketchy but useful.)

Trompf, Garry, *Melanesian Religion*. Cambridge, 1991. (The only general textbook on Melanesian religion available; the first half of the work considers traditional religious life, while the second half considers mission history, cargo cults, black theologies, etc.)

Williamson, Robert, *Religious and Cosmic Beliefs of Central Polynesia*. 2 vols, Cambridge, 1933. (Older but indispensable survey of traditional Polynesian beliefs.)

Cosmos

Gillison, Gillian, *Between Culture and Fantasy: a New Guinea Highlands Mythology*. Chicago and London, 1993. (The best recent consideration of mythology in a Melanesian culture – the highland Gimi – though rather unclear about the role of the unconscious.)

Grimble, Arthur, *Tungaru Traditions: Writings on the Atoll Culture of the Gilbert Islands* (ed. H. E. Maude). Melbourne, 1989. (Important ethnographic materials posthumously published.)

Handy, Craighill, *Polynesian Religion*. Bernice P. Bishop Museum Bulletin 34. Honolulu, 1927. (Somewhat out of date, but still one of the best comparative studies of traditional Polynesian worldviews.)

Kamakau, Samuel, *Ka Po'e Kahiko: the People of Old*, trans. M. K. Pukui, ed. D. B. Barrère, Honolulu, 1991. (Among the most detailed of collections of Polynesian traditions, in this case of Hawaii.)

Lawrence, Peter and Meggitt, Mervyn (eds), *Gods, Ghosts and Men in Melanesia*. Melbourne, 1965. (An older, solid collection of articles on traditional Melanesian worldviews by a team of reputable anthropologists.)

Payback

Baal, Jan van, *Dema: Description and Analysis of the Marind-Anim Culture (South New Guinea)* (Koninklijk Instituut voor Taal, - Land- en Volkenkunde: Translation Series 9), The Hague, 1966. (The most detailed of all Melanesian ethnographies, analysing the motifs for Marind headhunting.)

Meggitt, Mervyn, *Blood is Their Argument: Warfare among the Mae Enga Tribesmen of the New Guinea Highlands* (Explorations in World Anthropology). Palo Alto, Calif., 1977. (Important monograph on the principles of revenge warfare.)

Trompf, Garry, *Payback: the Logic of Retribution in Melanesian Religions*. Cambridge, 1992. (The analysis of an important theme in Melanesian religious life; a third of the work considers traditional religions.)

Valeri, Valerio, *Kinship and Sacrifice: Ritual and Society in Ancient Hawaii*, trans. P. Wissing. Chicago, 1985. (A clever historical reconstruction of a Polynesian sacrificial cult.)

Power

Guiart, Jean, *Structure de la chefferie en Mélanésie du Sud*. Tranx et Mémoires de l'Institut d'ethnologie 66. Paris, 1963. (One of the important studies of chieftainship patterns in Melanesia.)

Stephen, Michele (ed.), *Sorcerer and Witch in Melanesia*. Melbourne, 1987. (Excellent collation on important themes in Melanesian traditional religions.)

Williamson, Robert, *Religion and Social Organization in Central Polynesia*, ed. R. Piddington. Cambridge, 1937. (An older yet useful introduction to chieftain societies and the management of sacral power in traditional Polynesia, though bettered on particular groups e.g. by D. Oliver on Tahiti.)

Creative participation

Firth, Raymond, *Art and Life in New Guinea*. London and New York, 1979. (A solid introduction to western Melanesian art by a famous anthropologist.)

Herdt, Gilbert and Stephen, Michele (eds), *The Religious Imagination in New Guinea*. New Brunswick, NJ, 1989. (A needed entrée into the Melanesian world of the imaginal.)

Schmitz, Carl, *Oceanic Art: Myth, Men and Image in the South Seas*. New

York, 1969. (The best introduction to Pacific island art and its sacral significations.)

Becoming spirit

Burrows, Edwin and Spiro, Melford, *An Atoll Culture*. New Haven, Conn., 1957. (The most famous ethnography of Micronesian survivalism.)

Leenhardt, Maurice, *Do Kamo: Person and Myth in a Melanesian World*, trans. B. M. Gulati. Chicago and London, 1979. (A famous older and very sensitive work by a French Protestant missionary anthropologist who worked on New Caledonia. Later at the Sorbonne, the Chair he vacated was taken by Claude Lévi-Strauss.)

Moss, Rosalind, *The Life after Death in Oceania and the Malay Archipelago*. Oxford, 1925. (Somewhat superficial, but the only general account of beliefs about life after death in the Pacific islands.)

5 Cults of intrusion

General

Siikala, Jukka, *Cult and Conflict in Tropical Polynesia*. Academia Scientarum Fennicae, FF Communications 99/2). Helsinki, 1982. (Easily the best general analysis of new religious movements in Polynesia. The account of the Tahitian Mamaia movement is excellent.)

Steinbauer, Friedrich, *Melanesian Cargo Cults*, trans. M. Wohlwill, St. Lucia, 1979. (A useful survey to the most famous new religious movements of the Pacific.)

Trompf, Garry (ed.), *Islands and Enclaves: Nationalisms and Separatist Pressures in Island and Littoral Contexts*. New Delhi, 1993. (Includes six chapters relevant to religious study on ethnicity, protest and rebellion in the Pacific.)

Cults of victory and prosperity

Gunson, Neil, 'An Account of the Mamaia or Visionary Heresy of Tahiti, 1826–1841'. *Journal of the Polynesian Society* 71 (1962): 209ff. (The best introduction to the earliest new religious movement in the Pacific islands.)

Trompf, Garry (ed.), *Prophets of Melanesia*, Port Moresby and Suva, 1986 edn. (Various articles on indigenous responses to colonialization.)

Of kings and cargo

Burridge, Kenelm, *Mambu: a Melanesian Millennium*. London, 1960. (A brilliant analysis of a Tangu cargo cult.)

Clark, Paul, *Hauhau: the Pai Marire Search for Maori Identity*. Auckland, 1975. (Includes good coverage of the Maori King movement and the role of religion in Maori reactions to White dominion.)

Inspirations of world war

Lawrence, Peter, *Road Belong Cargo*. Manchester, 1964. (A masterly study of one cargo cult from the war era.)
Worsley, Peter, *The Trumpet Shall Sound: a Study of 'Cargo' Cults in Melanesia*. London, 1970. (A famous reference work on cargo cultism by a neo-Marxist scholar. It is especially good for developments during the Pacific War.)

Your own church

Ernest, Manfred, *Winds of Change: Rapidly Growing Religious Groups in the Pacific Islands*, Suva, 1994. (Very recent 'sectarianisms' surveyed).
Gesch, Patrick, *Initiative and Initiation: a Cargo Cult-type Movement in the Sepik against Its Background in Traditional Village Religion*. Studia Instituti Anthropos 33, St Augustin, 1985. (The most detailed study of a Melanesian cargo cult and the processes whereby it became an independent church.)
Trompf, Garry, 'Independent Churches of Melanesia', *Oceania* 54 (1983): 51–72; 122–32. (The only survey of Melanesian independent churches).

6 Missions, Christianity and modernity

General

Boutilier, James; Hughes, Daniel; and Tiffany, Sharon (eds), *Mission Church and Sect in Oceania*. Ann Arbor, Mich., 1978. (Useful articles on missions and their consequences across the Pacific.)
Forman, Charles, *The Island Churches of the South Pacific*. American Society of Missiology Series 5. Maryknoll, NY, 1982. (A very handy historical and contemporary survey of the Christian churches across Oceania.)
Quanchi, Max, and Adams, Ron (eds), *Culture Contact in the Pacific*. Cambridge, 1992. (Helpful introduction to patterns of Pacific contact history.)
Wagner, Herwig (ed.), *Papua Neuguinea: Gesellschaft und Kirche*. Erlanger Taschenbücher 93. Neuendettelsan and Erlanger, 1989. (Helpful survey of mission history and social developments in connection with it.)

Missions to savages

Garrett, John, *To Live among the Stars: Christian Origins in Oceania*, and *Footsteps in the Sea: Christianity in Oceania to World War II*. Geneva and Suva, 1982, 1992. (Together, the best broad survey of the early missionization of the island Pacific.)
Gunsen, Neil, *Messengers of Grace: Evangelical Missionaries in the South Seas 1797–1860*. Melbourne and Oxford, 1978. (A groundbreaking work on early missionaries to Polynesia and Melanesia.)
Wagner, Herwig, and Reiner, Hermann (eds), *The Lutheran Church in*

Papua New Guinea. 1886–1986. Adelaide, 1986. (Splendid coverage of the mission history of a particular tradition in a particular Pacific country, using German sources hitherto unavailable.)

Islanders as missionaries

Crocombe, Marjorie (ed.), *Cannibals and Converts: Radical Change in the Cook Islands.* Suva, 1983. (Editing of writings by the famous Rarotongan missionary Maretu, with an assessment of the crucial role Cook Islanders made in the Christianization of the Pacific.)
Crocombe, Ronald and Marjorie (eds), *Polynesian Missions in Melanesia.* Suva, 1982. (The only survey of this topic, and solid.)

Indigenous Christianity

Barker, John (ed.), *Christianity in Oceania: Ethnographic Perspectives.* ASAO Monographs 12. Lanham, New York and London, 1990. (The only collection on varied expressions of indigenous Christianity across Oceania.)
Loeliger, Carl and Trompf, Garry (eds), *New Religious Movements in Melanesia.* Port Moresby and Suva, 1985. (To work on cargo cults this collection adds studies of various other movements expressing indigenous Christianity in Melanesia.)

Pacific theologies

Pattel-Gray, Anne and Trompf, Garry, 'Styles of Aboriginal and Melanesian Theology'. *International Review of Mission* 82/326 (1993): 167–88. (The only general and up-to-date survey of both Aboriginal and Melanesian theologies.)
Trompf, Garry (ed.), *The Gospel is Not Western: Black Theologies from the Southwest Pacific.* Maryknoll, NY, 1987. (Black theologies in the making: a selection of voices from all Melanesian countries, with Australian Aboriginal thinkers represented as well.)
World Vision, *South Pacific Theology: Papers from the Consultation on Pacific Theology, Papua New Guinea, January, 1986.* Oxford, 1986. (A good collection of more conservative theologies from across Oceania.)

Index

Printed in the United States
100956LV00002B